GOOD CHEAP EATS
DINNER IN 30 MINUTES
(OR LESS!)

Also by Jessica Fisher

Good Cheap Eats
Best 100 Juices for Kids
Not Your Mother's Make-Ahead and Freeze Cookbook

GOOD CHEAP EATS
DINNER IN 30 MINUTES
(OR LESS!)

JESSICA FISHER

The Harvard Common Press
Boston, Massachusetts

The Harvard Common Press
www.harvardcommonpress.com

Printed in China
Printed on acid-free paper

Library of Congress Cataloging-in-Publication Data
Fisher, Jessica (Jessica Getskow)
  Good cheap eats dinner in 30 minutes (or less!) / Jessica Fisher. -- First edition.
    pages cm
  Includes index.
  ISBN 978-1-55832-816-7 (acid-free paper)
  1. Quick and easy cooking. 2. Low budget cooking. I. Title. II. Title: Good cheap
eats dinner in thirty minutes (or less!) .
  TX833.5.F575 2015
  641.5'52--dc23
                                                              2014041989

Special bulk-order discounts are available on this and other Harvard Common
Press books. Companies and organizations may purchase books for premiums or
resale, or may arrange a custom edition, by contacting the Marketing Director at
the web address above.

Book design by Elizabeth Van Itallie
Text photographs by Jessica Getskow Fisher
Front cover photograph by Rick Starkman Photography

10 9 8 7 6 5 4 3 2

To my husband and children,
for loving me and supporting me in
all my crazy endeavors

Contents

Introduction: The Quick-Fix Dinner

Wouldn't it be nice to bypass the long line at the drive-through, to skip the frozen food aisle at the grocery store, and to avoid long hours in the kitchen? What about eating delicious, healthy, wholesome meals on a regular basis? It sounds like a dream. How in the world could this be possible when we are all so pressed for time?

There are lots of things that clamor for our attention these days: family, work, school, community, friends, and, of course, our various modes of entertainment. We are inundated with more opportunity and infor-mation than ever before. In most respects this is good, but what happens in real life is that we feel busier than the generations before us. There is always more to do in this Information Age.

Along with all this newfangled technol-ogy come more and more food innovations that have us opening boxes and cans, dump-ing prepared things onto a plate, or eating on the run. Yet sprouting up through all this is the blossoming understanding that pro-cessed foods are, in fact, *not* the best thing since sliced bread. More and more, folks are concluding that home cooking is cheaper and healthier.

Let's be real. How can you quickly get a meal on the table? How can a busy-night supper happen without making "a run for the border" or passing through the Golden Arches? How can we reconcile healthy intentions with real-life schedules?

With easy-to-prep ingredients and time-saving strategies, you can get a delicious, healthy, home-cooked meal on the table in just half an hour. That's quicker than I can find my car keys and get through the take-out line at the local burger joint. Thirty minutes: We can all do that!

Why 30-Minute Meals?

Whether you are a college student carrying a heavy load, a busy professional, a full-time homemaker, a working parent, or an active retiree, chances are that you desire a quick, healthy meal. I know I do.

I've got six kids 18 and under. As you can imagine, ours is a busy household. Between home-school activities, my husband's and my work schedules, and the kids' various les-sons, classes, practices, and games, our after-noons and evenings are far from humdrum.

When the kids were all little, dinner together was something we made a priority every night, never fail. As they've grown, we've held on to this family ritual, adjusting mealtimes to fit with our varying outside obligations. This means that I might have only a 60-minute window to get supper on the table between my son's science class and my daughters' swim lesson. Things have gotten a little tricky!

Dinner needs to be a quick fix.

While your life might not mirror mine, I'll hazard a guess that you've got nights when you want dinner on the table, like, five minutes ago. You might be tempted to grab a frozen pizza or run out for fast food instead of bustling about the kitchen. I am, too, sometimes. I've learned, however, that we eat more healthfully and more economically when I take the time to buckle down in the kitchen and give 30 minutes of my time toward dinner prep. What results is delicious and nutritious—and also offers a small taste of home.

You've got 30 minutes. Put down the tablet, switch off the computer, turn up the music, and get thee to the kitchen.

About This Book

This book is a result of my efforts to get a quality, home-cooked meal on the table before a little one starts whining or a big one is late for karate. (Did you know that the sensei will close the door on you if you're late for karate?)

Dinner doesn't have to come out of a box. With a few tricks and some simple organizational techniques, you can pull off a great meal in the time it takes to watch a sitcom—including commercials. The tricks are all laid out for you here. Throughout the book, you will find my 101 top tips for saving time in the kitchen. Heed them well, and you can always enjoy good food.

The 200 recipes here are designed to be easy, flavorful, quick to prepare, and kid-friendly. In most cases, they are also frugal meals. That's how I roll. I'm a pretty thrifty shopper, but I'm not averse to spending a little extra for something that will cook quickly and keep us away from so-called fast food. In the end, we still save money compared with the cost of eating out.

What you'll find in this book are menus composed of pairs of recipes rather than one-dish suppers or three-course meals. A one-dish meal can be a quick fix, but sometimes it feels incomplete, like it's lacking in variety. And given how quickly 30 minutes can go by, a three-course meal seems too cumbersome for every day. I'm the queen of biting off more than I can chew, so with two-course dinners I keep things exciting without being too complicated.

In each menu, the "main event" is always listed first, but you can decide how you want to serve the courses. Sometimes I've paired an obvious main dish with a side to serve on the same plate, such as Honey-Broiled Ham Steak and Cheater Cheesy Potatoes (page 50); other times it's an appetizer and a one-dish main course, such as the Red Pepper Hummus and Greek Beef Wraps with Tzatziki (page 196). In some instances, I pair a main dish with a salad that you can serve before, after, or at the same time, such as the Biscuit Pizza with Sausage and Peppers and Marinated Olive and Tomato Salad (page 146). And in some cases the two dishes are "equal" and you'll just want to serve them side by side, such as the Bacon and Brie Samwiches and Vegetable Soup with Thyme (page 55).

The recipes in each menu are designed to complement one another, but you should feel free to mix and match them to suit your own taste buds. I've tried to create versatile recipes that lend themselves to many possible combinations. Many recipes can stand alone instead of being part of a menu, and the recipe notes offer lots of alternative serving suggestions. Often a salad or side dish can be quickly and easily adapted into a main dish by adding grilled meat or fish, so please feel free to make yours a one-dish dinner if that suits the day. No matter what you do, dinner will be on the table in a flash!

Each meal in this book will serve at least four adults. For many meals, leftovers will keep well, and you can save even more time by enjoying them the next day for lunch or reheated for supper later in the week. Some dishes take well to preparing and freezing in advance, giving you a bulk-cooking option to save even more precious time.

At my house, we love to end a meal with a bite of something sweet. It doesn't have to be a big, fancy dessert, just a little treat to cap off the meal and help it feel complete. At the end of the book, you'll find a roundup of quick-to-prepare desserts. Present them with style and no one will know you didn't spend hours in the kitchen.

If you're a visual person, you'll be pleased to know that there is a database of photographs of recipes in this book located at GoodCheapEats.com/gallery30/, in addition to the photos that appear in these pages.

Label It!

Since my youngest daughter has a food allergy, we take care to read labels and adapt recipes so that she can enjoy them safely. Even though a food item might not contain the allergen in question, the risk of cross-contamination at the factory or restaurant is often a concern. Cooking most foods at home allows us to save money as well as ensure a healthy and safe diet for her. I know many other families have ingredient concerns of their own, whether it be an allergen or an intolerance of certain ingredients.

I know from experience that when I'm strapped for time, I want to easily and quickly scan a recipe to see if it is going to suit our family's needs. Many of the recipes in this book are marked with the following labels to help you know at a glance how they can fit into the bigger picture of your life, schedule, and dietary preferences.

Meatless: Making meals without meat is a great way to eat more healthfully and economically—and save time as well. Many meatless meals can be ready in the blink of an eye, especially when using quick-fix ingredients such as eggs or canned beans.

Dairy-free: Many recipes can easily be adapted for dairy-free eating by making substitutions for butter or cow's milk. Those that are already naturally dairy-free are indicated as such.

Gluten-free: If you already cook gluten-free, you know how to adapt recipes. The labels here will help friends and family prepare a gluten-free meal. Please keep in mind that manufacturers hide gluten in crazy places, so be sure to read all ingredient labels to ensure, for example, that there is no gluten hiding in your bacon, soy sauce, corn tortillas, or chili powder. Naturally gluten-free recipes are labeled as such, though countless others can easily be adapted to work without gluten.

Make-ahead: While all the recipes in this book can be made in 30 minutes or less, there's an added advantage to making food a few hours before serving time. It allows you flexibility in your kitchen schedule as well as provides the option to pack the food for picnics, work lunches, and other on-the-go meals. And, quite honestly, after a hard day, spending even half an hour in the kitchen can seem intimidating. With make-ahead meals, you can do the prep work the night before or first thing in the morning and then come home in the evening knowing that supper will be on the table just a few minutes after you walk in the door.

Freezer-friendly: I am a huge fan of freezer meals—after all, I wrote the book on it! If you liked my first book, *Not Your Mother's Make-Ahead and Freeze Cookbook,* then you'll appreciate the freezer-friendly options peppered throughout this book. In many instances, you can make a double batch of a favorite meal and stash half in the freezer for a busy night weeks or even months down the road. Booyah! Extra time saved. Freezer cooking is also a fantastic way to save money, as you can buy ingredients in bulk when they are on sale.

About Ingredients

Whenever possible, I've chosen ingredients that are readily available and super convenient to use. I lean on items like bagged shredded cabbage or jarred minced ginger or garlic to help me save time in the kitchen. I look at these items as whole-foods convenience items. Spooning out the ginger instead of peeling and grating it buys me an extra five minutes (plus cleanup time).

Some days, that five minutes is the difference between survival and losing my cool.

Often convenience might cost a little more. In the situations where I had to choose between time and money in these recipes, I've chosen Door Number One: saving time. For instance, buying a bag of prewashed baby spinach is a much easier alternative to hand washing bulk spinach that's full of sand and grit. The latter may be cheaper, but the convenience of the bagged variety wins this busy mama's heart every time. Time is money, right? Cooked shrimp or bacon may be a bit more costly than their uncooked counterparts, but the speed they bring to meal prep is well worth it to me, particularly if it helps me avoid eating out, which is always more expensive than eating at home. As with all my shopping, I look for these convenience items on sale and stock up when I see a great price. I build my meal plans around what's on special and thereby get the best of both worlds. All this being said, if you prefer to buy ingredients that aren't precooked and take a few extra minutes in the kitchen, go right ahead and do that.

While these meals definitely count as from-scratch recipes, you will notice a small handful of commercial items in the ingredients lists, like barbecue sauce and enchilada sauce. I can and do make my own most often, but I realize that this may not be everyone else's favorite option. Feel free to make your own when time allows, but by all means grab a bottle of your favorite prepared sauce to get supper on the table more quickly.

As far as meat is concerned, I've focused on the cuts that cook the most quickly. You won't find roasts and whole chickens in this book, as they take more than half an hour to cook in a conventional oven. Instead, I turn to boneless chicken pieces, beef steaks, and pork chops and tenderloin, as well as ground meats and charcuterie. And, of course, sea-

food almost always cooks up fast.

When it comes to chopping vegetables, I've given you the option of skipping the measuring cup to help you stay under our 30-minute target. Half of a medium onion equals about 1 cup chopped onion. Half of a bell pepper yields about ½ cup chopped pepper. Once you get an idea of how your vegetables "measure up," you can skip the step of piling them in the cup and just get on with your recipe. For those who prefer to be exact, the ingredients lists offer both options, but know that recipes like these tend to be very forgiving. Just be sure to measure exactly for all baking recipes.

Tools of the Trade

There are certain tools that will help you save time in the kitchen. While there are feasible alternative methods to using each one, I think that the time they save more than justifies the space they take up in my kitchen.

Immersion blender: The only regret that I have about my "stick" blender is that I didn't buy it sooner. It has proven to be a rock star in the kitchen, helping me achieve smooth sauces and soups without dirtying another pan or spilling all over the counter.

Stand blender: A good, sturdy stand blender is a great resource for making smoothies and other blended drinks quickly and efficiently.

Food processor: I've had a food processor for over 20 years—as long as my marriage. My husband and my food processor are necessities in my life. They both help me slice and chop vegetables, but the latter does it much more quickly. (Sorry, honey!) The food processor also quickly shreds cheese, purees sauces, and makes fast work of pie crust and other pastry dough.

Rice cooker: Rice is so versatile and one of my favorite quick-cooking grains. While I love baking rice (see page 26), I still rely on my rice cooker as a hands-free helper in the kitchen.

Good knives: I can't stress enough the importance of good knives. I'm not sure there's anything more annoying than hacking through a piece of meat with a dull, junky knife. Not only is it slow work, but it's also dangerous—dull knives are more likely to contribute to kitchen accidents than sharp ones. Invest in a good-quality chef's knife, bread knife, and paring knife, and keep your knives sharpened.

Quality cutting boards: I love big cutting boards. They allow me ample workspace so that I can do all my chopping for a sauté or salad in one spot. Be sure you have enough boards so that you can switch them between working with meats and vegetables to avoid cross-contamination.

Pots and pans: You don't need a full suite of cookware. Choose some key pieces, like a stockpot, a 12-inch nonstick skillet, and a large saucepan, and buy the highest quality you can afford. Good-quality cookware will save you time by being a pleasure to cook with as well as easy to clean. It's just easier to prepare high-quality meals with high-quality cookware.

Baking dishes: The recipes in this book call for different baking dishes on occasion, like rimmed baking sheets, ramekins, 9 x 13-inch baking dishes, and muffin pans. Having the right pan for a job will help you prepare a recipe quickly.

Meat thermometer: Meats are easy to overcook. When we do that, we waste time we could be spending eating or doing something else pleasurable, and the result isn't as appetizing, which is a waste of money. Using an instant-read meat thermometer will let you know exactly when your meat is ready.

My hope is that this book will help put an end to the age-old question of "What's for dinner?" May you find yourself skipping the fast-food lane and instead coming home to quickly and easily prepare a healthy, delicious meal. When kids, spouse, or housemates ask, "When will dinner be ready?" may your answer be a confident "In a half hour."

Quick Casseroles, Bakes, and Broils

We tend to think that baking involves a long, drawn-out process. I am pleased to report that, aside from the initial preheat time—something that some modern ranges can completely bypass—using the oven or broiler is a fast and easy way to get dinner on the table.

These casseroles, bakes, and broils are designed so that both dishes on the menu can share space in the oven or that one will cook on the stovetop or be mixed in the salad bowl while the other bakes in the oven.

GOLDEN RULES OF MEAL PLANNING

Meal planning is one winning strategy for helping you save time and money in the kitchen. Everyone does meal planning, but some people do it in line at the burger joint. If you don't already, make your plans just a bit more in advance so that you can ensure that you have the ingredients necessary and that you're ready to get cooking when it's time.

Here are some golden tips to help you create winning meal plans:

1. Know what you like.

Don't plan things that you know your family won't eat. It's an exercise in frustration and a waste of your time and money. While I'm all for experimentation and trying new things, do this judiciously to better use your resources.

2. Take stock.

If you know what you have, you won't spend time and money buying more of that thing. Take an inventory before you go shopping to make sure you don't buy duplicates. Maybe you don't even need to shop this week!

3. Make an emergency meals list.

Real quick! Jot down 10 meals that you know like the back of your hand and that are quick to prepare. Add the ingredients for those meals to your grocery list and keep them in stock for those nights when you need a backup plan.

4. Create a formula for the week.

Remember when TV sitcom moms would talk about "meatloaf night"? They planned a certain type of meal for each night of the week. It was a weekly rotation that they knew fit their budgets and schedules. Do the same but update it for the twenty-first century: tacos, pizza, pasta, curry, stir-fry. Choose one type of meal for each night of the week. You'll likely have a common grocery list each week (saves time!), and you'll have endless variety since there are so many fun combinations to make within each of those themes.

5. Plan for leftovers.

Make good use of leftovers. They are typically good for up to three or four days, under proper storage. Plan to use up leftovers and take the night off from cooking.

MENU

Chili Stacks

California Winter Salad

I grew up in Southern California, near Los Angeles, where Latin flavors dominated during my childhood. As a result, my comfort foods are typically of the Mexican-inspired variety. The same goes for my husband. This meal reflects flavors of home for us both.

Chili Stacks

SERVES 4 TO 6

`GLUTEN-FREE` `MAKE-AHEAD`

My mom was a working mom in the 1980s, and she needed quick meals to feed us five kids. This was one of our favorites, so I dug up Mom's old recipe and made a few tweaks to it. *Voilà!* An easy and filling meal that comes together quickly. I'm guessing that's one of the reasons Mom served it so often.

1 pound ground beef or turkey
¼ medium onion, chopped (about ½ cup)
1 (14.5-ounce) can petite diced tomatoes, with their juices
½ cup tomato sauce
1 tablespoon chili powder
1 teaspoon salt
½ teaspoon dried oregano
½ teaspoon ground cumin
6 corn tortillas
2 cups shredded Monterey Jack or cheddar cheese

TOPPINGS (OPTIONAL)
Chopped fresh cilantro
Sliced scallions
Sliced black olives

1. Preheat the oven to 350°F. Spray a pie plate with nonstick cooking spray.

2. In a large nonstick skillet, brown the beef and onion over medium-high heat until the meat is cooked through and the onion turns translucent, 5 to 7 minutes.

3. Add the tomatoes, tomato sauce, chili powder, salt, oregano, and cumin and cook for another 3 minutes.

4. Layer a tortilla, some meat sauce, and some cheese in the prepared baking dish. Repeat the layers until all the ingredients are used.

5. Bake until the cheese is melted and bubbly, about 15 minutes. Serve wedges of the casserole with the toppings of your choice.

MAKE IT AHEAD: Prepare the recipe through step 4. Wrap and chill until you are ready to bake, up to 24 hours. Add about 10 minutes to the baking time since the dish will be cold.

#1

MAKE A CLEAN SWEEP

Quit rummaging around in your fridge, looking for that elusive ingredient you need that's hiding behind last week's leftovers. Stop making extra trips to the store every time stuff goes bad because you didn't see it to use it. Clean your fridge to save yourself time and frustration. If your refrigerator is tidy and organized, you'll enjoy cooking more and be able to create meals in a quicker time frame.

California Winter Salad

SERVES 4

`MEATLESS` `DAIRY-FREE` `GLUTEN-FREE` `MAKE-AHEAD`

Winters in the Golden State are pretty mellow. We enjoy sunshine and warm temps while the rest of the country shivers. Sorry about that! It's also the season when citrus and avocados flourish. This salad shines with those flavors, so even if you don't live in the land of eternal summer, at least you can enjoy this salad. Feel free to top the salad with grilled chicken or shrimp for a complete one-dish main-course salad.

1 ruby red grapefruit
1 large orange
¼ cup olive oil
1 teaspoon minced garlic
Freshly ground black pepper
1 (6-ounce) bag baby spinach
1 large avocado, pitted, peeled, and sliced
¼ cup slivered almonds
2 scallions, chopped

1. Using a sharp knife, slice off the blossom and stem ends of the grapefruit. Stand the fruit up on one end. Following the curve of the fruit, cut away the peel and pith. Continue around the fruit until all the peel and pith have been removed. Then cut along the sections of the fruit, removing the flesh from the membranes. Save 2 tablespoons of the juice to make the dressing; you should be able to squeeze extra juice from the fruit's membranes. Repeat with the orange, again saving 2 tablespoons of the juice.

2. In a small jar or bowl, combine the citrus juices, olive oil, garlic, and pepper to taste. Cap the jar and shake, or whisk vigorously to combine.

3. Place the baby spinach in a large salad bowl. Toss it with enough dressing to coat.

4. Divide the dressed greens among four salad plates. Top each plate with an equal portion of grapefruit sections, orange sections, avocado slices, slivered almonds, and scallions. Serve with additional dressing on the side.

MAKE IT AHEAD: The dressing and citrus sections can be stored in separate covered containers in the refrigerator for up to 2 days.

Seasoned Turkey Meatloaf

Out-of-the-Box Rice Pilaf

We don't generally think of comfort food as being quick to prepare—unless it's a run through a favorite take-out line. But this meat-loaf and rice pilaf to-tally fit the bill. Add a steamed vegetable on the side and you will feel nurtured and nourished.

Seasoned Turkey Meatloaf

SERVES 4 TO 6

`DAIRY-FREE` `MAKE-AHEAD` `FREEZER-FRIENDLY`

I've always loved turkey meatloaf, especially in the context of friends offering me comfort. Many are the times that I've dined impromptu at a friend's house and been served meatloaf and a large helping of love. Here's to bringing comfort into your own home in 30 minutes or less!

1¼ pounds ground turkey
1½ cups fresh bread crumbs
1 large egg, beaten
1½ tablespoons onion flakes
¼ teaspoon paprika
¼ teaspoon garlic powder
¼ teaspoon rubbed sage
¼ teaspoon fine sea salt
¼ teaspoon freshly ground black pepper

1. Preheat the oven to 425°F. Grease a 9 x 13-inch baking pan with nonstick cooking spray.

2. In a large bowl, combine the turkey, bread crumbs, egg, onion flakes, paprika, garlic powder, sage, salt, and pepper. Mix until all components are well incorporated.

3. Form the mixture into a 4 x 9-inch loaf in the center of the baking pan.

4. Bake until the center reaches an internal temperature of 165°F, about 20 minutes.

MAKE IT AHEAD: The formed loaf can be covered and refrigerated for up to a day, or wrapped well in aluminum foil and frozen for up to 2 months. Thaw in the refrigerator overnight before baking. Add 5 to 10 minutes to the baking time if the dish is very cold.

WHAT A CRUMB!

Homemade bread crumbs are cheap and easy to make. You don't need to settle for overly salted boxed crumbs with added preservatives. You'll be surprised what little time it takes to run a couple of slices of day-old bread through the food processor or blender. *Voilà!* Fresh bread crumbs at the ready.

Out-of-the-Box Rice Pilaf

SERVES 4 TO 6

`GLUTEN-FREE`

Rice pilaf is so easy to make; why would you ever want to buy a boxed mix made with all kinds of preservatives and extra sodium? A little secret: Those boxed-mix companies make you do many of the things you'd have to do anyway if you were making it from scratch. They simply have you make a pilaf without fresh ingredients. Now you can beat the box.

4 tablespoons (½ stick) butter
1 cup long-grain white rice
½ cup orzo
1 teaspoon dried herbes de Provence
3 cups chicken broth
2 scallions, chopped
2 tablespoons chopped fresh parsley
Fine sea salt and freshly ground black pepper

1. In a large skillet with a lid, melt the butter over medium heat. Add the rice and orzo. Sauté until the rice becomes opaque and the orzo browns lightly, 2 to 4 minutes.

2. Add the herbes de Provence and stir. Stir in the chicken broth and bring to a low boil. Cover and reduce the heat to low. Cook until the liquid is absorbed, about 20 minutes.

3. Fluff with a fork and fold in the scallions and parsley. Season to taste with salt and pepper.

Denver Oven
Omelet

Butter Lettuce
Salad with
Apples and
Gruyère

An omelet and a
salad make the
perfect lunch or
supper across the
pond. We Americans
have been slow to
catch on, relegating
omelets merely to
breakfast time. You'll
be pleasantly sur-
prised how quickly
this meal comes
together and how
tasty it is! (You have
my permission to eat
it for breakfast, too.)

Denver Oven Omelet

SERVES 4

DAIRY-FREE GLUTEN-FREE MAKE-AHEAD FREEZER-FRIENDLY

My parents often made Denver omelets for me when I was growing
up, using onions and peppers from the garden along with smoky
ham. Since there were so many of us, I had to wait my turn for an
omelet—which seemed like an eternity. Baking the omelet in the
oven cuts the wait time and allows everyone to enjoy the meal
together.

1 tablespoon olive oil
¼ medium onion, chopped (about ½ cup)
½ cup chopped white mushrooms
½ medium green bell pepper, chopped (about ½ cup)
1 cup chopped ham
6 large eggs, beaten

1. Preheat the oven to 425°F. Grease a 9-inch deep-dish pie plate.

2. In a large nonstick skillet, heat the oil over medium-high heat
until shimmering. Add the onion and mushrooms and cook until the
onion starts to turn translucent and the mushrooms start to lose
their liquid, about 5 minutes.

3. Add the bell pepper and ham and continue cooking until the pepper has softened and the ham is hot, about 5 minutes.

4. Transfer the ham and vegetable mixture to the prepared pie plate.
Pour the eggs over the top and bake until set, 10 to 12 minutes.

MAKE IT AHEAD: Once the vegetables are cooked, allow them to cool before
pouring the eggs over the top. Wrap the dish and chill in the refrigerator overnight. To freeze, place the dish on a level surface in the freezer and freeze until
firm, about 2 hours. Wrap well and store in the freezer for up to 1 month. Thaw
in the refrigerator before baking. The dish may take 5 to 10 minutes longer to
cook depending on how cold it is.

BE PREPARED!

If you spend a few minutes each morning thinking about the day's meal prep, you'll be ready when it comes time to actually make that meal. Check that you have the ingredients on hand, lay out the tools you'll need, and fill in the gaps accordingly.

Butter Lettuce Salad with Apples and Gruyère

SERVES 4

`MEATLESS` `GLUTEN-FREE` `MAKE-AHEAD`

I love the combination of sweet-tart apples and nutty Gruyère cheese. I first tasted it as a college student in France. It is delicious atop this salad of delicate butter lettuce. Make it a complete meal by adding grilled chicken.

2 tablespoons balsamic vinegar
½ teaspoon dried tarragon
Fine sea salt and freshly ground black pepper
¼ cup olive oil
1 (7-ounce) bag butter lettuce
2 medium apples (any kind), cored and chopped
½ cup small-cubed Gruyère cheese
⅓ cup slivered almonds
¼ cup finely chopped red onion

1. In a small jar or bowl, combine the balsamic vinegar, tarragon, and salt and pepper to taste. Cap the jar and shake, or whisk to combine. Add the olive oil and shake or whisk again.

2. Place the butter lettuce in a large salad bowl. Toss it with enough dressing to coat.

3. Divide the dressed greens among four salad plates. Top each plate with an equal portion of the apple, cheese, almonds, and red onion. Serve with additional dressing on the side.

MAKE IT AHEAD: The dressing can be stored in a covered container in the refrigerator for up to 4 days.

No-Brainer
Baked Rice

Chinese take-out
was never so easy as
this great fake out.
Both components
cook in the oven.
Start the rice first
and then slide the
pan of chicken and
vegetables into the
oven alongside.
Dinner will be ready
faster than it takes
to find the number
of the local take-out
place.

Hands-Free Cashew Chicken

SERVES 4

`DAIRY-FREE` `GLUTEN-FREE`

My kids love Chinese food, or at least what we call "Chinese food"
here in the United States. Since my youngest has a peanut and
walnut allergy, we don't get take-out very often anymore. The kids
were pleasantly flabbergasted when I first served them this dish.
"It tastes just like Panda!" (And, like all good take-out, this tastes
great reheated the next day.) Serve over or alongside the rice.

1 pound chicken tenders
1 (9-ounce) package fresh snow peas
½ cup cashews
4 scallions, chopped
½ cup chicken broth
2 tablespoons soy sauce
2 tablespoons dry sherry
1 tablespoon cornstarch
1 tablespoon honey
1 teaspoon minced garlic
1 teaspoon toasted sesame oil
⅛ teaspoon red pepper flakes
Toasted sesame seeds, for garnish (optional)

1. Preheat the oven to 425°F. Grease a 9 x 13-inch baking pan with
nonstick cooking spray.

2. Place the chicken tenders in the pan. Scatter the snow peas,
cashews, and scallions over the chicken.

3. In a small bowl, combine the chicken broth, soy sauce, sherry,
cornstarch, honey, garlic, sesame oil, and red pepper flakes, whisking to blend thoroughly. Pour this mixture over the chicken and
vegetables in the pan.

4. Bake until the chicken is cooked through and the sauce is thick
and bubbly, about 15 minutes. Sprinkle with sesame seeds, if
you wish.

While homemade broth and stocks are economical and tasty, they take time to make—and thaw, if stored in the freezer. Keeping a few cartons of broth in the pantry makes a go-to convenience shortcut for me when I'm pressed for time. Be sure to buy organic for the best quality.

No-Brainer Baked Rice

SERVES 4

MEATLESS **DAIRY-FREE** **GLUTEN-FREE**

What a revelation to bake rice! I had no idea how easy it was until I started exploring different ways to cook rice quickly. My kids like this better than the stovetop or rice cooker varieties. I love it that I can cook rice while I already have the oven heated for something else. Double duty equals double win. If you use chicken broth, omit the salt.

2 cups long-grain white rice
½ teaspoon salt
4 cups boiling water or chicken broth

1. Preheat the oven to 425°F. Grease a 9 x 13-inch baking pan with nonstick cooking spray.

2. Spread the rice in the pan in an even layer. Sprinkle the salt over the top.

3. Pour in the boiling water and cover the pan immediately with heavy-duty aluminum foil, sealing the edges.

4. Bake the rice for 20 minutes, or until done to your liking. Fluff with a fork and serve.

A casserole and a
vegetable side dish
hark back to an
earlier time when
dinner was served
promptly at 6 with
all family members
washed up and
presentable. Perhaps
the homemaker
had prepped it in
the morning after
running the daily
errands. Today our
schedules have us
going hither and
yon. But that doesn't
mean we can't cozy
up with a comforting
casserole at the end
of the day. This meal
comes together in a
flash and fills up all
the hungry spaces.

Black Bean Tortilla Casserole

SERVES 4 TO 6

MEATLESS **GLUTEN-FREE** **MAKE-AHEAD**

This dish features some of my family's favorite flavor combinations:
black beans, cheddar cheese, corn tortillas, and salsa verde. Mix it
up quickly and slide it into the oven—it will transform into hot, bubbly comfort food in no time. The casserole is delicious with cooked
chicken mixed in as well.

2 cups sour cream
1 (12-ounce) jar salsa verde
1 tablespoon chili powder
12 corn tortillas, torn into pieces
2 (15-ounce) cans black beans, drained
3 cups shredded cheddar cheese
2 scallions, chopped

TOPPINGS
Sliced avocado
Chopped fresh cilantro
Chopped tomatoes

1. Preheat the oven to 400°F. Grease a 9 x 13-inch baking pan with
nonstick cooking spray.

2. In a large bowl, combine the sour cream, salsa verde, and chili
powder. Add the tortillas, beans, and 2 cups of the shredded cheese.

3. Spoon the mixture into the prepared pan. Sprinkle the remaining
1 cup cheese over the top. Sprinkle the scallions over the cheese.

4. Bake until hot and bubbly, 20 to 25 minutes. Pass the toppings
at the table.

MAKE IT AHEAD: The casserole can be prepared through step 3, covered, and
refrigerated for up to 24 hours. Add 10 minutes or so to the baking time since
the dish will be cold.

Growing fresh basil, mint, and parsley in containers is practically foolproof. It allows you to grab a handful of fresh herbs to include in recipes whenever you like. A few quick chops will ensure great flavor in seconds.

Cilantro-Lime Carrots

SERVES 4

MEATLESS **GLUTEN-FREE**

Bagged baby carrots are not technically "baby," since they are cut from "adult" carrots, but they are perfectly sized for quick cooking and serving. These are seasoned with a bit of lime juice and cilantro, making for an excellent foil to a Mexican-inspired casserole or main dish.

1 pound baby carrots
¼ teaspoon fine sea salt, plus a pinch
2 tablespoons butter
1 tablespoon fresh lime juice
1 tablespoon chopped fresh cilantro
¼ teaspoon ground cumin
⅛ teaspoon freshly ground black pepper

1. Place the carrots in a saucepan and cover with water. Add a pinch of salt and cover. Cook over medium-high heat until the carrots are tender, 8 to 10 minutes.

2. Drain the carrots and place in a bowl. Add the butter, lime juice, cilantro, cumin, remaining ¼ teaspoon salt, and the pepper to the carrots. Stir well, taste, and adjust the seasonings. Serve hot.

Creamy
Baked Eggs

Spicy and Sweet
Potatoes

Eggs really are an incredible food; it's not just a commercial jingle. They are an inexpensive, power-packed ingredient that tastes great any time of day. Coupled with sweet potatoes, they form a meal that will soothe you after a hard day's work. Start the potatoes first and then add the egg dishes to the oven.

Creamy Baked Eggs

SERVES 4

`GLUTEN-FREE`

I didn't have baked eggs until I was an adult and was left wondering how I had missed this awesomeness for so long. Creamy, cheesy, meaty, with a kick of scallion, these eggs with prosciutto are happiness on a plate.

4 tablespoons heavy cream
8 large eggs
1 ounce prosciutto, chopped
¼ cup shredded Romano cheese
2 scallions, chopped
1 tablespoon chopped fresh basil
Fine sea salt and freshly ground black pepper

1. Preheat the oven to 350°F. Grease four small ramekins, baking dishes, or individual quiche pans with nonstick cooking spray.

2. Spoon 1 tablespoon cream into each dish. Crack 2 eggs into each dish, being careful not to break the yolks. Sprinkle the eggs with the prosciutto, cheese, scallions, and basil. Season to taste with salt and pepper.

3. Bake until the whites are set and the yolks reach your preferred texture, 15 to 20 minutes.

Spend some time discarding those kitchen items you no longer use or need, like that badly scratched nonstick skillet or that spaghetti measurer. Not only will you spend less time hunting for the thing you want amid things you don't, but it will also be easier to put things away, thanks to newly reclaimed storage space. An easy-to-use kitchen is a well-used kitchen.

Spicy and Sweet Potatoes

SERVES 4

MEATLESS **DAIRY-FREE** **GLUTEN-FREE**

Use a food processor fitted with a slicing blade to make quick work of slicing the potatoes. For larger sweet potatoes, cut them in halves or thirds so they will fit into the machine.

2 long, skinny sweet potatoes, thinly sliced crosswise
2 tablespoons olive oil
1 teaspoon garlic powder
1 teaspoon fine sea salt
½ teaspoon ground cumin
½ teaspoon paprika
½ teaspoon ground ancho chile powder
¼ teaspoon black pepper

1. Preheat the oven to 350°F. Line a large baking sheet with parchment paper or a silicone baking mat.

2. Place the potatoes in a large bowl. Add all of the remaining ingredients and toss to coat.

3. Spread the potatoes in a single layer on the prepared baking sheet. Bake until tender, 20 to 25 minutes.

Cheese enchiladas are a favorite supper of mine. I could easily eat them on a weekly basis. There's just something about that luscious combination of corn tortillas, cheese, and hot chiles. A side of beans and a little salad put me in my happy place.

Three-Cheese Enchiladas

SERVES 4 TO 6

`MEATLESS` `GLUTEN-FREE` `MAKE-AHEAD` `FREEZER-FRIENDLY`

These enchiladas come together quickly and easily. They are so packed with flavor that you won't miss the meat. I've offered several options for softening the tortillas before rolling them, but I prefer the traditional frying.

12 corn tortillas
Vegetable oil for frying (optional)
8 ounces cream cheese, softened
1 (4-ounce) can chopped green chiles
4 to 6 scallions, chopped (about ½ cup)
1 cup shredded pepper Jack cheese
1 cup shredded cheddar cheese
2 cups favorite enchilada sauce
1 (2.25-ounce) can sliced black olives, drained

1. Preheat the oven to 350°F. Grease a 9 x 13-inch baking pan with nonstick cooking spray.

2. Soften the tortillas by heating them in the microwave or in a hot dry skillet, or by frying them in an inch of hot oil until softened and a bit leathery. If frying, drain them on paper towels before proceeding.

3. In a small bowl, combine the cream cheese, green chiles, scallions, ¾ cup of the pepper Jack, and ¾ cup of the cheddar cheese.

4. Divide the cheese mixture among the tortillas and roll them up. Place each rolled enchilada, seam side down, in the prepared pan.

5. Pour the enchilada sauce over the top. Sprinkle the remaining cheeses over the top. Sprinkle the olives over the top.

6. Bake until hot and bubbly, about 15 minutes.

MAKE IT AHEAD: Prepare the recipe through step 5. Wrap and store in the refrigerator for up to 24 hours or in the freezer for up to 2 months. Thaw in the refrigerator before baking. Add 5 to 10 minutes to the baking time to accommodate the colder dish.

DON'T WASH THE MEASURES EVERY TIME

Some clean freak is probably gonna freak. But if you don't have food allergies to worry about, using the same measuring spoon multiple times for different dry ingredients can save you time. Just wipe it with a clean cloth and put it away.

Spicy Pintos

SERVES 6 TO 8

`MEATLESS` `DAIRY-FREE` `GLUTEN-FREE` `MAKE-AHEAD` `FREEZER-FRIENDLY`

When I made these the first time, FishBoy11 turned up his nose. He assumed that he wouldn't like the onion and jalapeño. He was wrong. Even Mr. Picky admits that these are scrumdiddliumptious. This recipe makes a lot of beans, perfect as a hearty side dish or for filling burritos or topping tostadas. Freeze any leftovers for an easier dinner night later in the month. If you prefer a little more heat, leave the seeds in the jalapeño.

1 tablespoon vegetable oil
¼ cup finely chopped onion
1 tablespoon chopped seeded jalapeño
Fine sea salt and freshly ground black pepper
2 (29-ounce) cans pinto beans, drained
1 teaspoon ground cumin
½ teaspoon dried oregano
½ teaspoon garlic powder
½ teaspoon ground ancho chile powder

1. In a large nonstick skillet or saucepan, heat the oil over medium heat until shimmering. Cook the onion and jalapeño until softened, about 2 minutes. Season to taste with salt and pepper.

2. Add the beans and mash them slightly. Stir in the cumin, oregano, garlic powder, and ancho chile powder. Simmer until hot and bubbly, about 5 minutes.

MAKE IT AHEAD: The beans can be stored in a covered container in the refrigerator for up to 4 days or in the freezer for up to 2 months. Thaw in the refrigerator before reheating.

MENU

Crustless Potato-
Leek Quiche

Carrot Cups

A few years ago we
started a weekly
subscription service
for organic local
produce. Since then
I have learned so
much about eating
seasonally! At first
it was rough to go
without tomatoes
and cucumbers in
winter, but slowly
I've learned what
works when. This
is the perfect meal
for winter when you
crave a fresh vegeta-
ble. The combination
of quiche and carrot
salad is refresh-
ing but still hearty
enough for cooler
days.

Crustless Potato-Leek Quiche

SERVES 4

`MEATLESS` `GLUTEN-FREE` `MAKE-AHEAD` `FREEZER-FRIENDLY`

This quiche comes together quickly, thanks to frozen shredded
hash browns. I buy a brand that is just potatoes, with no salt or
other additives, making it an excellent staple to keep on hand for
quick-fix meals.

1 tablespoon butter
½ large leek, thinly sliced (about 2 cups)
2 cups frozen shredded hash browns, no need to thaw
1 teaspoon minced garlic
Fine sea salt and freshly ground black pepper
1 cup shredded cheddar cheese
6 large eggs
1 cup half-and-half
1 teaspoon Dijon mustard
½ teaspoon dried thyme

1. Preheat the oven to 425°F. Grease a 9-inch deep-dish pie plate.

2. In a large nonstick skillet, melt the butter over medium-high heat.
Cook the leek, potatoes, and garlic in the butter until the leek is tender and starting to brown and the potatoes are hot, 2 to 3 minutes.
Season generously with salt and pepper. Transfer the vegetables to
the prepared dish.

3. Sprinkle the cheese over the vegetables.

4. In a large bowl, beat the eggs. Add the half-and-half, mustard,
and thyme and whisk to combine. Pour this mixture over the cheese
and vegetables.

5. Bake until the eggs are set and a tester inserted in the
center comes out clean, 20 to 25 minutes. Serve hot or at room
temperature.

MAKE IT AHEAD: Once the vegetables are cooked, allow them to cool before
sprinkling with cheese and pouring the egg mixture over the top. Wrap the pie
plate and chill in the refrigerator overnight. To freeze, place the dish on a level
surface in the freezer until set, about 2 hours. Wrap well and store in the freezer
for up to 1 month. Thaw in the refrigerator before baking. You may need to add
5 to 10 minutes to the baking time, depending on how cold the dish is.

8

If you buy organic produce, save time by not peeling all your produce. Just scrub well with a vegetable brush. Organic carrots and potatoes, for example, can easily be scrubbed and the whole thing eaten.

Carrot Cups

SERVES 4

`MEATLESS` `DAIRY-FREE` `GLUTEN-FREE` `MAKE-AHEAD`

I first tasted carrot salad in France as an *entrée*, or the "entrance" to the meal—the appetizer, as we would say in the United States. It was a delightful way to start things off. This dish is a take on the one that I enjoyed so many years ago.

4 large carrots, peeled and shredded (about 2 cups)
1 tablespoon chopped fresh parsley
1 tablespoon red wine vinegar
1 teaspoon Dijon mustard
¼ teaspoon paprika
Fine sea salt and freshly ground black pepper
3 tablespoons olive oil
4 large butter lettuce leaves
12 pitted black olives

1. In a large bowl, combine the carrots and parsley.

2. In a small jar or bowl, combine the vinegar, mustard, paprika, and salt and pepper to taste. Cap the jar and shake, or whisk to combine. Add the oil and shake or whisk again.

3. Pour the dressing over the carrots and toss to mix.

4. Place one lettuce leaf on each salad plate. Divide the carrot mixture among the plates, piling it into each leaf. Top with 3 olives each.

MAKE IT AHEAD: The dressing can be stored in a covered container in the refrigerator for up to 4 days.

Lemon-Balsamic
Broccoli

Stuffed chicken breast and broccoli on a bed of rice sounds like either a lot of work or a mediocre TV dinner, doesn't it? It doesn't have to be either. With a few shortcuts, you can have a healthy, home-cooked meal that's worthy of candlelight and a glass of wine. Start the rice cooker, get the chicken cooking, and then add the pan of broccoli to the oven.

Chicken Breasts Stuffed with Goat Cheese

SERVES 4

MAKE-AHEAD **FREEZER-FRIENDLY**

Boneless, skinless chicken breast halves are currently weighing in at about 1 pound at my local grocer's. This is far more than a single serving. To stretch the meat and keep portions under control, I fillet each breast half. This makes a nice thin cutlet, perfect for rolling around a savory filling. If your chicken breasts are more of a vintage size, use four and pound them thin with a mallet.

2 large boneless, skinless chicken breast halves
Fine sea salt and freshly ground black pepper
4 ounces soft goat cheese
2 tablespoons chopped fresh basil
½ teaspoon minced garlic
Zest of 1 lemon
¾ cup panko bread crumbs

1. Preheat the oven to 400°F. Grease a 9 x 13-inch baking pan with nonstick cooking spray.

2. Fillet each chicken breast. With the thicker side of the breast facing the knife, hold the meat flat on the cutting board and cut horizontally, creating two thin cutlets. Season the chicken with salt and pepper to taste.

3. In a small bowl, combine the goat cheese, basil, garlic, and lemon zest. Divide the mixture into four equal portions and place one portion on each chicken cutlet.

4. Roll up the chicken around the cheese mixture, tucking in the sides as you roll.

5. Spread the bread crumbs on a plate. Roll each chicken piece in the bread crumbs and place, seam side down, in the prepared baking dish.

6. Bake until the chicken is cooked to an internal temperature of 165°F and the juices run clear, about 20 minutes.

MAKE IT AHEAD: The chicken can be prepared through step 5, covered, and refrigerated for up to 24 hours. Add a few minutes to the baking time to allow for a very cold dish.

9

When juicing citrus
fruits, allow them
to come to room
temperature first.
Juicing will go
more quickly and
yield more juice.
In a pinch, you can
microwave the whole
fruit briefly or place
it in warm water for
a few minutes.

Lemon-Balsamic Broccoli

SERVES 4

`MEATLESS` `DAIRY-FREE` `GLUTEN-FREE`

My family loves broccoli. There are rarely any leftovers, especially when I season it well, as in this dish. Roasting broccoli gives it fabulous flavor and is a hands-free process. If you don't keep balsamic on hand, feel free to use red wine vinegar instead.

1 (12-ounce) bag broccoli florets or 1 head broccoli, cut into florets
2 tablespoons olive oil
1 tablespoon fresh lemon juice
1 tablespoon balsamic vinegar
Fine sea salt and freshly ground black pepper

1. Preheat the oven to 400°F.

2. Place the broccoli in a 9 x 13-inch baking dish. Drizzle on the olive oil, lemon juice, and balsamic vinegar. Season to taste with salt and pepper. Toss to coat.

3. Roast until the broccoli is tender and browned in spots, about 15 minutes.

MENU

Teriyaki
Meatballs

Swiss Chard and
Mushroom Sauté

To bring balance to
my diet—and to my
tendency to carbo-
load—I often serve
low-carb meals. This
supper of meatballs,
greens, and mush-
rooms fits the bill,
but you can add a
cooked grain to the
plate if you like.

Teriyaki Meatballs

MAKES 24 MEATBALLS

`DAIRY-FREE` `GLUTEN-FREE` `MAKE-AHEAD` `FREEZER-FRIENDLY`

These meatballs mix up quickly with plenty of flavor. Using a quick-release scoop helps speed up the process, and their small size ensures quick cooking.

- 1¼ pounds ground turkey
- ¼ medium onion, chopped (about ½ cup)
- ¼ cup quick-cooking oats
- 1 tablespoon soy sauce
- 1 tablespoon rice vinegar
- 1 teaspoon minced garlic
- 1 teaspoon ground ginger
- ⅛ teaspoon red pepper flakes

1. Preheat the oven to 375°F. Line a rimmed baking sheet with aluminum foil and spray the foil with nonstick cooking spray.

2. In a large bowl, combine all of the ingredients.

3. Using a quick-release scoop, form 24 meatballs 1 to 1½ inches in diameter and place them on the prepared baking sheet. Bake until cooked through and lightly browned, 15 to 20 minutes.

MAKE IT AHEAD: You can shape the meatballs and refrigerate them in a covered container for up to 1 day. Baked meatballs can be cooled, wrapped, and frozen for up to 2 months.

Swiss Chard and Mushroom Sauté

SERVES 4

`MEATLESS` `DAIRY-FREE` `GLUTEN-FREE`

Sautéed mushrooms and Swiss chard are a delight. Swiss chard is one of the more delicate greens, so don't overcook it—just wilt it gently.

2 tablespoons olive oil
4 ounces white mushrooms, sliced (about 1 cup)
2 shallots, sliced
1 teaspoon minced garlic
1 large bunch Swiss chard, chopped
¼ cup water
Fine sea salt and freshly ground black pepper

1. In a large skillet with a lid, heat the oil over medium-high heat until shimmering. Add the mushrooms, shallots, and garlic and cook, stirring, until the mushrooms start to brown and the shallots start to turn translucent, about 5 minutes.

2. Add the chard and water to the pan and turn the heat to high. Cover the skillet and cook for 5 minutes. Uncover and continue cooking until the liquid is evaporated and the chard is wilted, a few minutes more. Season to taste with salt and pepper.

STOCKING THE QUICK-FIX KITCHEN ON A BUDGET

When strapped for time and faced with the choice between buying a quicker but more expensive ingredient and a cheaper one, I find it hard to go for the pricier item. Thrifty Me wants it both ways. If I plan right, I can.

Here's how to stock your pantry with quick-fix, budget-friendly items:

1. Watch for sales.

Every week your grocery store releases a sales flyer. On the front cover it will typically feature the lowest-priced items for the week. These are called loss leaders, and are basically shopper's bait. They use those to entice you to visit their store and buy a bunch of other things (that aren't on sale) while you're there.

Stock up on the items that you know you will use in a reasonable amount of time. Then, when you want to prepare a certain recipe, you'll have the ingredient in your possession already. You'll save time and money by building a practical stockpile.

2. Check the clearance section.

You'd be surprised at the great treasures you can find in the clearance aisle of the grocery store. Visit it regularly, as the selection changes often. Items here are typically just being discontinued or they're seasonal items whose time has passed, but the quality is still fine.

3. Compare prices.

If you spend a little time comparing the prices of the same items at different stores, you'll find out which places give you the best deal on the things you buy regularly. This may be different for everyone, depending on what you like to eat. But you can stock your pantry economically if you source wisely.

4. Skimp somewhere else.

Maybe food is your hobby or something that you really don't mind spending money on. Go for it. Just skimp somewhere else so that you can still keep the budget in check.

5. Get *Good Cheap Eats*.

If you're interested in trimming your grocery budget but aren't sure where to start, be sure to grab a copy of my cookbook, *Good Cheap Eats: Everyday Dinners and Fantastic Feasts for $10 or Less*. It provides you with 200 budget-friendly recipes as well as tips and tricks for saving more money on food costs. And don't forget to check the Good Cheap Eats blog for daily updates.

MENU

MENU

Chicken
Fajita Bake

Baby Greens with
Chipotle-Lime
Dressing

I love the utter
simplicity of this
menu. Toss a bunch
of things in a baking
pan. Toss some more
things in a salad
bowl. Serve with
tortillas. Awesome-
sauce.

Chicken Fajita Bake

SERVES 4

`DAIRY-FREE` `GLUTEN-FREE` `MAKE-AHEAD`

This delicious dish has similar flavors to fajitas but is much easier to
put together. It's perfect for a night when you want quick and easy.

1 pound chicken tenders
1 (15.25-ounce) can black beans, drained
½ medium onion, sliced from root to blossom end
1 red bell pepper, cored and sliced
½ cup favorite salsa, plus more for serving
Flour or corn tortillas, for serving

1. Preheat the oven to 400°F. Grease a 9 x 13-inch baking pan with
nonstick cooking spray.

2. Distribute the chicken, beans, onion, and bell pepper evenly in
the pan. Spoon the salsa over the top. Stir gently.

3. Bake until the chicken is cooked through and the vegetables are
tender, 20 to 25 minutes.

MAKE IT AHEAD: The dish can be prepped through step 2, covered, and refrigerated for up to 8 hours. Add a few minutes to the baking time to allow for a
cold pan.

11

Making a salad is not difficult, but laziness can get in the way. One strategy to combat this is to make a salad bar. If I prep a ton of vegetables, greens, and dressings, and package them for the fridge, I've got salad fixings whenever I want them. And salads come together in a snap!

Baby Greens with Chipotle-Lime Dressing

SERVES 4

`MEATLESS` `DAIRY-FREE` `GLUTEN-FREE` `MAKE-AHEAD`

I love the salad at a certain fast-food burrito restaurant. This is my take on that citrus dressing that makes you want to lick the bowl. At home, feel free to do just that.

2 tablespoons fresh lime juice
1 teaspoon honey
½ teaspoon minced garlic
¼ teaspoon ground chipotle chile powder
Fine sea salt and freshly ground black pepper
¼ cup olive oil
1 (5-ounce) bag baby greens
1 medium carrot, peeled and sliced
6 radishes, sliced
2 scallions, sliced
2 tablespoons roasted salted pepitas (pumpkin seeds)

1. In a small jar or bowl, combine the lime juice, honey, garlic, chile powder, and salt and pepper to taste. Cap the jar and shake, or whisk to combine. Add the olive oil and shake or whisk again.

2. Place the greens in a large salad bowl. Toss them with enough dressing to coat.

3. Divide the dressed greens among four salad plates. Top each plate with an equal portion of the carrots, radishes, scallions, and pepitas. Serve with additional dressing on the side.

MAKE IT AHEAD: The dressing can be stored in a covered container in the refrigerator for up to 4 days.

Roast Chicken
and Veggies

Red Quinoa with
Chickpeas

Our family is work-
ing on improving
our diet. For me
that means serving
more vegetables
even though my kids
would prefer to load
up on carbs. This
meal provides plenti-
ful veg as well as lots
of protein from the
quinoa and chicken.
Be sure to start the
quinoa first, as it's
the longer-cooking
recipe of the two.

Roast Chicken and Veggies

SERVES 4

DAIRY-FREE **GLUTEN-FREE** **MAKE-AHEAD**

I love roasting vegetables in the oven. They take on a more complex element of flavor compared with their steamed, sautéed, or
raw counterparts. Here they cook alongside the chicken, seasoned
generously with a family-favorite spice blend.

1 pound boneless, skinless chicken breast, cut into bite-size pieces
1 (12-ounce) bag broccoli florets or 1 head broccoli, cut into florets
1 medium red bell pepper, cored and cut into 1-inch chunks
1 medium yellow bell pepper, cored and cut into 1-inch chunks
1 (9-ounce) package fresh snow peas
8 ounces white mushrooms, sliced (about 2 cups)
⅓ cup olive oil
1 to 2 tablespoons Jamie's Spice Mix (page 163) or other favorite
   seasoning blend

1. Preheat the oven to 425°F. Grease a 9 x 13-inch baking pan with
nonstick cooking spray.

2. Place the chicken, broccoli, bell peppers, snow peas, and mushrooms in the baking dish. Drizzle the olive oil over the top and toss
to coat. Season generously with the spice mix and toss again.

3. Bake until the chicken is cooked through and the vegetables are
tender, 20 to 25 minutes.

MAKE IT AHEAD: The dish can be prepped through step 2, covered, and refrigerated
for up to 8 hours. Add a few minutes to the baking time to allow for a cold pan.

12

If you saw the wonderful Pixar foodie film *Ratatouille*, you will be familiar with the beautiful Colette, the only woman in the restaurant kitchen. Her refrain, "Keep your station clear or I will kill you," is a little forceful, but it's an important message. Clearing and washing up as you go will make your kitchen time safer, healthier, more fun, and yes, quicker. So, keep your station clear, okay?

Red Quinoa with Chickpeas

SERVES 4

DAIRY-FREE GLUTEN-FREE

Quinoa is a pseudo-cereal, meaning that it's technically a seed but acts and feels like a grain. It's high in protein and cooks quickly, making it a great side dish for quick suppers. Quinoa comes in a number of colors; red quinoa offers a beautiful contrast to the garbanzo beans. Feel free to use regular quinoa if that's what you have on hand. This dish is also a great side for the Baked Tomato-Basil Tilapia on page 47.

2 tablespoons olive oil
1 cup red quinoa
½ teaspoon minced garlic
2 cups chicken broth
⅛ teaspoon freshly ground black pepper, or more to taste
1 cup canned chickpeas, rinsed and drained
Fine sea salt (optional)

1. In a large skillet with a lid, heat the oil over medium-high heat until shimmering. Add the quinoa and garlic and cook until fragrant, 1 to 2 minutes.

2. Add the chicken broth and pepper and stir. Bring to a low boil. Cover and reduce the heat to medium. Simmer until the liquid is absorbed, about 12 minutes.

3. Stir in the chickpeas, cover, and cook for another 15 minutes to allow the beans to heat through and blend with the other ingredients. Adjust the seasonings and serve.

Baked Tomato-
Basil Tilapia

Roasted
Butternut Squash

This meal is incredibly easy to put together and just happens to be paleo-friendly. Buy packages of peeled and cubed squash to save time and energy wrestling with a whole squash. If you like, add a green salad on the side.

Baked Tomato-Basil Tilapia

SERVES 4

`DAIRY-FREE` `GLUTEN-FREE`

My mom cooked fish in the microwave when I was growing up, so baked fish is not a dish I learned to make as a child. In my adult home, we've usually relegated fish to the grill. It's only in recent years that I've tried baking it, and I've been quite pleased with the results.

> 4 tilapia fillets
> 4 teaspoons Jamie's Spice Mix (page 163) or other favorite
>   seasoning
> 2 medium tomatoes, chopped
> 2 tablespoons chopped fresh basil
> Lemon wedges, for serving

1. Preheat the oven to 425°F. Grease a 9 x 13-inch baking pan with nonstick cooking spray.

2. Place the fillets in the pan. Sprinkle evenly with the spice mix. Top the fillets with the chopped tomatoes, distributing them evenly over the fish.

3. Bake until the fish pulls apart easily, 12 to 15 minutes. Sprinkle with the fresh basil and serve with lemon wedges.

#13

SPICE IT UP

There's no doubt about it—busting out the measuring spoons and all the jars of spices takes time. Wouldn't it be so much faster just to open a packet of commercial seasoning mix? Better yet, save time and money when you make a set of custom spice blends to use in recipes. I buy spices in bulk and then mix them up in different ways. See pages 162 and 163 for some of my favorite home-made seasoning mixes that add flavor without taking up excess time.

Roasted Butternut Squash

SERVES 4

MEATLESS **DAIRY-FREE** **GLUTEN-FREE**

This roasted squash is a delicious side dish on its own, but it also works well atop salads.

> 2 (12-ounce) packages cubed butternut squash
> ¼ cup olive oil
> 1 tablespoon Jamie's Spice Mix (page 163)
> Fine sea salt and freshly ground black pepper

1. Preheat the oven to 425°F. Grease a 9 x 13-inch baking pan with nonstick cooking spray.

2. Place the squash in the prepared pan. Drizzle on the oil and season with the spice mix. Toss to coat.

3. Roast until the squash is tender and browned in spots, about 25 minutes. Season to taste with salt and pepper and serve.

MENU

MENU

Honey-Broiled
Ham Steak

Cheater Cheesy
Potatoes

We typically have
a big ham and a
hot potato dish on
Christmas Eve. I
spend hours in the
kitchen preparing
this special meal.
However, this
version takes the
work right out of
this combination
while leaving all of
its festiveness. My
kids were stunned:
"It smells like
Christmas in here!"
Add some steamed
broccoli or green
beans and your
dinner plate will be
complete.

Honey-Broiled Ham Steak

SERVES 4

DAIRY-FREE **GLUTEN-FREE**

Ham steaks are a quick and easy way to enjoy ham any time of
year. About ½ inch thick, they are super quick to cook, a welcome
contrast to the half ham I roast each year at Christmastime. The
honey-mustard glaze is delicious.

  1 (1-pound) ham steak
  1 tablespoon honey
  1 teaspoon Dijon mustard
  ⅛ teaspoon ground cloves

1. Preheat the broiler. Line a small broiler-safe baking dish with
aluminum foil and spray the foil with nonstick cooking spray.

2. Put the ham in the prepared dish and broil for 3 minutes.

3. In a small bowl, combine the honey, mustard, and cloves. Flip the
ham and spread the mixture over the ham. Return the pan to the
broiler and cook until glazed, 4 to 5 minutes.

14

THIS SPUD'S FOR YOU

Frozen chopped potatoes can help you make quick work in the kitchen. Stir them into soups, stews, and other dishes. What a time saver not to have to peel and chop at suppertime!

Cheater Cheesy Potatoes

SERVES 4 TO 6

MEATLESS

One of our family's favorite dishes is a cheesy potato casserole that I bake in the oven for a full 90 minutes. You might be familiar with one version or another of this dish—some folks call them "church potatoes." Here I've reduced the cooking time by using frozen shredded potatoes and cooking the mixture on the stovetop. You won't get a crusty top, but it's still delish! If allowed, my husband would eat the whole potful himself.

4 tablespoons (½ stick) butter
¼ cup unbleached all-purpose flour
1 cup chicken broth
½ cup milk
2 cups shredded Monterey Jack cheese
1½ teaspoons FishMama Spice (page 162), or more to taste
1 (30-ounce) bag frozen shredded potatoes, no need to thaw
4 scallions, chopped
Fine sea salt and freshly ground black pepper (optional)

1. In a large pot, melt the butter over medium-high heat. Whisk in the flour and stir until well mixed, hot, and bubbly, 1 to 2 minutes.

2. Gradually whisk in the chicken broth and milk, stirring until smooth and thickened, 5 to 10 minutes. Add the cheese, a handful at a time, whisking until smooth. Stir in the spice mix.

3. Stir in the potatoes and scallions and stir until combined. Cook, stirring occasionally to prevent sticking, until the potatoes are hot and bubbly, about 15 minutes. Adjust the seasonings and serve hot.

Breakneck Sandwiches and Burgers

These days, sandwiches don't have to be two slices of white bread with some bologna stuck in between. With the rise of the five-dollar foot-long sub and upscale delis and sandwich shops, the humble sandwich has become a veritable work of art. Thanks to its easy, tasty, and versatile nature, my family gives sandwich night a regular spot in the meal-planning rotation.

These breakneck sandwiches and burgers are made from wholesome ingredients and packed with flavor. They taste amazing and come together in no time. For sure, they make sandwich night something to look forward to.

THE BENEFITS OF THE QUICK FIX

"There is more to life than simply increasing its speed."—Mahatma Gandhi

Since I started curating this collection of 30-minute meals, it's been such a joy to prep meals for my family. It's not that it wasn't fun before, but meal prep took a little more time. Now when my husband says, "How much longer until we eat?" I have a ready answer.

While I love getting supper on the table in a short amount of time, I don't believe that everything in life should be done quickly. I want my kids' childhoods to last a good long while. I want to enjoy time with my husband. I want to savor a good book. And sometimes, I don't mind puttering in the kitchen for hours on end because it can be fun and relaxing.

I know from experience that the quick-fix supper benefits me in many ways. Let me count them for you:

1. Time is saved.

This is an obvious perk. I've been known to spend two hours on one meal. If supper takes you 30 minutes (or less) to prepare, you save time. That's a profit of 90 minutes that I could use on something else, like playing a game with my kids, calling my mom, or getting a pedicure.

2. It's easy to include helpers.

If you've got folks around (spouse, children, roommates) who could help in the kitchen, they'll be more likely to jump in if they know they won't be held captive for the entire evening. A quick-fix meal encourages camaraderie in the kitchen, which is also great for building relationships and both learning and teaching new skills.

3. You can enjoy a more leisurely meal.

In our busy world, suppertime can feel rushed, particularly when you've already taken a bunch of time to cook. You are fed up and want to leave the kitchen. If prep work is short and sweet, you'll be ready to relax and enjoy your meal.

4. Cooking is more fun.

Too many times, I've spent a lengthy amount of time in the kitchen and become frazzled and frustrated. There are other things I want to do, but I sometimes feel stuck. When you plan a quick fix, the cooking process itself becomes more fun. And if something is enjoyable, you'll do it more often. If you cook and eat at home more often, you will save money and eat more healthfully.

See? The quick fix scores big time.

We are huge Tolkien
fans at our house,
and love the idea
of a happy hearth
and delicious food. I
created this meal in
honor of our friends
in *The Lord of the
Rings*. Feel free to
share a pint with the
adults in your crowd
for a meal perfect for
hobbits.

Bacon and Brie Samwiches

SERVES 4

This sandwich is named after Samwise Gamgee, Frodo's faithful companion. We know he would appreciate this bite of bread and cheese with bacon. I find precooked bacon to be a great convenience. It adds that little bit of flavor without a lot of mess or time. It's a bit more expensive than uncooked, so feel free to start with regular uncooked bacon if you prefer. Just zap it quickly in the microwave or simply take a little extra time to cook it with the onions and mushrooms. You can sub in another melting cheese, like Jack or cheddar, if you'd like.

1 tablespoon olive oil
8 ounces precooked bacon, chopped
1 medium onion, sliced from stem to root end
4 ounces white mushrooms, sliced (about 1 cup)
1 tablespoon chopped fresh herbs (such as dill, tarragon, rosemary, thyme, or oregano; can be one kind or a mixture) or 1 teaspoon dried
Fine sea salt and freshly ground black pepper
Butter, for the bread (if using a griddle)
8 slices sourdough bread
4 ounces Brie cheese, thinly sliced

1. In a large nonstick skillet, heat the oil over medium-high heat and add the bacon, onion, and mushrooms. Cook until the bacon starts to crisp, the onion is translucent, and the mushrooms are tender, about 15 minutes. Stir in the herbs. Season to taste with salt and pepper.

2. Heat a panini press or stovetop griddle. If using a griddle, butter one side of each slice of bread. Assemble the sandwiches, butter side out, by layering cheese slices and the bacon mixture between two slices of bread.

3. Cook in the panini press or on the griddle until the bread is toasted on both sides and cheese is melted.

15

STICK IT

Invest in a stick blender. When I first saw immersion blenders come on the market in the 1980s, I thought they were a joke. Why would you want something like that? It wasn't until I got fed up with pouring hot liquids into a food processor—and often spilling them—that I decided to give the stick blender a try. There was no looking back. Those suckers rock.

Vegetable Soup with Thyme

MAKES ABOUT 6 CUPS

MEATLESS **DAIRY-FREE** **GLUTEN-FREE** **MAKE-AHEAD** **FREEZER-FRIENDLY**

I love the convenience of frozen vegetables. Not only are they usually packed at the peak of perfection, but they're prepped and ready to go. This soup comes together in a flash, leaving you more time to enjoy eating it. If you've got garden vegetables like Sam Gamgee does, take a few extra minutes to chop things yourself.

2 tablespoons olive oil
½ medium onion, chopped (about 1 cup)
1 (1-pound) bag mixed frozen vegetables (corn, peas, carrots, green beans), no need to thaw
4 cups vegetable broth
1 teaspoon fine sea salt
¾ teaspoon dried thyme
½ teaspoon sweet paprika
¼ teaspoon freshly ground black pepper

1. In a large stockpot, heat the oil over high heat until shimmering. Add the onion and cook, stirring, until translucent, about 5 minutes.

2. Add the mixed vegetables, broth, salt, thyme, paprika, and pepper. Bring to a low boil. This may take up to 10 minutes.

3. Reduce the heat and simmer, partially covered, until the vegetables are tender, about 12 minutes.

4. Remove from the heat. Using an immersion blender, blend the soup until very smooth. Alternatively, you can puree the soup in batches in a food processor or blender, being sure to vent the lid according to the manufacturer's directions. Adjust the seasonings and serve.

MAKE IT AHEAD: The soup may be cooled and stored in a covered container in the refrigerator for up to 4 days or in the freezer for up to 2 months. Thaw in the refrigerator before reheating.

MENU

Hot Ham
and Swiss
Sandwiches

Easy Wedge
Salad with Blue
Cheese and Sun-
Dried Tomatoes

As a child, my favorite meal in the whole wide world was found at Bob's Big Boy: the hot ham and Swiss combo with a blue cheese salad on the side. Bob's went out of business long ago, but it lingers in my memory. This meal is an updated recreation of that childhood classic.

Hot Ham and Swiss Sandwiches

SERVES 4

`MAKE-AHEAD`

Hot sandwiches feel so much "more" than the cold variety. They take just a few minutes longer, but the effort really packs a punch, especially when the bun develops crispy edges and the cheese gets all gooey. This is that kind of sandwich.

4 onion rolls, split horizontally
4 slices Swiss cheese
8 ounces thinly sliced ham
½ cup mayonnaise
2 tablespoons chopped dill pickles
1 scallion, finely chopped
1 teaspoon Dijon mustard
¼ teaspoon dried dill
¼ teaspoon sweet paprika
Fine sea salt and freshly ground black pepper
Tomato slices, for topping
Lettuce leaves, for topping

1. Preheat the oven to 350°F.

2. Lay out the bottom halves of the rolls on a baking sheet. Place one slice of cheese on each roll bottom. Divide the ham among the rolls and place atop the cheese. Top the ham with the other halves of the rolls. Bake until the sandwiches are hot and the cheese is melted, about 10 minutes.

3. In a small bowl, stir together the mayo, pickles, scallion, mustard, dill, and paprika. Season to taste with salt and pepper.

4. Remove the tops of the sandwiches and spread the mayonnaise mixture on the underside of each. Layer tomato slices and lettuce on each sandwich and replace the tops.

MAKE IT AHEAD: The mayonnaise spread can be stored in a covered container in the refrigerator for up to 1 day.

16

If you know that
you're going to need
certain vegetables
chopped for to-
night's dinner, con-
sider buying them
from the grocery
store's salad bar. The
work is all done for
you, and you can
even weigh and por-
tion it while you're at
the store.

Easy Wedge Salad with Blue Cheese and Sun-Dried Tomatoes

SERVES 4

`MEATLESS` `GLUTEN-FREE` `MAKE-AHEAD`

The wedge salad is a classic, harking back to early cookbooks of the 1920s. It was ubiquitous on dinner tables in the '50s and '60s and then sort of disappeared except for at high-end steakhouses. Since I'm a huge fan of both blue cheese and time-saving techniques, this salad is one of my favorites. Core a head of iceberg lettuce, rinse and drain it, cut it into quarters, and *voilà*! You just need a few toppings to make it fab.

1 head iceberg lettuce, quartered
½ cup julienned sun-dried tomatoes, drained if using jarred
½ cup crumbled blue cheese
1 cup mayonnaise
1 cup buttermilk
4 scallions, chopped
½ teaspoon freshly ground black pepper

1. Divide the lettuce quarters among salad plates. Divide the tomatoes and blue cheese among the lettuce wedges.

2. In a small bowl, whisk together the mayonnaise and buttermilk until smooth. Add the scallions and black pepper. Drizzle the dressing over the salads and serve with additional dressing on the side.

MAKE IT AHEAD: The dressing can be stored in a covered container in the refrigerator for up to 4 days.

As a teenager, I was
able to put away not
one, but two of those
double-burgers with
the special sauce, let-
tuce, cheese, pickles,
onions on a sesame
seed bun. I had a
ravenous appetite,
and those burgers
were a quick fix for
my hunger.

Making a better
burger at home has
been a triumph. Not
only does it contain
better ingredients,
but the flavors are
richer. Time spent?
Nominal.

Better than Big Mac's Burgers

SERVES 4

`MAKE-AHEAD`

Replacing mediocre ingredients with high-quality whole foods can
revolutionize a burger experience. Each bite tastes real and full
of flavor. There's no going back. Make these on a grill pan on your
stovetop, or fire up the outdoor grill if you prefer.

> 1 pound ground beef
> Jamie's Spice Mix (page 163), as needed
> 4 slices cheddar cheese
> 1 tablespoon olive oil
> ½ medium onion, sliced
> ½ cup mayonnaise
> 2 tablespoons ketchup
> 4 whole-wheat sesame seed buns, toasted or grilled if desired
> 2 cups shredded lettuce
> Sliced dill pickles, for topping

1. Divide the ground beef into four equal portions and form each
one into a thin patty. Make a slight indentation in the center to
prevent shrinkage. Season the patties generously with Jamie's
Spice Mix.

2. Preheat a stovetop grill pan over medium-high heat or an outdoor grill for a medium-hot fire. Cook the patties on the grill pan
or grill over direct heat until cooked through to your liking. Place
a slice of cheese on each one and continue cooking just until the
cheese melts.

3. Meanwhile, in a small nonstick skillet, heat the oil over medium-
high heat and cook the onion until very soft, about 7 minutes.

4. In a small bowl, combine the mayonnaise, ketchup, and 1 tablespoon Jamie's Spice Mix. Stir well.

5. To assemble the burgers, place one cheeseburger on each
bottom bun half. Layer on the sautéed onion, lettuce, pickles, and
sauce, and cover with the top bun half.

MAKE IT AHEAD: Form the hamburger patties and make the mayonnaise spread
up to 1 day in advance; store them in separate covered containers in the
refrigerator.

Make smoothies with frozen fruit instead of fresh. They are already prepped and ready to go and you won't need to add ice. Frozen fruit is packed at its peak of ripeness, so you can be sure that the flavor and nutrition are locked in.

Tangy Strawberry Shakes
SERVES 4

`MEATLESS` `GLUTEN-FREE` `MAKE-AHEAD` `FREEZER-FRIENDLY`

What's a burger meal without a shake? Make your meal complete with a sip of this fruity delightfulness. It's a lightly spiced, yogurt-based shake full of strawberries.

1 (6-ounce) bag frozen strawberries, slightly thawed
1 pint vanilla Greek frozen yogurt
2 cups milk
½ teaspoon ground cinnamon
½ teaspoon ground nutmeg
Honey Syrup (recipe follows; optional)

1. Place the strawberries, frozen yogurt, milk, cinnamon, and nutmeg in a blender and blend until smooth.

2. Taste for sweetness, and stir in a drizzle of honey syrup if too tart. Serve immediately.

MAKE IT AHEAD: Freeze individual shakes in freezer-proof plastic containers for up to 2 months. Let thaw at room temperature until slushy, and stir to recombine.

honey syrup
MAKES 1 CUP

`MEATLESS` `DAIRY-FREE` `GLUTEN-FREE` `MAKE-AHEAD`

Honey syrup is great to have on hand for sweetening cold beverages.

½ cup honey
½ cup boiling-hot water

Pour the honey into a small heatproof jar. Add the hot water and stir until the honey dissolves.

MAKE IT AHEAD: Allow the syrup to cool before placing the cap on; store the syrup in the refrigerator for up to 1 week.

My mom is pretty remarkable. She raised five kids on a tight budget, while teaching full time and earning her doctorate. She doesn't typically make her requests known except when it comes to fish and cilantro, two of her favorite ingredients. A huge seafood fan, she ate a Filet-O-Fish sandwich every week during her pregnancy with me. It was her one indulgence. I've updated that meal and added a cilantro-laden slaw on the side. This one's for you, Mom.

Veronica's Fillet of Fish Sandwiches

SERVES 4

`DAIRY-FREE` `MAKE-AHEAD`

A home-fried fish sandwich really doesn't take that long to make, and it's so much healthier than one you would buy at a fast-food joint. Coated with almond meal, these fillets are full of flavor, especially when served with homemade tartar sauce.

Olive oil, for frying
1 large egg
½ cup almond meal
4 cod fillets, about 3 ounces each
Fine sea salt and freshly ground black pepper
⅓ cup mayonnaise
2 tablespoons chopped dill pickles
Zest of 1 lemon
1 teaspoon dried dill
4 hamburger buns

1. Cover the bottom of a large nonstick skillet with a thin layer of oil. Heat over medium-high heat until shimmering.

2. Beat the egg in a shallow bowl and put the almond meal in another shallow bowl. Dip each cod fillet in the beaten egg, letting the excess drip off, and then dredge in the almond meal. Season to taste with salt and pepper.

3. Fry the fillets in the hot oil, turning once, until the fish can be easily pulled apart, about 10 minutes, lowering the heat to medium if necessary to prevent the crust from burning.

4. In a small bowl, stir together the mayonnaise, pickles, lemon zest, and dried dill. Season to taste with salt and pepper.

5. Assemble sandwiches by placing one fillet on each hamburger bun and topping with sauce.

MAKE IT AHEAD: The mayonnaise spread can be stored in a covered container in the refrigerator for up to 1 day.

Use kitchen shears to quickly cut herbs, scallions, and other fine items. Many a parent has also used them to quickly cut pancakes and pizza for toddlers.

Not Creamy Coleslaw

SERVES 4

MEATLESS **DAIRY-FREE** **GLUTEN-FREE** **MAKE-AHEAD**

Coleslaw is the classic traditional accompaniment to fried fish. This one goes outside the norm by eschewing a mayonnaise dressing in favor of a vinaigrette. The result is a refreshing, lighter-tasting slaw. The abundant cilantro adds great flavor.

1 (10- to 12-ounce) bag shredded cabbage (about 5 cups)
2 medium carrots, peeled and shredded (about 1 cup)
3 scallions, chopped
⅓ cup chopped fresh cilantro
½ cup rice vinegar
1 tablespoon honey or sugar
1 teaspoon Dijon mustard
¼ teaspoon freshly ground black pepper
¼ cup vegetable oil

1. In a large bowl, combine the cabbage, carrots, scallions, and cilantro.

2. In a small jar or bowl, combine the vinegar, honey, mustard, and pepper. Cap the jar and shake, or whisk to combine. Add the oil and shake or whisk again.

3. Pour the dressing over the salad mixture and toss to combine.

MAKE IT AHEAD: Make the slaw and the dressing up to 3 days in advance and store in separate covered containers in the refrigerator. Or, if you prefer, you can store the slaw already dressed; the vegetables will soften if you do this.

MENU

Turkey-Cheddar Melts with Golden Onions and Spicy Mayo

Quick Tomato Bisque

This turkey-cheddar melt embodies my formula for a great hot sandwich. Between slices of rye bread we tuck layers of cheddar cheese, a generous helping of grilled onions, thickly sliced turkey breast, tomato slices, fresh spinach, and a spicy brown mustard–mayo spread. Partner it with a cup of tomato soup and you're more than good to go.

Start the soup and the onion topping at the same time. While the soup simmers, make the mayo and assemble the sandwiches. Let the sandwiches cook while you blend and cream the soup.

Turkey-Cheddar Melts with Golden Onions and Spicy Mayo

SERVES 4

MAKE-AHEAD

The order of the components makes a big difference to the success of this sandwich. The cheese is on the bottom with only the bread separating it from the heating element. The sautéed onions go next—they won't fall out of the sandwich because they are stuck to the melted cheddar. The spinach goes near the top, right next to the creamy spread. As the spread heats up, it blends nicely with the spinach. And of course, spinach can stand the heat better than lettuce. It's all in the design, people!

1 tablespoon olive oil
1 medium onion, chopped
Fine sea salt and freshly ground black pepper
½ cup mayonnaise
1 generous tablespoon spicy brown mustard
4 slices rye bread
4 slices cheddar cheese
8 ounces thickly sliced turkey breast
1 large tomato, sliced
4 to 8 spinach leaves

1. In a large nonstick skillet, heat the oil over medium-high heat until shimmering. Cook the onion, stirring occasionally, until golden brown, about 10 minutes. Season to taste with salt and pepper.

2. In a small bowl, combine the mayonnaise and mustard. Set aside.

3. Preheat a panini press or stovetop griddle.

4. Layer the sandwiches as follows: rye bread, cheese, onions, turkey slices, tomato slices, and spinach. Spread the desired amount of mayo mixture across one side of the top bread slice. Place it mayo side down onto the spinach.

5. Grill the sandwiches on the panini press or griddle. Serve hot.

MAKE IT AHEAD: Make the sautéed onions and the mayonnaise spread up to 1 day in advance and store in separate covered containers in the refrigerator.

#19

LUNCHABLES

By making lunches ahead of time, you avoid that last-minute rush before shooing the kids out the door in the morning or having to interrupt a midday activity in order to go cook something up or grab take-out. Spend time making lunches in advance and save time later.

Quick Tomato Bisque

SERVES 4

`MEATLESS` `GLUTEN-FREE` `MAKE-AHEAD` `FREEZER-FRIENDLY`

Tomato soup has become a favorite in my adult years. I never had it as a child, but I'm making up for lost time. This soup is a great accompaniment to grilled cheese sandwiches and panini, but it can also stand on its own, especially if you've got some buttered soda crackers on hand. Yum-o!

2 tablespoons olive oil
½ medium onion (about 1 cup chopped)
1 celery rib, diced
1 medium carrot, peeled and diced
2 (14.5-ounce) cans diced tomatoes, with their juices
¼ cup dry sherry
¼ cup heavy cream
2 tablespoons chopped fresh basil
Fine sea salt and freshly ground black pepper

1. In a stockpot, heat the oil over medium-high heat until shimmering. Cook the onion, celery, and carrot until the onion starts to turn translucent, about 5 minutes.

2. Add the tomatoes and sherry, reduce the heat to low, and simmer for 15 minutes.

3. Remove from the heat. Using an immersion blender, blend the soup until very smooth. Alternatively, you can puree the soup in batches in a food processor or blender, being sure to vent the lid according to the manufacturer's directions.

4. Return the soup to the pot, stir in the cream, and gently heat through over low heat. Stir in the fresh basil and season to taste with salt and pepper.

MAKE IT AHEAD: The soup may be stored in a covered container in the refrigerator for up to 4 days or in the freezer for up to 2 months.

A sloppy joe with a side of beans and a green salad is a classic summertime feast. But let's face it: It's pretty good in the wintertime, too. Serve it with a Mexican twist and the old becomes new again.

Taco Joes

SERVES 4 TO 6

MAKE-AHEAD　**FREEZER-FRIENDLY**

I love the versatility of the joe sandwich. Sloppy or otherwise, it comes together quickly, and its preparation allows you to stretch the amount of meat you use for economy's sake. This mixture is absolutely delicious—it's like a taco in a bun. Feel free to serve it on Mexican-style bolillo or telera rolls, if you like.

1 pound ground beef
1 (8-ounce) can tomato sauce
1 to 2 tablespoons Basic Taco Seasoning Mix (page 163) or other favorite seasoning
2 cups shredded cheddar cheese
2 cups shredded cabbage
Salsa, such as Serrano Pico de Gallo (page 189), for serving
Sliced pickled jalapeños, for serving
4 to 6 hamburger buns

1. In a large nonstick skillet, cook the beef over medium-high heat until no longer pink, 5 to 7 minutes. Add the tomato sauce and taco seasoning mix. Simmer for 5 minutes.

2. To assemble the sandwiches, layer the meat mixture, cheese, cabbage, salsa, and jalapeños on each hamburger bun. Serve immediately.

MAKE IT AHEAD: The meat mixture can be stored in a covered container in the refrigerator for up to 4 days or in the freezer for up to 2 months. Thaw in the refrigerator overnight before reheating.

20

Colored grocery
bags or baskets
are a great tool for
organizing the deep
freeze. Not only do
they provide sepa-
rate compartments
for different kinds
of items, but their
colors also help you
locate what you need
quickly.

Smoky Chili Beans

SERVES 4

`DAIRY-FREE` `GLUTEN-FREE` `MAKE-AHEAD` `FREEZER-FRIENDLY`

This dish offers the smoky flavor of baked beans without the sweetness. These beans are great as a side dish but are also tasty in
burritos or atop tostadas. You can, of course, use regular uncooked
bacon here, taking the extra time to fry it in the pan.

1 tablespoon olive oil
½ medium onion, chopped (about 1 cup)
2 slices precooked bacon
1 (40-ounce) can pinto beans, drained
¼ to ½ cup water
1 teaspoon ground chipotle or ancho chile powder
1 teaspoon minced garlic
Fine sea salt and freshly ground black pepper

1. In a large nonstick skillet or saucepan, heat the oil over medium-
high heat until shimmering. Add the onion and bacon and cook until
the onion turns translucent and the bacon starts to crisp up, 5 to
7 minutes.

2. Stir in the beans, water, chile powder, garlic, and salt and pepper
to taste. Simmer for 10 minutes.

MAKE IT AHEAD: The beans can be stored in a covered container in the refrigerator for up to 4 days or in the freezer for up to 2 months. Thaw in the refrigerator
before reheating.

A hot roast beef sandwich is an ever-popular deli offering, particularly when accompanied by fries or onion rings. Instead of those side items, green up the combination a bit with fried zucchini. Prepare the sandwich filling and keep it warm on the stove while you fry the fritters. Assemble and serve.

Hot Roast Beef and Pepper Subs

SERVES 4

I've always loved a good roast beef sandwich, be it cold or hot, spicy or mild. This grinder full of flavorful beef, tasty veggies, and gooey cheese is a crowd pleaser.

4 sub rolls
1 tablespoon olive oil
1 medium onion, sliced
1 green bell pepper, cored and sliced
1 jalapeño, cored and sliced lengthwise
½ teaspoon dried Italian herb blend
Fine sea salt and freshly ground black pepper
1 pound thinly sliced roast beef, coarsely chopped
4 slices provolone cheese, cut in half

1. Preheat the oven to 350°F. Place the rolls in the oven to warm, about 5 minutes.

2. In a large nonstick skillet, heat the oil over medium-high heat until shimmering. Add the onion, bell pepper, jalapeño, herbs, and salt and pepper to taste. Cook, stirring, until the onion turns translucent and the pepper softens, 5 to 7 minutes.

3. Add the chopped beef and cook, stirring, until the meat is hot, about 5 minutes.

4. When the rolls are warm, split them almost all the way through, leaving a small hinge. Lay 2 cheese slice halves on each roll. Divide the meat and vegetable mixture among the rolls.

#21

TURN UP
THE HEAT

Increasing the cooking temperature of foods can shorten your cooking time. Veggies, seafood, and grains can roast at higher temps and may taste even better than long, slow cooking.

Zucchini Fritters

SERVES 4

MEATLESS **DAIRY-FREE**

These crispy little cakes of zucchini and leeks, dipped in homemade ranch dressing, are a delicious side dish for all kinds of suppers and a great snack all on their own. They will turn zucchini haters into lovers—I promise! The leeks get crispy when fried, adding great texture and a flavor reminiscent of onion rings. You can substitute shredded onion for the leek, if you prefer.

2 medium zucchini
¼ large leek, chopped (about 1 cup)
2 large eggs, beaten
1 cup panko bread crumbs
1 teaspoon kosher salt
½ teaspoon paprika
Freshly ground black pepper
Vegetable oil, for frying
Creamy Buttermilk Ranch Dressing (page 129) or sour cream,
    for dipping (optional)

1. Shred the zucchini using a box grater or the shredding disk in a food processor. Squeeze the zucchini to get rid of any extra liquid. (I do this in a nut milk bag, but you can also use layers of cheesecloth or a thin dishtowel.)

2. In a large bowl, combine the zucchini, leek, eggs, panko, salt, paprika, and pepper to taste.

3. Heat ½ inch of oil in a large nonstick skillet over medium-high heat.

4. Form the zucchini mixture into 2-inch patties. Fry the patties in batches in the hot oil until golden brown, 2 to 3 minutes per side.

5. Drain the fritters on paper towels. Serve immediately with dipping sauce.

Veggie and Feta
Torpedoes

BBQ French Fries

Years ago, when I
worked in a public
high school, my
friend Tami, a fellow
teacher, and I would
bring each other
lunch. One week
Tami would cook for
both of us, and the
next week I would.
In this way, we got
to have the best of
both worlds: a great
home-cooked meal
as well as time off
from the kitchen.
This menu is mod-
eled after one Tami
made for me so
many years ago.

Veggie and Feta Torpedoes

SERVES 4

MEATLESS **MAKE-AHEAD**

These sandwiches can be served hot or cold. For a different twist,
assemble them in pitas or on lavash.

    4 sub rolls
    1 tablespoon olive oil
    ½ medium onion, sliced into rings
    1 red bell pepper, cored and sliced into rings
    1 small zucchini, sliced
    4 ounces white mushrooms, sliced (about 1 cup)
    1½ tablespoons plus ½ teaspoon Greek Spice Blend (page 163)
    ⅓ cup plain Greek yogurt
    ¼ cup crumbled feta cheese
    1 large tomato, sliced
    1 medium cucumber, sliced
    12 leaves baby spinach

1. Preheat the toaster oven or broiler. Split the rolls, lay them out on
a tray, and toast lightly.

2. In a large nonstick skillet, heat the oil over medium-high heat
until shimmering. Sauté the onion, bell pepper, zucchini, and mushrooms until the onion is translucent and starting to brown and the
other vegetables are tender, about 10 minutes. Season with 1½
tablespoons of the Greek seasoning.

3. In a small bowl, combine the Greek yogurt, feta cheese, and the
remaining ½ teaspoon Greek seasoning.

4. Layer the ingredients in the rolls as follows: sautéed vegetable
mixture, tomato slices, cucumber slices, and spinach. Spread the
desired amount of yogurt spread across the inside of the roll top
and close.

MAKE IT AHEAD: Make the vegetable mixture and the yogurt spread up to 2 days
in advance and store in separate covered containers in the refrigerator.

22

Many local grocers provide online ordering and home delivery. With a few clicks of a mouse, you can choose your groceries and set a time for the local store to deliver the goods. I've tried it out, and it was amazing to grocery shop in my jammies.

BBQ French Fries

SERVES 4

MEATLESS **DAIRY-FREE** **GLUTEN-FREE**

I love the flavors of BBQ potato chips. They are one of my true weaknesses. I was thrilled when I was able to re-create those tastes in a French fry. How good can it get?

For the quickest fix, I use frozen French fries. Look for a brand that uses just potatoes, with few added ingredients. If you've got time to spare, you can use fresh potatoes. Toss them with olive oil and the seasoning mix and increase the baking time until they are crisp on the outside and tender on the inside.

¾ teaspoon sugar
½ teaspoon chili powder
½ teaspoon fine sea salt
½ teaspoon sweet paprika
½ teaspoon garlic powder
½ teaspoon onion powder
⅛ teaspoon cayenne pepper
⅛ teaspoon ground cinnamon
⅛ teaspoon ground ginger
1 (24-ounce) bag unseasoned frozen French fries

1. Preheat the oven according to the French fry package instructions. Line a rimmed baking sheet with aluminum foil.

2. In a small bowl, combine the sugar, chili powder, salt, paprika, garlic powder, onion powder, cayenne, cinnamon, and ginger.

3. Lay out the fries in a single layer on the prepared baking sheet. Sprinkle the seasonings on generously. Toss to distribute and spread out again.

4. Bake according to the package instructions. Add additional seasoning after baking, if desired.

Spicy Sausage
Burgers

Creamy Coleslaw

If we weren't already married, this meal would make my husband propose all over again. (He said so.) The burgers are full of flavor and spice, and the coleslaw adds a bit of fresh crunch and extra fiber. It all comes together for a perfect backyard barbecue or game day feast.

Spicy Sausage Burgers

SERVES 4

`DAIRY-FREE` `MAKE-AHEAD`

Just the idea of this burger makes me start to drool. Spicy sausage, sautéed onions and peppers, and an herbed mayo? Excuse me while I go get a napkin. If you prefer things less spicy, feel free to use mild sausage.

1 pound bulk spicy Italian sausage
1 tablespoon olive oil
½ medium onion, sliced into rings
1 green bell pepper, cored and sliced into rings
Fine sea salt and freshly ground black pepper
½ cup mayonnaise
1 teaspoon dried basil
½ teaspoon dried oregano
½ teaspoon minced garlic
4 kaiser rolls
Tomato slices, for topping
Lettuce leaves, for topping

1. Divide the sausage into four equal portions and form each one into a thin patty. Make a slight indentation in the center to prevent shrinkage.

2. Heat a large nonstick skillet over medium-high heat or preheat an outdoor grill for a medium-hot fire. Cook the patties on the hot skillet or grill over direct heat until cooked through, 5 to 7 minutes.

3. Meanwhile, in a separate nonstick skillet, heat the oil over medium-high heat and cook the onion and bell pepper until very soft and starting to brown, about 7 minutes. Season to taste with salt and pepper.

4. In a small bowl, combine the mayonnaise, basil, oregano, and garlic. Stir well.

5. To assemble the burgers, place one burger on a bottom bun half. Layer on the tomatoes, lettuce, and sauce, and top with the bun.

MAKE IT AHEAD: Form the patties and make the mayonnaise spread up to 1 day in advance; store them in separate covered containers in the refrigerator.

23

Read the full recipe that you're about to prepare before you start cooking. Make sure you understand all that you'll need to do as well as what tools and ingredients you need. Oftentimes, skimming a recipe can cause us to miss a step, have to backtrack, or, worse, start all over. Do it right the first time.

Creamy Coleslaw

SERVES 4

`MEATLESS` `DAIRY-FREE` `GLUTEN-FREE` `MAKE-AHEAD`

Homemade coleslaw comes together in a heartbeat and easily beats those soggy, overdressed commercial brands. This serves as a creamy, cooling foil to the spicy burgers.

1 (1-pound) bag coleslaw mix
4 scallions, chopped
1 tablespoon chopped fresh cilantro or dill
½ cup mayonnaise
2 tablespoons cider vinegar
½ teaspoon ground cumin
⅛ teaspoon ground ancho chile powder
Fine sea salt and freshly ground black pepper

1. In a large bowl, combine the coleslaw mix, scallions, and cilantro.

2. In another bowl, whisk together the mayonnaise, vinegar, cumin, and chile powder. Whisk until smooth.

3. Pour the dressing over the vegetable mixture and toss to coat. Season to taste with salt and pepper.

MAKE IT AHEAD: The slaw can be stored in a covered container in the refrigerator for up to 2 days.

Spring Street Clubs

Berry-Cherry-Banana Smoothies

As young parents, we bought a house in a town two hours away from our friends and families. We really knew no one in our new town, and Bryan didn't even have a job! Call us wild and crazy, but we fell in love with the little town of Paso Robles and its quaint downtown, historic Carnegie library, and the gazebo in the park that runs along Spring Street. A few blocks' walk scored us great food, including delicious sandwiches and smoothies. This is a meal from our olden days.

Spring Street Clubs

SERVES 4

`MAKE-AHEAD`

This was one of my first meals after giving birth to our second child, FishBoy14. I was craving a club sandwich the whole time in the hospital, so as soon as we headed home, Bryan stopped and picked one up for me. Just what the doctor ordered! While I don't think that third layer of bread is necessary in a homemade club sandwich, the frilly toothpicks, on the other hand, do make the sandwich taste better! If you've got them, use them to hold your club together.

    8 slices sourdough sandwich bread
    8 slices precooked bacon
    8 ounces sliced turkey breast
    8 ounces sliced ham
    4 ounces sliced sharp cheddar cheese
    1 large tomato, sliced
    About 1 cup shredded lettuce
    Mayonnaise, as desired
    Fine sea salt and freshly ground black pepper

1. Toast the bread lightly.

2. For each sandwich, layer on one slice of the bread the bacon, turkey, ham, cheese, tomato, and lettuce. Spread mayonnaise on the top slice. Season to taste with salt and pepper and place it mayo side down on the sandwich.

24

NEVER RUN OUT OF MILK

If you inevitably run out of milk before you need to shop for other items, stock up on shelf-stable milk and cream so that you have a backup for those nights when you don't have enough in the fridge for a recipe. I also keep dry milk powder on hand to use in baking recipes.

Berry-Cherry-Banana Smoothies

SERVES 4

MEATLESS **GLUTEN-FREE** *MAKE-AHEAD* **FREEZER-FRIENDLY**

Smoothies, when made with real ingredients and not sugar-laden ice creams and sorbets, totally count as food, albeit drinkable. This smoothie, full of fresh fruit and healthful dairy, makes a great beverage to sip with a sandwich or as a snack on its own. If you use fresh rather than frozen cherries, you might want to add a couple of ice cubes to the blender.

2 bananas
1 cup fresh or frozen pitted cherries
1 cup mixed frozen berries
1 cup plain yogurt
1 cup milk

Place all of the ingredients in a pitcher and blend until smooth. Serve immediately.

MAKE IT AHEAD: Freeze individual smoothies in freezer-proof plastic containers for up to 2 months. Thaw on the counter until slushy, and stir to recombine.

Pan Bagnat

Summer Vegetable Salad

We honeymooned in France, visiting my French friends in their ancestral village of Collioure, near the French-Spanish border. I ate my first *pan bagnat* along the shores of the Mediterranean Sea. This meal, bursting with the flavors of the southern coast of France, shouts with cheers of summer.

Hard-cook the eggs first (or ahead of time), then prep the vegetables. You can assemble the sandwiches and salad while the eggs cool. Peel and slice them last. If you've got extra vegetables after prepping the sandwiches, toss them into the salad.

Pan Bagnat

SERVES 4

DAIRY-FREE

There's great debate about what exactly goes into a *pan bagnat*. On Facebook I have access to my adoptive French "family," their friends, my high-school French teacher, and friends I made while living abroad. This version is our consensus—and a delicious one it is.

> 4 large eggs
> Fine sea salt
> 2 French baguettes
> 2 (6.5-ounce) cans olive oil–packed tuna, drained, oil reserved
> Freshly ground black pepper
> 2 medium tomatoes, sliced
> 1 green bell pepper, cored and thinly sliced
> ½ small red onion, thinly sliced
> 2 cups baby greens

1. Place the eggs in a large saucepan and cover with water. Add a pinch of salt and bring to a boil. Cover and turn off the heat. Allow the eggs to sit in the hot water for 12 minutes. Plunge them immediately into a bowl of ice water.

2. Cut each baguette in half crosswise and then split each half horizontally, leaving a small hinge. Divide the tuna among the baguettes, breaking up any large chunks. Drizzle with some of the reserved oil. Season to taste with salt and pepper. Layer on the tomatoes, bell pepper, onion, and greens.

3. Peel the eggs and slice them thinly. Place atop the greens. Drizzle additional oil on the top insides of the baguettes. Close the sandwiches and serve.

25

There has been more than one occasion when I've unnecessarily planned a huge, elaborate meal that took hours to pull off. I'm not talking holiday feasts, but just a regular weeknight dinner when my people would have been more than happy to eat spaghetti and meatballs, not three different courses. Remember that simple meals can be just as delicious as elaborate ones, and they take less time.

Summer Vegetable Salad

SERVES 4

`MEATLESS` `DAIRY-FREE` `GLUTEN-FREE` `MAKE-AHEAD`

If you have a summer garden or get a weekly CSA delivery, you'll appreciate this salad, free of greens but packed with flavor and crunch.

1 large cucumber, peeled and chopped
1 small zucchini, sliced
1 red bell pepper, cored and cut into 1-inch chunks
10 grape tomatoes, halved
8 pitted black olives
2 scallions, chopped
2 tablespoons chopped fresh basil
¼ cup red wine vinegar
1 teaspoon minced garlic
1 teaspoon Dijon mustard
Fine sea salt and freshly ground black pepper
¼ cup olive oil

1. In a large salad bowl, combine the cucumber, zucchini, bell pepper, tomatoes, olives, scallions, and basil.

2. In a small jar or bowl, combine the vinegar, garlic, mustard, and salt and pepper to taste. Cap the jar and shake, or whisk to combine. Add the oil and shake or whisk again.

3. Pour the dressing over the salad mixture and toss to coat.

MAKE IT AHEAD: Make the dressing and the salad up to 3 days in advance and store in separate covered containers in the refrigerator. Or, if you prefer, you can store the salad already dressed; the vegetables will just be softer at serving time.

A patty melt and
a tomato salad:
Sounds like a vin-
tage meal from the
1950s, doesn't it?
Yet the flavors and
textures of this meal
never go out of style.
Sauerkraut is a fa-
vorite food from my
childhood. Despite
my children's pa-
ternal DNA, I have
successfully passed
on the love of 'kraut
to them. This meal
makes it shine.

Reuben-Style Patty Melts

SERVES 4

Typically a Reuben sandwich is a grilled sandwich on rye bread,
featuring corned beef, Swiss cheese, Russian dressing, and sauerkraut. I don't like corned beef, so I did a patty melt mash-up with
the other Reuben players. Superyum, as they say. For a quicker
dish, skip the rye bread and griddling step and serve this fabulous
combo on hamburger buns.

1 pound ground beef
Fine sea salt and freshly ground black pepper
½ cup mayonnaise
2 tablespoons ketchup
Zest of 1 lemon
1 tablespoon chopped dill pickles
½ teaspoon paprika
Butter, for the bread
8 slices rye bread
4 slices Swiss cheese
1 cup sauerkraut, drained

1. Divide the ground beef into four portions and form each into an
oblong patty, similar in size and shape to the rye bread. Season to
taste with salt and pepper.

2. Heat a large nonstick skillet over medium-high heat and cook the
burgers until no pink remains, about 10 minutes.

3. Meanwhile, in a small bowl, combine the mayonnaise, ketchup,
lemon zest, dill pickles, and paprika. Season to taste with salt and
pepper. Stir well.

4. Heat a stovetop griddle over medium-high heat. Butter one side
of each piece of bread. Build each sandwich with one slice of bread
(butter side out), a slathering of sauce, a cooked patty, one slice of
Swiss cheese, and ¼ cup sauerkraut. Top with the remaining bread
slice, butter side out. Cook on the hot griddle until the bread is
crisp and toasty and the cheese is melted. Serve with extra sauce
for dipping.

While peeling and chopping garlic doesn't take that long, preminced garlic still saves precious minutes during meal prep. A jar keeps for quite some time in the fridge, so you don't need to worry about garlic heads sprouting or getting either wimpy or bitter in the pantry.

Basil-Tomato Salad

SERVES 4

MEATLESS **DAIRY-FREE** **GLUTEN-FREE**

My dad grew an abundance of tomatoes in the backyard when I was a kid. I didn't appreciate that fact until I was an adult with a backyard garden of my own. A homegrown tomato is superb! Summer salads can be as simple—and stupendous—as slicing tomatoes and drizzling them with a flavorful dressing. Use fresh-from-the-garden tomatoes and basil if you can swing it. The flavors will just explode with summer.

4 medium tomatoes, thickly sliced
⅓ cup olive oil
Juice of 1 lemon
6 large basil leaves
1 teaspoon minced garlic
Fine sea salt and freshly ground black pepper

1. Place the tomato slices in overlapping circles on a serving plate.

2. Combine the olive oil, lemon juice, basil, and garlic in a blender and blend until very smooth. Drizzle the tomatoes with the vinaigrette. Season to taste with salt and pepper.

Speedy Soups and Stews

Soups have a reputation for needing long simmering, so folks tend to turn to processed and overly salted canned soups. Stop it, already. You can easily make a homemade soup in a very short time.

I almost always pair soup with a tasty homemade bread. To my way of thinking, the enticement of biscuits, savory muffins, or garlic bread wins over any reluctant soup eater pretty easily. (Kids and some husbands, I'm looking at you.) That being said, the stuffed peppers on page 88 will go great with some of the other soups in the chapter as well. Sandwiches and salads are also great pairings for soup.

Soup Night is one of my favorite nights of the week. Not only is it a quick and easy meal to prepare, but it is also one that signals comfort and relaxation. Practically every generation that's gone before us has enjoyed a bite of bread and some soup for the evening meal. Why should we be any different?

This meal is the
perfect stick-to-
your-ribs comfort
food. Serve the
stuffed peppers as
an unexpected and
wonderful appetizer,
and be sure to pass
the bread basket
alongside the soup.

Minute Minestrone with Chicken

MAKES ABOUT 8 CUPS

DAIRY-FREE **MAKE-AHEAD** **FREEZER-FRIENDLY**

Minestrone is my husband's favorite soup. Our traditional version of
the Italian stew-soup cooks long on the stovetop, but this shortcut
rendition comes together in a flash.

2 tablespoons olive oil
½ medium onion, chopped (about 1 cup)
4 ounces white mushrooms, sliced (about 1 cup)
2 celery ribs, chopped
2 medium carrots, peeled and sliced
1 medium zucchini, chopped
½ medium green bell pepper, cored and chopped (about ½ cup)
1 tablespoon minced garlic
4 cups chicken broth
4 cups water
1 (15-ounce) can tomato sauce
1 (15-ounce) can cannellini beans, drained
½ cup quick-cooking barley
8 ounces boneless, skinless chicken breast, cut into bite-size pieces
2 teaspoons dried basil
½ teaspoon dried marjoram
⅛ teaspoon red pepper flakes
Fine sea salt and freshly ground black pepper
8 ounces small pasta, like shells or elbows

1. In a large stockpot, heat the oil over medium-high heat until
shimmering. Add the onion and mushrooms and cook until the
onion starts to turn translucent, about 5 minutes.

2. Add the celery, carrots, zucchini, bell pepper, and garlic. Cook
until the onion is translucent and the mushrooms have lost their
liquid, about 3 minutes.

3. Add the broth, water, tomato sauce, beans, barley, chicken, basil,
marjoram, pepper flakes, and salt and pepper to taste. Bring to a
low boil. (This may take up to 10 minutes.)

4. Add the pasta and cook until the chicken is cooked through and
the pasta is tender, another 8 minutes or so. Adjust the seasonings
and serve.

MAKE IT AHEAD: The soup can be cooled and stored in a covered container
in the fridge for up to 4 days or in the freezer for up to 2 months. Thaw in the
refrigerator overnight before reheating.

Sausage-Stuffed Peppers

SERES 4

`GLUTEN-FREE` `MAKE-AHEAD`

My husband, Bryan, can eat the whole plate of these spicy stuffed peppers himself! They are that good. If you've got voracious eaters, consider taking a few more minutes to make a double batch. I use spicy yellow hot peppers, but you can use the thinner and milder banana peppers if you like. Likewise, feel free to use mild sausage if you prefer less heat.

4 large yellow hot or banana peppers, split lengthwise and cored
8 ounces bulk spicy Italian sausage
½ cup shredded mozzarella cheese
1 teaspoon olive oil
1 teaspoon minced garlic
1 cup tomato sauce
1 teaspoon dried Italian herb blend

1. Preheat the oven to 400°F. Grease a small rimmed baking sheet.

2. Place the peppers on the baking sheet, cut sides up.

3. Divide the sausage into eight equal portions. Place one portion in each pepper half. Top each with 1 tablespoon mozzarella cheese, patting it down to make it adhere.

4. Bake the peppers until the meat is cooked, the cheese is melted and gooey, and the peppers start to brown slightly and wrinkle, about 20 minutes.

5. Meanwhile, in a small saucepan, heat the oil over medium-high heat until shimmering. Add the garlic and cook for 1 minute. Add the tomato sauce and Italian herbs, and simmer until the peppers are done. Serve the peppers with the sauce on the side.

MAKE IT AHEAD: Prep the peppers through step 3, cover, and store in the fridge for up to 1 day.

Quickest Chili
in the West

Jalapeño Cheese
Toasts

A hearty chili supper
always brings smiles
at our house. It's fill-
ing and full of flavor.
Best of all, my home-
made version comes
together easily and
economically—and
without the whop-
ping sodium count
of the canned vari-
ety. While the chili
simmers, assemble
the jalapeño toasts.

Quickest Chili in the West

MAKES ABOUT 12 CUPS

`GLUTEN-FREE` `MAKE-AHEAD` `FREEZER-FRIENDLY`

This chili is super easy to pull together. Simply gather all the ingredients, mix it up, and simmer for about 20 minutes before serving.
(Bonus: It can also cook all day on low in the slow cooker if your
30 minutes is only available in the morning.)

1 pound ground beef or turkey
1 (28-ounce) can crushed tomatoes
1 (28-ounce) can pinto beans, drained
2 (15-ounce) cans black beans, drained
1 (15-ounce) can hominy, rinsed and drained
1 to 2 cups water
¼ cup chili powder
1 tablespoon onion flakes
1 tablespoon dried oregano
1 tablespoon dried parsley
1 tablespoon garlic powder
Fine sea salt and freshly ground black pepper

TOPPINGS
Salsa of your choice
Grated cheese of your choice
Sour cream

1. In a large stockpot, brown the ground beef over high heat, about
7 minutes.

2. Add the crushed tomatoes, beans, and hominy. Thin with water
to the consistency you like. Stir in the chili powder, onion flakes,
oregano, parsley, garlic powder, and salt and pepper to taste.
Simmer for 20 minutes over medium-low heat.

3. Serve with salsa, cheese, and sour cream for topping.

MAKE IT AHEAD: The chili can be cooled and stored in a covered container in the
fridge for up to 4 days or in the freezer for up to 2 months. Thaw in the refrigerator overnight before reheating.

#28

VIVA LA SALSA!

Keep jarred salsa on hand at all times to add a quick zip of flavor to chili, soup, guacamole, egg dishes, and so on. Fresh salsa is easy to make, but having a jar in reserve can really save the day—or the dinner.

Jalapeño Cheese Toasts

MAKES 8 TOASTS

`MEATLESS` `MAKE-AHEAD`

This is garlic bread turned on its head. Delicious and spicy, these toasts are a perfect accompaniment to soup or salad. Feel free to reduce the amount of jalapeño for less heat.

4 ciabatta sandwich rolls, split horizontally
6 tablespoons (¾ stick) butter, softened
2 tablespoons chopped seeded jalapeño
1 teaspoon minced garlic
1 cup shredded cheddar cheese
1 cup shredded Monterey Jack cheese

1. Preheat the broiler.

2. Lay out the roll halves in a single layer on a large rimmed baking sheet.

3. In a small bowl, combine the butter, jalapeño, garlic, and both cheeses.

4. Spread the mixture over the roll halves. Broil until hot and bubbly, 3 to 5 minutes.

MAKE IT AHEAD: The spicy butter-cheese mixture can be stored in a covered container in the refrigerator for up to 3 days or in the freezer for up to 2 months.

MENU

Vegetable
Alphabet Soup

Cheesy Scallion
Biscuits

Soup and bread is a classic quick fix. While many folks purchase canned soups and packaged biscuits for such a meal, these easy from-scratch recipes elevate the supper of the common man to something special. This simple soup pleases kids of all ages, and cheesy biscuits make a perfect accompaniment.

Vegetable Alphabet Soup

MAKES ABOUT 10 CUPS

MEATLESS   **DAIRY-FREE**   **MAKE-AHEAD**   **FREEZER-FRIENDLY**

I grew up eating canned soups. One of my favorites was the vegetable variety with the ABCs floating in it. This is a healthier, happier recreation of that childhood favorite. You can use 4 cups of frozen mixed vegetables instead of the corn, peas, green beans, and carrots. Either way, there's no need to thaw the veggies before adding them to the pot.

2 tablespoons olive oil
½ medium onion, chopped (about 1 cup)
1 teaspoon minced garlic
6 to 8 cups vegetable broth, depending on how thin or thick you like your soup
1 cup frozen corn kernels
1 cup frozen peas
1 cup frozen cut green beans
1 large carrot, peeled and diced (about 1 cup)
1 cup tomato sauce
1 teaspoon dried dill
½ teaspoon paprika
Pinch of cayenne pepper
Fine sea salt and freshly ground black pepper
1 cup alphabet pasta

1. In a large stockpot, heat the oil over high heat until shimmering. Add the onion and garlic and sauté until the onion starts to turn translucent, 3 to 5 minutes. Watch for scorching.

2. Add the broth, scraping up any browned bits.

3. Add the corn, peas, green beans, carrot, tomato sauce, dill, paprika, cayenne, and salt and black pepper to taste. Bring to a low boil. (This may take up to 10 minutes.)

4. Add the pasta and cook until tender, another 7 minutes or so. Adjust the seasonings and serve.

MAKE IT AHEAD: The soup can be cooled and stored in a covered container in the fridge for up to 4 days or in the freezer for up to 2 months. Thaw in the refrigerator overnight before reheating.

29

Label containers of oats, rice, and flour. You don't have time to guess whether that's bread flour or pastry flour. Labels take out the guesswork and save you time, and possibly the expense of mistakes.

Cheesy Scallion Biscuits

MAKES 20 TO 22 SMALL BISCUITS

MEATLESS **MAKE-AHEAD** **FREEZER-FRIENDLY**

My kids love these! They remind them of some they've enjoyed at a popular seafood restaurant. Only we don't have to wait for a table, and I know exactly what ingredients we're eating. These drop biscuits come together quickly, particularly if you use a food processor to whiz the dough together. If you can't find whole-wheat pastry flour, feel free to use all unbleached all-purpose flour.

1 cup unbleached all-purpose flour
1 cup whole-wheat pastry flour
½ cup shredded cheddar cheese
2 tablespoons chopped scallions
1 tablespoon baking powder
½ teaspoon salt
¼ teaspoon paprika
4 tablespoons (½ stick) cold butter, cut into cubes
1 cup buttermilk

1. Preheat the oven to 450°F. Line a baking sheet with parchment paper or a silicone baking mat.

2. In a food processor fitted with a metal blade, combine both flours, the cheese, scallions, baking powder, salt, and paprika. Pulse a few times.

3. Add the butter cubes. Pulse until coarse crumbs are formed. Pour the mixture into a bowl. Add the buttermilk and stir until a sticky batter forms.

4. Using a quick-release scoop, scoop up about 2 tablespoons of dough and place the biscuits on the prepared baking sheet. Bake until golden brown, 10 to 12 minutes.

MAKE IT AHEAD: The baked and cooled biscuits can be stored in an airtight container at room temperature for up to 2 days or in the freezer for up to 2 months.

Living near the
coast, our family
loves to head to the
local fish restaurant
for supper. It's a little
pricey, and there's
almost always a wait.
Making homemade
chowder and cheese
toasts is a quick and
delicious way to get
our fix without the
wait—or the high
price.

Shrimp Chowder

MAKES ABOUT 10 CUPS

`MAKE-AHEAD` `FREEZER-FRIENDLY`

I always keep a few bags of frozen shrimp on hand to toss into
soups and salads. They make the meal feel like a million bucks
without much effort at all. Stock up when you see a sale so you
don't pay the premium price.

All my kids love this chowder, even the child who otherwise scorns
seafood. You can also make it with fish instead of shrimp. I've found
that frozen cod chunks cost much less than whole pieces of fish.

2 tablespoons olive oil
½ medium onion, chopped (about 1 cup)
2 medium russet potatoes, peeled and chopped (about 1½ cups)
2 celery ribs, chopped (about ½ cup)
1 large carrot, peeled and chopped (about ¾ cup)
½ medium red bell pepper, cored and chopped (about ½ cup)
1 tablespoon Cajun Spice Blend (page 162)
6 cups chicken broth
1 cup milk
2 tablespoons butter, softened
¼ cup unbleached all-purpose flour
12 ounces peeled medium shrimp, thawed if frozen
Fine sea salt and freshly ground pepper

1. In a large stockpot, heat the oil over high heat until shimmering.
Add the onion and cook until the onion starts to turn translucent,
3 to 5 minutes. Watch for scorching.

2. Add the potatoes, celery, carrot, bell pepper, and spice blend and
lower the heat to low. Cook, stirring, to caramelize the vegetables a
bit, about 5 minutes.

3. Add the broth, scraping up any browned bits. Stir in the milk.
Bring to a low boil.

4. Meanwhile, in a small bowl, combine the butter and flour into a
smooth paste. Add this by small spoonfuls to the stockpot, whisking after each addition to help thicken the soup. Simmer until the
soup has thickened slightly.

5. Add the shrimp and cook until cooked through, about 10 minutes. Adjust the seasonings and serve.

MAKE IT AHEAD: The soup can be made through step 4 and stored in a covered
container in the fridge for up to 4 days or in the freezer for up to 2 months.
Thaw in the refrigerator overnight and reheat before adding the shrimp.

30

BAG THE BAGUETTE

When making bruschetta or other baguette-based appetizers, search your grocery's baked goods section for a presliced baguette. You can often find cubed bread as well, which works great for egg bakes and bread pudding, as well as making croutons. These bags are often offered at a discount on the day-old shelf, so you can save some money, too.

Garlicky Brie Toasts

SERVES 4

MEATLESS

French baguettes are brushed with a garlic-infused olive oil and topped with a slice of Brie cheese. A few minutes under the broiler creates a quick and delicious accompaniment for soups and stews.

½ baguette, about 9 inches long
1 tablespoon olive oil
1 teaspoon minced garlic
4 ounces Brie cheese

1. Preheat the broiler.

2. Slice the baguette on the bias into eight 1-inch-thick slices. Place the slices on a baking sheet.

3. In a small bowl, combine the olive oil and garlic. Brush this mixture over the bread slices.

4. Slice the Brie into eight equal portions. Place one portion on each slice of bread.

5. Broil until the cheese bubbles and the bread is toasted, about 5 minutes. Watch carefully to avoid burning. Serve immediately.

Confetti Chili

Pumpkin Biscuits

Fall weather and football games practically beg you to mix up something hot and filling. And what says fall more than a bowl of bubbling stew and something with a little hint of pumpkin? This meal fits the bill on both counts. Please the crowd at your next tailgate party or bonfire supper with this festive fall fare.

Confetti Chili

MAKES ABOUT 10 CUPS

MEATLESS **DAIRY-FREE** **GLUTEN-FREE** **MAKE-AHEAD** **FREEZER-FRIENDLY**

Wow your family with this quick-fix chili loaded with vegetables and bright colors. My kiddos gobble this down, even the picky people. If you have salsa verde on hand, it offers great flavor. If not, tomato sauce works just as well. Serve with any traditional chili toppings of your choice.

    1 tablespoon vegetable oil
    1 medium onion, chopped
    1 green bell pepper, cored and chopped
    1 (15-ounce) can pinto beans, drained
    1 (15-ounce) can black beans, drained
    1 (15-ounce) can kidney beans, drained
    1 (15.5-ounce) hominy, rinsed and drained
    1 (14.5-ounce) can petite diced tomatoes, with their juices
    1 cup salsa verde or tomato sauce
    2 tablespoons chili powder
    1 teaspoon ground cumin

1. In a large stockpot, heat the oil over high heat until shimmering. Add the onion and bell pepper and cook, stirring, until the onion turns translucent and the peppers are tender, about 5 minutes. Watch carefully to prevent scorching.

2. Add the beans, hominy, tomatoes, salsa verde, chili powder, and cumin. Bring to a low boil, cover, and simmer for 15 minutes.

MAKE IT AHEAD: The chili can be cooled and stored in a covered container in the fridge for up to 4 days or in the freezer for up to 2 months. Thaw in the refrigerator before reheating.

31

QUICK MIX

I love having dry biscuit, pancake, and waffle mixes on hand. It saves me precious minutes at baking time. I make several batches at once while I have all the dry ingredients out and store the mixes in labeled quart jars. Assembly-line mix making doesn't take me as long as it would to make five batches on five different days.

Pumpkin Biscuits

MAKES 12 BISCUITS

MEATLESS **MAKE-AHEAD** **FREEZER-FRIENDLY**

These drop biscuits are light and fluffy without all the work of traditional biscuits. They are unsweetened, allowing them to meld well with savory foods. I serve them with honey and butter. They remind both FishPapa and me of sopaipillas, a classic Southwestern fried bread that is served as a foil for spicy foods. Use plain canned pumpkin here, not pumpkin pie filling, which has sugar and spices added.

2 cups unbleached all-purpose flour
1 tablespoon baking powder
½ teaspoon fine sea salt
½ teaspoon ground cinnamon
½ teaspoon ground nutmeg
1 cup canned pumpkin puree
1 large egg, beaten
½ cup milk
¼ cup vegetable oil

1. Preheat the oven to 450°F. Line a baking sheet with parchment paper or a silicone baking mat.

2. In a medium-size bowl, whisk together the flour, baking powder, salt, cinnamon, and nutmeg. In a large bowl, whisk together the pumpkin puree, egg, milk, and oil.

3. Pour the dry mixture over the wet mixture. Stir gently until a sticky batter forms.

4. Spoon the batter into 12 mounds on the prepared baking sheet. Bake until golden brown, 10 to 12 minutes.

MAKE IT AHEAD: The baked and cooled biscuits can be stored in an airtight container at room temperature for up to 2 days or in the freezer for up to 2 months.

Stews are hearty and filling fare, perfect for chillier days. This French-inspired meal features the flavors of a long-cooked cassoulet with the ease and speed of a weeknight meal. Start the rice cooker at the beginning of your cooking session so that the rice is ready to serve with the stew and herbed broccoli.

Quick Chicken and Sausage White Bean Stew

SERVES 4 TO 6

`DAIRY-FREE` `GLUTEN-FREE` `MAKE-AHEAD` `FREEZER-FRIENDLY`

Traditional cassoulet is a long-simmering French dish of white beans and varied meats. I've simplified its preparation greatly by relying on chicken and sausage and using canned beans instead of dried. The result is a quick cheater's version that pleases the palate. If you have regular bacon on hand rather than the precooked kind, just cook it in the pan before adding the chicken.

1 tablespoon olive oil
2 mild Italian sausage links
1 pound boneless, skinless chicken breast, cut into bite-size pieces
1 teaspoon dried herbes de Provence
Fine sea salt and freshly ground black pepper
3 slices precooked bacon, chopped
½ medium green bell pepper, cored and chopped
½ medium onion, chopped (about 1 cup)
1 teaspoon minced garlic
½ cup brown ale or chicken broth
2 (15-ounce) cans cannellini beans, drained
Hot cooked rice, for serving

1. In a large nonstick skillet, heat the oil over medium-high heat until shimmering. Add the sausages and cook until brown on all sides and cooked through, about 7 minutes. Remove from the pan and slice the sausages.

2. Season the chicken with the herbes de Provence and salt and pepper to taste. Add to the skillet, and then add the bacon, bell pepper, onion, and garlic. Cook, stirring, until the chicken is cooked through, about 5 minutes.

3. Pour in the ale or broth and stir, scraping up any browned bits.

4. Add the beans and return the sausage to the skillet. Simmer until heated through and the flavors have blended a bit. Serve over hot cooked rice.

MAKE IT AHEAD: The stew can be cooled and stored in a covered container in the fridge for up to 4 days or in the freezer for up to 2 months. Thaw in the refrigerator overnight before reheating.

32

Bulk buying is great
when you go through
a lot of a certain
ingredient. But
sometimes buying
just the right amount
of something, such
as at the meat or deli
counter, will help
you save time as
well. If the sausage is
the exact portion for
your recipe, there's
no need to weigh
or divide it before
you get cooking.
You can still benefit
from bulk pricing
at the counter or in
the bulk bins, but
you don't have to
worry about using a
larger prepackaged
amount.

Herbed Lemon Broccoli

SERVES 4 TO 6

MEATLESS **DAIRY-FREE** **GLUTEN-FREE**

This broccoli dish comes together effortlessly. A friend of ours made
something similar for my children years ago, and they gobbled it
down. Since then, none of them can resist broccoli prepared this way.

6 cups broccoli florets (from about 2 medium heads)
1 cup water
2 tablespoons olive oil
1 tablespoon finely chopped onion
1 teaspoon minced garlic
2 tablespoons fresh lemon juice
1 teaspoon chopped fresh basil or ½ teaspoon dried basil
Pinch of red pepper flakes
Fine sea salt and freshly ground black pepper

1. Place the broccoli and water in a large nonstick skillet. Cover and
cook over medium-high heat for 10 minutes. Drain the broccoli and
return it to the skillet, pushing it to one side.

2. Add the oil, onion, and garlic to the other side of the skillet and
raise the heat to high. Cook, stirring, until the onion starts to turn
translucent and the garlic is fragrant, 2 to 3 minutes. Toss the
broccoli with the garlic and oil in the skillet. The broccoli should be
tender but not too soft.

3. Drizzle the broccoli with the lemon juice. Sprinkle with the basil
and red pepper flakes, season to taste with salt and pepper, and
serve warm.

Old wives' tale or
not, I maintain that
chicken noodle soup
is good for a cold
and for the soul.
Whenever I ask
one of my children
for his or her soup
choice, the answer
is good ol' chicken
noodle. Herbed
toasts, redolent with
garlic, complete the
FishMama Cure.

Simply Chicken Noodle Soup

MAKES ABOUT 10 CUPS

`DAIRY-FREE` `MAKE-AHEAD` `FREEZER-FRIENDLY`

I like using fine egg noodles for this soup because they remind me
of those boxed soup mixes I enjoyed as a kid. The flavor and quality
of this soup, though, are far superior to those of my childhood.

  1 pound boneless, skinless chicken breast, cut into bite-size pieces
  1 teaspoon rubbed sage
  1 teaspoon dried tarragon
  1 teaspoon dried thyme
  Fine sea salt and freshly ground black pepper
  1 tablespoon olive oil
  ⅓ cup sliced leeks
  1 teaspoon minced garlic
  8 cups chicken broth
  1 (6-ounce) package fine egg noodles
  ½ cup frozen peas and carrots, no need to thaw

1. Season the chicken with the sage, tarragon, thyme, and salt and
pepper to taste.

2. In a large stockpot, heat the oil over medium-high heat until
shimmering. Add the chicken, leeks, and garlic to the pot. Cook, stirring, until the chicken is cooked and the leeks are soft, about
5 minutes. Transfer the mixture to a bowl and tent with aluminum
foil to keep warm.

3. Add the chicken broth to the pot, scraping up any browned bits.
Bring to a boil. Return the chicken mixture to the pot, add the noodles and veggies, and cook until the noodles are tender, 4 minutes
or so. Adjust the seasonings and serve.

MAKE IT AHEAD: The soup can be cooled and stored in a covered container
in the fridge for up to 4 days or in the freezer for up to 2 months. Thaw in the
refrigerator overnight before reheating.

33

This may come as a no-brainer to some of you; to others it is a timely reminder. If you go to bed with a clean kitchen, you will wake up to a clean kitchen— barring an invasion of crumb-scattering zombies, of course. Waking up to a clean kitchen starts your morning and the rest of your time in said kitchen on a positive tone. You'll be more likely to fix a quick and healthy breakfast than to drive through a fast-food joint on the way to work.

Easy Herbed Garlic Bread

SERVES 4 TO 6

MEATLESS **DAIRY-FREE**

Garlic bread never lasts long at our house. We have to ration it. I suppose I should just give up and make a double batch. Serving great bread with soup is a good way to encourage reluctant soup eaters to dig in. This bread does the job.

1 baguette, thinly sliced
¼ cup olive oil
1 teaspoon minced garlic
¼ teaspoon dried oregano
¼ teaspoon dried basil

1. Preheat the broiler. Lay out the baguette slices on a large baking sheet.

2. In a small bowl, combine the oil, garlic, oregano, and basil. Brush the bread slices with the oil mixture.

3. Broil until lightly toasted, 3 to 5 minutes. Serve warm.

We often eat a
veggie-centric meal
in order to curb
spending. Preparing
mostly vegetables
also helps me
get dinner on the
table lickety-split.
Soup and bread
night takes a fun,
flavorful twist with
a fresh pea soup
dotted with bacon
and bagels topped
with tomatoes and
cucumbers. There's
plenty of fresh
flavors to enjoy here.

Sweet Pea Soup

MAKES ABOUT 8 CUPS

DAIRY-FREE **GLUTEN-FREE** **MAKE-AHEAD** **FREEZER-FRIENDLY**

Split pea soup is one of my favorites, but it takes a little forethought to make, what with cooking the dried beans and all. This recipe condenses 2 hours in the kitchen to just 30 minutes by using frozen petite peas instead. The result is this super fresh and spring-like soup. It's still full of flavor but with a lighthearted spin.

    4 slices precooked bacon, chopped
    2 tablespoons olive oil (optional)
    ½ medium onion, chopped (about 1 cup)
    1 (1-pound) bag frozen petite peas, no need to thaw
    2 medium Yukon Gold potatoes, peeled and chopped (about 2 cups)
    1 large carrot, peeled and sliced
    4 cups vegetable broth
    ½ teaspoon dried tarragon
    ½ teaspoon dried thyme
    ½ teaspoon dried marjoram
    Fine sea salt and freshly ground black pepper

1. In a large stockpot, heat the bacon over high heat until crisp. Remove from the pan with a slotted spoon and drain on paper towels.

2. If the bacon didn't render much fat, add the oil and heat until shimmering. Add the onion and cook until translucent, about 5 minutes. Watch carefully to prevent scorching.

3. Add the peas, potatoes, carrot, broth, tarragon, thyme, marjoram, and salt and pepper to taste. Bring to a low boil. Reduce the heat and simmer until the vegetables are very tender, 15 to 20 minutes.

4. Remove the pot from the heat. Using an immersion blender, puree the soup until very smooth. Alternatively, you can puree the soup in batches in a food processor or blender, being sure to vent the lid according to the manufacturer's directions. If you prefer a thinner soup, add a little water. Adjust the seasonings, sprinkle with the bacon, and serve.

MAKE IT AHEAD: The soup can be cooled and stored in a covered container in the fridge for up to 4 days or in the freezer for up to 2 months. Thaw in the refrigerator overnight before reheating.

34

I buy American Neufchâtel cheese, a lighter cream cheese. It has a lower fat content and higher moisture content than regular cream cheese, making it easily spreadable and ready to use for recipes without waiting for it to soften.

Tomato- and Cucumber-Topped Bagels

SERVES 4 TO 8

MEATLESS **MAKE-AHEAD**

Bagels mean "fun food" at our house. Because of their expense—and my children's ability to inhale a dozen at one sitting—I don't buy them often, so they make any meal a special occasion when I do. I prepare a custom schmear that takes this fun food over the top. In this case, the bagels are spread with a seasoned cream cheese and topped with fresh basil, cucumbers, and tomatoes. Delish! The result is a delightful open-face sandwich to enjoy along with the soup.

    4 bagels, split
    8 ounces cream cheese, softened
    2 scallions, chopped
    ⅛ teaspoon freshly ground black pepper
    ¼ cup thinly sliced fresh basil leaves
    1 medium cucumber, peeled and thinly sliced
    2 medium tomatoes, sliced

1. Lightly toast the bagels in the toaster or under the broiler.

2. In a small bowl, combine the cream cheese, scallions, and pepper. Mix well.

3. Spread a thin layer of the cream cheese mixture on each bagel half. Sprinkle the basil over the cream cheese. Layer with the cucumbers, and then the tomatoes. Serve immediately.

MAKE IT AHEAD: The cream cheese mixture can be stored in a covered container in the refrigerator for up to 4 days.

MENU

Loaded Potato Soup

Garlic-Herb Mini Breads

I've been making some rendition of this meal since we were newlyweds. It was something of a gamble, since Bryan told me early on that he didn't like creamy soups. Well, he sure likes this one, as do the kids. Loading up the soup with bacon and cheese makes it all the more fun. It's easy to stretch, making it a quick meal to serve a crowd. Please, pass the bread basket.

Loaded Potato Soup

MAKES ABOUT 8 CUPS

`MEATLESS` `GLUTEN-FREE` `MAKE-AHEAD`

This soup features all the flavors of a loaded baked potato: sour cream, scallions, cheese, and bacon, as well as all the comforts of a soup. It's practically perfection in a bowl. If you're feeding a crowd, it's easy to make a double batch.

1 tablespoon olive oil
½ medium onion, chopped (about 1 cup)
1 teaspoon minced garlic
5 large russet potatoes, peeled and chopped (about 6 cups)
4 cups chicken broth
1 cup half-and-half
1 teaspoon kosher salt
¼ teaspoon freshly ground black pepper
¼ teaspoon dried parsley

TOPPINGS
Shredded cheese of your choice
Sour cream
Sliced scallions or fresh chives
Crumbled cooked bacon

1. In a large stockpot, heat the oil over high heat until shimmering. Add the onion and garlic and sauté until the onion starts to turn translucent, 3 to 5 minutes. Watch for scorching.

2. Add the potatoes and broth and bring to a low boil. Reduce the heat and simmer until the potatoes are very tender, about 15 minutes.

3. With a potato masher, mash the potatoes in the pot, leaving some chunks. Stir in the half-and-half, salt, pepper, and parsley. Simmer until thickened, 5 to 10 minutes. Serve with the toppings in separate bowls for passing at the table.

MAKE IT AHEAD: The soup can be cooled and stored in a covered container in the fridge for up to 4 days.

You can easily and
quickly soften butter
in the microwave.
Run the machine for
20 seconds at a time
at 10 percent power
until you have the
texture you prefer.
You can do the same
thing with cream
cheese.

Garlic-Herb Mini Breads

MAKES 12 MUFFINS

MEATLESS | **MAKE-AHEAD** | **FREEZER-FRIENDLY**

Though baked in a muffin pan, these are more like a biscuit-type
bread. They bake quickly in muffin form, allowing for fresh bread on
a quick-fix night. Serve them slathered with plenty of butter.

1 cup milk
½ cup vegetable oil
2 large eggs
2 cups unbleached all-purpose flour
1 teaspoon sugar
1 teaspoon baking powder
1 teaspoon baking soda
1 teaspoon fine sea salt
1 teaspoon garlic powder
1 teaspoon dried Italian herb blend

1. Preheat the oven to 400°F. Line a 12-cup muffin pan with paper
liners.

2. In a large bowl, whisk together the milk, oil, and eggs. Add the
flour, sugar, baking powder, baking soda, salt, garlic powder, and Italian herbs. Fold gently to combine.

3. Divide the batter among the 12 paper cups. Bake until the mini
breads are golden and a tester inserted in the center of one comes
out clean, 15 to 20 minutes.

MAKE IT AHEAD: The cooled mini breads can be stored in an airtight container
at room temperature for up to 2 days or in the freezer for up to 2 months.

Swift Salads

I have always been a salad girl. Of anything to eat in the world, I would choose a salad. A bed of greens, slices of veg, chunks of cheese, and hunks of protein? I'm all over that.

These main-dish salads range all over the globe, taking their inspiration from China, India, the Middle East, Europe, Latin America, and the good ol' USA. I love them all.

Chicken,
Avocado, and
Orange Salad

Mangolada
Smoothies

I try to eat health-
fully. Some days are
better than others.
When I have the
fixings for this salad
and smoothie combo,
well, just call me
Mrs. Healthy Super-
woman. Bright, fresh,
and rich flavors are
all at play here.

Chicken, Avocado, and Orange Salad

SERVES 4

DAIRY-FREE GLUTEN-FREE MAKE-AHEAD

I love this flavor combination of spicy chicken, buttery avocado, and tart juicy orange, all punctuated with the crunch of nuts and radish. The flavors play so well together and offer a clean, nutritious meal-time option that is filling but not heavy.

DRESSING
2 tablespoons cider vinegar
1 teaspoon minced garlic
Fine sea salt and freshly ground black pepper
¼ cup olive oil

1 teaspoon paprika
¼ teaspoon ground ginger
¼ teaspoon dried dill
¼ teaspoon garlic powder
¼ teaspoon onion powder
¼ teaspoon salt
⅛ teaspoon freshly ground black pepper
⅛ teaspoon cayenne pepper
1 pound boneless, skinless chicken breast, cut into bite-size pieces
1 tablespoon olive oil
1 (6-ounce) bag chopped romaine lettuce
2 oranges, peel and pith removed, sliced into rounds
2 avocados, pitted, peeled, and sliced
½ cup roasted unsalted cashews
4 watermelon radishes, sliced
2 scallions, chopped

1. In a small jar or bowl, combine the vinegar, garlic, and salt and pepper to taste. Cap the jar and shake, or whisk to combine. Add the olive oil and shake or whisk again.

2. In a small bowl, combine the paprika, ginger, dill, garlic powder, onion powder, salt, black pepper, and cayenne. Sprinkle this mixture generously over the chicken pieces.

3. In a large nonstick skillet, heat the oil over medium-high heat until shimmering. Add the chicken and cook, stirring occasionally, until the chicken is cooked through and lightly browned, about 10 minutes. Remove from the heat.

4. Place the romaine in a large salad bowl and toss with enough of the dressing to coat the lettuce. Divide the salad among four dinner plates. Divide the orange rounds, avocado slices, cashews, radishes, and scallions among the plates.

5. Distribute the chicken evenly among the salads. Serve with additional dressing on the side.

MAKE IT AHEAD: The chicken and dressing can be stored in separate covered containers in the refrigerator for up to 4 days. The chicken is just as good cold on the salad as it is hot, but you can warm it quickly in the microwave if you'd like.

Mangolada Smoothies

MAKES ABOUT 4 CUPS

MEATLESS DAIRY-FREE GLUTEN-FREE MAKE-AHEAD FREEZER-FRIENDLY

I'm a huge fan of coconut and pineapple. This smoothie takes those piña colada flavors and combines them with mango for a tropical, fruity, frosty treat that's good for you!

- 2 cups frozen mango chunks
- 1 (8-ounce) can pineapple chunks, with their juices
- 1 (14-ounce) can light coconut milk

Combine the mango, pineapple, and coconut milk in the pitcher of a blender. Blend until smooth. Serve immediately.

MAKE IT AHEAD: Freeze individual smoothies in freezer-proof plastic containers for up to 2 months. Thaw on the counter until slushy, and stir to recombine.

MENU

Asian Steak
Salad

Vegetable
Wonton Soup

Soup and salad are
perfect meal part-
ners. They offer a
variety of textures,
flavors, and tem-
peratures so that
you never get bored.
Here the classic duo
gets an Asian spin,
and the salad takes
center stage with the
soup acting as the
side.

Asian Steak Salad

SERVES 4

DAIRY-FREE **GLUTEN-FREE** **MAKE-AHEAD**

I love the flavors of Chinese take-out; here I've adapted them for a refreshing but filling steak salad.

1 teaspoon garlic powder
½ teaspoon onion powder
½ teaspoon Chinese five-spice powder
1 pound top sirloin steak
2 tablespoons fresh lime juice
1 tablespoon soy sauce
1 tablespoon toasted sesame oil
1 tablespoon sriracha sauce
1 teaspoon chopped fresh ginger
¼ cup vegetable oil
6 ounces baby spinach
1 medium carrot, peeled and shaved into strips
½ medium cucumber, peeled and sliced
2 scallions, chopped
¼ cup chopped fresh cilantro

1. Preheat an outdoor grill for a medium-hot fire or the oven broiler.

2. In a small bowl, combine the garlic powder, onion powder, and Chinese five-spice powder. Season the steak generously with the mixture.

3. Cook the steak on the grill over direct heat or under the broiler, turning once, until it reaches your preferred doneness (an internal temperature of 145°F for medium-rare or up to 170°F for well-done), 10 to 15 minutes. Let the steak rest, tented with aluminum foil, while you make the dressing.

4. In a small jar or bowl, combine the lime juice, soy sauce, sesame oil, sriracha, and ginger. Cap the jar and shake, or whisk to combine. Add the vegetable oil and shake or whisk again.

5. Place the spinach in a large salad bowl and toss with enough of the dressing to coat the leaves. Divide the spinach among dinner plates. Divide the carrot, cucumber, scallions, and cilantro among the plates.

6. Distribute the steak evenly among the salads. Serve with additional dressing on the side.

MAKE IT AHEAD: The steak and dressing can be stored in separate covered containers in the refrigerator for up to 4 days. The steak is great served cold on the salad (and reheating the steak may overcook it).

36

Meaty sauces can develop rich flavor with slow cooking. However, a bit of soy sauce or beef broth added to the sauce mimics that richer flavor and allows you a shorter cooking time.

Vegetable Wonton Soup

SERVES 4

MEATLESS **DAIRY-FREE**

This Chinese-inspired soup is delightful, a perfect antidote for the blues. Frozen wontons make the process easy, but the soup will still be fresh and tasty, thanks to the abundance of vegetables included.

1 tablespoon vegetable oil
6 ounces white mushrooms, sliced (about 1½ cups)
2 medium carrots, peeled and sliced (about 1 cup)
1 teaspoon minced garlic
4 cups vegetable broth
1 tablespoon soy sauce
1 (12-ounce) package frozen vegetable wontons, no need to thaw
3 cups shredded napa cabbage
1 cup snow peas
2 scallions, chopped
Chopped fresh cilantro, for garnish (optional)

1. In a large stockpot, heat the oil over high heat until shimmering. Add the mushrooms, carrots, and garlic and cook until the mushrooms lose their liquid and start to brown.

2. Stir in the vegetable broth and soy sauce, scraping up any browned bits. Bring the soup to a low boil.

3. Add the wontons, cabbage, snow peas, and scallions and simmer until the wontons are heated through, about 12 minutes. Garnish with the cilantro, if you like.

Rainbow Ravioli Salad

Garlic-Basil Asparagus

Real men do eat salad, particularly when it's full of cheesy ravioli and abundant textures and flavors. This meatless meal is a surprise—no one will feel like there's something missing. Beef it up (so to speak) by adding some grilled chicken or chopped salami. If you can't find mini ravioli or prefer to go dairy-free, this salad is delicious made with tri-color rotini.

Rainbow Ravioli Salad

SERVES 4

MEATLESS **MAKE-AHEAD**

FishPapa, who claims not to care for certain ingredients in this salad, gobbles it down. His declaration: "Fantastic!" The mix of colors and flavors is *that* good. It's perfect hot-weather good cheap eats.

1 pound mini cheese ravioli
1 (12-ounce) jar marinated artichoke hearts, drained
4 ounces white mushrooms, sliced (about 1 cup)
1 cup snow peas
½ red bell pepper, cored and cut into matchsticks
2 Roma tomatoes, chopped
½ cup sliced black olives
½ small red onion, chopped (about ⅓ cup)
¼ cup chopped fresh basil or 1 generous tablespoon dried basil
¼ cup white wine vinegar
1 teaspoon minced garlic
Fine sea salt and freshly ground black pepper
¼ cup olive oil

1. Bring a large pot of salted water to a boil over high heat. Cook the ravioli according to the package directions just until al dente. Drain, rinse with cool water, and set aside to cool.

2. In a large bowl, combine the artichoke hearts, mushrooms, snow peas, bell pepper, tomatoes, olives, onion, and basil.

3. In a small jar or bowl, combine the vinegar, garlic, and salt and pepper to taste. Cap the jar and shake, or whisk to combine. Add the oil and shake or whisk again.

4. Add the ravioli to the bowl with the vegetables. Add the dressing and toss gently to mix. Adjust the seasonings and serve at room temperature.

MAKE IT AHEAD: The salad can be stored in a covered container in the refrigerator for up to 4 days.

37

TONGS ARE TERRIFIC

Spring-loaded tongs are a must-have in my kitchen. I think I have four sets! I use them to sauté meats and vegetables, toss salads, turn items when frying, dip fish in batter, and serve cooked items. Not only do they help you work quickly, but they also reduce messes and help you avoid burns.

Garlic-Basil Asparagus

SERVES 4

MEATLESS | **GLUTEN-FREE**

I used to frequently overcook asparagus until it was a mushy mess (too much multitasking?). Once I started sautéing the asparagus instead of steaming it, that problem disappeared. By tossing the vegetable in oil and spices and cooking it quickly in the skillet, I've landed on a great side dish with little work—and no mushiness.

1 tablespoon olive oil
1 pound asparagus spears, trimmed
1 teaspoon minced garlic
1 tablespoon chopped fresh basil
1 tablespoon shredded Parmesan cheese
1 tablespoon fresh lemon juice

1. In a large nonstick skillet, heat the oil over medium-high heat until shimmering. Add the asparagus and garlic and toss to coat. Cook, using tongs to move the vegetables about the pan, until tender, 5 to 7 minutes.

2. Add the basil, Parmesan, and lemon juice and toss to coat. Serve hot.

Now that pack-
aged greens have
improved in quality,
salads are a great
way to fix a quick
and healthy meal,
whether you're eat-
ing at home or on
the go. This meal of-
fers a variety of dif-
ferent flavors: roast
beef, cheddar, veg-
etables, and rich and
tangy muffins. Prep
the muffins first,
and then assemble
the salad while the
savory breads bake.

Roast Beef and Cheddar Salad

SERVES 4

`GLUTEN-FREE` `MAKE-AHEAD`

I first made this salad with leftover roast beef, but good-quality sliced roast beef from the deli counter works just as well. Fresh basil, tomatoes, and cheddar round out this flavor-packed salad.

2 tablespoons red wine vinegar
1 teaspoon Dijon mustard
Fine sea salt and freshly ground black pepper
¼ cup olive oil
7 ounces romaine lettuce, chopped
8 ounces sliced roast beef, chopped
2 medium tomatoes, chopped
1 cup shredded cheddar cheese
1 cup canned chickpeas, rinsed and drained
4 scallions, chopped
2 tablespoons chopped fresh basil

1. In a small jar or bowl, combine the vinegar, mustard, and salt and pepper to taste. Cap the jar and shake, or whisk to combine. Add the olive oil and shake or whisk again.

2. Place the romaine in a large salad bowl and toss with enough of the dressing to coat the leaves. Divide the salad among four dinner plates. Divide the roast beef, tomatoes, cheddar cheese, chickpeas, scallions, and basil among the plates. Serve with additional dressing on the side.

MAKE IT AHEAD: The dressing can be stored in a covered container in the refrigerator for up to 4 days. The salad can be stored in a separate covered container in the refrigerator for up to 24 hours.

As a bargain shop-
per, I am fairly par-
ticular about where
I spend my grocery
money. I know which
stores offer the best
deals for the things
that I regularly buy.
Some weeks, I've
shopped at up to 10
stores, trying to get
rock-bottom pric-
ing. But when I've
got less time than
money, I don't stress
myself out cherry-
picking the grocery
sales. Instead, I
choose one or two
stores that generally
offer the best value
for the things I buy
and call it a day.

Tomato-Olive Muffins

MAKES 12 MUFFINS

MEATLESS **MAKE-AHEAD** **FREEZER-FRIENDLY**

One day when I was baking these savory muffins, my littlest daughter said, "I smell pizza!" These little breads, stuffed with olives and
sun-dried tomatoes, do evoke those aromas and flavors, making for
a fun way to fill the bread basket.

2½ cups unbleached all-purpose flour
2 teaspoons baking powder
½ teaspoon baking soda
½ teaspoon fine sea salt
¾ cup milk
½ cup olive oil
2 large eggs
2 tablespoons honey
2 tablespoons prepared pesto
½ cup chopped black olives
⅓ cup chopped sun-dried tomatoes, drained if using jarred

1. Preheat the oven to 400°F. Line a 12-cup muffin pan with paper
liners or spray with nonstick cooking spray.

2. In a medium-size bowl, whisk together the flour, baking powder,
baking soda, and salt.

3. In a large bowl, whisk together the milk, olive oil, eggs, honey,
and pesto. Fold the dry ingredients into the wet ingredients. Add the
olives and tomatoes and gently fold them in.

4. Divide the batter among the muffin cups. Bake until golden brown
and a tester inserted in the center of a muffin comes out with a few
crumbs attached, about 15 minutes. Cool on a rack.

MAKE IT AHEAD: Cooled muffins can be stored in an airtight container at room
temperature for up to 3 days or in the freezer for up to 2 months.

When we lived in
Santa Barbara years
ago, we participated
in our church's
fundraising dinners.
Rather than serve
soup or casseroles,
folks contributed
to a salad potluck,
dubbed "Salad's On."
Attending a Salad's
On meant you were
going to contribute
to a great cause at
the same time that
you were going to
have a great meal
of all-you-could-eat
salads and breads.
This dinner is our
version of a Salad's
On. Donations not
required.

Farfalle with Tomatoes, Olives, and Capers

SERVES 6 TO 8

MEATLESS **DAIRY-FREE** **MAKE-AHEAD**

This pasta salad is filling and tangy and totally delightful. My people gobble it down while my back's turned. I have to save a portion for myself beforehand if I want to make sure there's some left for me!

1 pound farfalle pasta
1 (6-ounce) can black olives, drained
½ cup julienned oil-packed sun-dried tomatoes, drained, ¼ cup oil reserved
1 (4-ounce) jar capers in brine, drained
2 tablespoons chopped fresh basil
¼ cup red wine vinegar
1 teaspoon minced garlic
Fine sea salt and freshly ground black pepper

1. Bring a large pot of salted water to a boil over high heat. Cook the farfalle according to the package directions just until al dente. Drain, rinse with cool water, and set aside to cool.

2. In a large bowl, combine the olives, tomatoes, capers, and basil.

3. In a small jar or bowl, combine the vinegar, garlic, and salt and pepper to taste. Cap the jar and shake, or whisk to combine. Add the reserved oil from the tomatoes and shake or whisk again.

4. Add the farfalle to the bowl with the vegetables. Add the dressing and toss gently to mix. Adjust the seasonings and serve at room temperature.

MAKE IT AHEAD: The salad can be stored in a covered container in the refrigerator for up to 4 days.

39

Fiddling with all
the different sized
measuring spoons
and cups takes time.
Learn the basics so
you can use the same
measure for many
ingredients.

¼ cup =
4 tablespoons

1 tablespoon =
3 teaspoons

⅓ cup =
5⅓ tablespoons
(or 5 tablespoons
plus 1 teaspoon)

Green Salad with Pears and Grapes

SERVES 4

MEATLESS **GLUTEN-FREE** **MAKE-AHEAD**

This is the perfect salad for late summer and early fall, when the fruits are at their peak. Fruit, robust cheese, and crunchy seeds make for a delicious salad topping.

2 tablespoons balsamic vinegar
½ teaspoon dried tarragon
½ teaspoon dry mustard
Fine sea salt and freshly ground black pepper
2 tablespoons olive oil
1 (6-ounce) bag baby greens
2 ripe pears, cored and thinly sliced
2 cups red grapes, halved
¼ cup shredded Parmesan cheese
¼ cup sunflower seeds
2 scallions, chopped

1. In a small jar or bowl, combine the vinegar, tarragon, dry mustard, and salt and pepper to taste. Cap the jar and shake, or whisk to combine. Add the olive oil and shake or whisk again.

2. Place the greens in a large salad bowl, and toss with enough of the dressing to coat the leaves. Divide the salad among four dinner plates. Divide the pears, grapes, cheese, sunflower seeds, and scallions among the plates. Serve with additional dressing on the side.

MAKE IT AHEAD: The dressing can be stored in a covered container in the refrigerator for up to 4 days.

MENU

Guac o'Clock
Tostadas

Cheesy
Jalapeños

Tostadas are a favorite food at our house. Any Mexican-style cuisine is, really, but tostadas hold a special place in our hearts. We ate a lot of tostadas while we were digging out of debt years ago. It's such a good cheap eat! This meal, complete with some cheese-stuffed jalapeños to start off the festivities, is a party waiting to happen.

Guac o'Clock Tostadas

SERVES 4 TO 8

MEATLESS **GLUTEN-FREE**

These tostadas are a salad version of the famous seven-layer dip. No need to double-dip since your "chip" is totally covered! Store-bought tostada shells provide a shortcut on busy nights, and the seasoned sour cream and homemade guacamole add plenty of flavor.

> 12 tostada shells
> 4 medium avocados, pitted and peeled
> 1 tablespoon fresh lime or lemon juice
> Fine sea salt and freshly ground black pepper
> Spiced Sour Cream (recipe follows)
> 1 (29-ounce) can favorite refried beans or 1 batch Spicy Pintos (page 33)
> 4 cups shredded lettuce
> 2 cups shredded cheddar cheese
> 3 medium tomatoes, finely chopped
> Chopped fresh cilantro
> Hot sauce, for serving (optional)

1. Heat the tostada shells according to the package directions.

2. In a small bowl, mash the avocados with a fork or potato masher until they are the texture you desire. Stir in the juice and season to taste with salt and pepper.

3. Spread a thin layer of sour cream on each tostada round, followed by a layer of refried beans, a layer of guacamole, some lettuce, cheese, tomatoes, and cilantro. Serve with hot sauce, if desired.

spiced sour cream

MAKES 1 CUP

MEATLESS **GLUTEN-FREE** **MAKE-AHEAD**

> 1 cup sour cream
> 1 teaspoon ground cumin
> 1 teaspoon garlic powder
> ⅛ teaspoon cayenne pepper

In a small bowl, combine all of the ingredients. Stir until smooth.

MAKE IT AHEAD: The sour cream can be stored in a covered container in the refrigerator for up to 3 days.

40

MANY HANDS MAKE LIGHT WORK

If you tend to be the sole cook in your household, then you might be spending more time in the kitchen than you need to. I'm not talking about cooking by yourself as a way to unwind. I'm referring to those nights when cooking seems like a chore. That drags on. And on. And someone, not to name names, is sitting around watching TV or playing a video game when they could be helping you out. Avoid the bitterness that might come from being the chief cook and bottle washer. Get some help! You'll get a chance to talk, the other members of your household can improve their kitchen skills, and you'll save time in the kitchen.

Cheesy Jalapeños

SERVES 4 TO 8

`MEATLESS` `GLUTEN-FREE` `MAKE-AHEAD`

These are a baked, meatless version of jalapeño poppers. If you prefer a less spicy pepper, you can use hot yellow peppers, which are a similar shape but not as fiery.

8 jalapeño or hot yellow peppers, split lengthwise and cored
4 tablespoons cream cheese, softened
½ cup shredded cheddar cheese
1 scallion, chopped
Fine sea salt and freshly ground black pepper
Chopped fresh cilantro, for garnish (optional)

1. Preheat the oven to 400°F. Lay the peppers, cut side up, on a rimmed baking sheet.

2. In a small bowl, mash together the cream cheese, cheddar cheese, and scallion. Season to taste with salt and pepper.

3. Fill each pepper with the cheese mixture.

4. Bake until hot and bubbly, 12 to 15 minutes. Sprinkle cilantro over each, if desired, and serve warm.

MAKE IT AHEAD: The peppers can be made through step 3, covered, and refrigerated for up to 1 day before baking. Leftovers freeze well and can be reheated in the broiler for a few minutes to rewarm.

Bacon and waffles
make a great break-
fast. Here, with a lit-
tle adjustment, they
make a great dinner,
too. All the flavors of
a BLT mingle in the
salad, while savory
cornbread waffles
provide a refresh-
ing and surprising
change to the bread
basket.

Avocado BLT Salad

SERVES 4

`MAKE-AHEAD`

This salad is happiness on a plate, with rich flavors coming from the bacon, avocados, croutons, cheese, and creamy dressing. It's all the great taste of a BLT in a salad instead. If you have a few extra minutes, cook the bacon fresh and make your own croutons from whatever day-old bread you have.

4 slices precooked bacon, chopped
8 ounces salad greens of your choice
2 medium carrots, peeled and shaved into strips
1 medium cucumber, sliced
2 cups halved cherry tomatoes
2 avocados, pitted, peeled, and sliced
2 cups croutons
1 cup cubed cheddar cheese
4 scallions, chopped
Creamy Buttermilk Ranch Dressing (page 129)

1. In a large nonstick skillet, heat the bacon over medium-high heat to crisp it up, 3 to 5 minutes. Drain on paper towels.

2. Divide the greens among four dinner plates. Divide the carrots, cucumber, tomatoes, avocado, bacon, croutons, cheddar, and scallions among the plates. Pass the ranch dressing at the table.

MAKE IT AHEAD: The salad (without the croutons) can be stored in a covered container in the refrigerator for up to 3 hours; add the croutons right before serving. The dressing can be stored in a covered container in the refrigerator for up to 4 days.

41

Don't feel as if you
need to be a short-
order cook at break-
fast time. Providing
a continental break-
fast bar saves you
precious morning
minutes and sup-
plies the needed sus-
tenance for the day.
Save yourself even
more morning time
by laying out the buf-
fet (bowls, spoons,
cereals, breads) the
night before.

Cornbread Waffles

MAKES ABOUT 8 WAFFLES

MAKE-AHEAD **FREEZER-FRIENDLY**

These waffles are a fun alternative to your typical cornbread. They're
rich in corn flavor, and the savory quotient is enhanced with cheddar
and scallions.

1½ cups milk
½ cup vegetable oil
2 large eggs, beaten
2 cups unbleached all-purpose flour
1 cup cornmeal
2 tablespoons baking powder
2 tablespoons sugar
¾ teaspoon salt
½ cup shredded cheddar cheese
2 scallions, chopped
Butter, for serving

1. Preheat the oven to 200°F. Heat a waffle iron according to the
manufacturer's instructions.

2. In a large bowl, combine the milk, olive oil, and eggs. In another
large bowl, combine the flour, cornmeal, baking powder, sugar, salt,
cheese, and scallions. Fold the dry ingredients into the wet ingredients to combine.

3. Cook the waffles in the waffle iron according to the manufacturer's instructions. Place finished waffles in the oven to keep warm
while you cook the remaining waffles. Serve with butter.

MAKE IT AHEAD: Cooled waffles can be stored in a covered container in the
refrigerator for up to 4 days or in the freezer for up to 2 months. Toast lightly
before serving to re-crisp.

EASY DRESSINGS IN A JIFFY

Making homemade salad dressings is unbelievably easy. They taste so much better than store-bought varieties and come together so quickly that there's really no reason to grab a bottle of commercial dressing.

Once you master the vinaigrette and the standard ranch dressing, you'll never need to buy the bottle. And your friends? They'll be begging you to bring the salad to the next get-together.

basic vinaigrette

MAKES ¾ TO 1 CUP

¼ cup vinegar or citrus juice, or a combination
1 teaspoon sweet paprika
½ teaspoon kosher salt
⅛ teaspoon freshly ground black pepper
Mix-ins (choose a few): 1 tablespoon jam;
    ½ teaspoon Dijon, yellow, or dry mustard;
    ½ teaspoon minced garlic; ¼ teaspoon
    favorite dried herbs such as basil, oregano,
    Italian herbs, herbes de Provence, or tarragon
½ to ¾ cup sunflower or olive oil

1. Place the vinegar, paprika, salt, and pepper in a Mason jar. Add the mix-ins of your choice. Cap the jar and shake until well combined.

2. Add the oil and cap again. Shake. Serve immediately, or chill until ready to serve.

creamy buttermilk ranch dressing

MAKES 1 CUP

½ cup buttermilk
½ cup mayonnaise
3 tablespoons chopped fresh parsley or
    1 tablespoon dried parsley
1 teaspoon minced garlic
½ teaspoon onion powder
¼ teaspoon freshly ground black pepper
Pinch of cayenne pepper

In a medium-size bowl, whisk together the buttermilk and mayonnaise until smooth. Stir in the parsley, garlic, onion powder, black pepper, and cayenne.

Pesto and shrimp are
a dynamic duo—and
make for a quick,
tasty supper in this
warm pasta salad.
Pass the bread bas-
ket and end the meal
as the French do:
with a few bites of
fruit and yogurt.

Pesto Shrimp Linguine Salad

SERVES 4

`MAKE-AHEAD`

This pasta salad is delicious warm, at room temperature, or chilled.
Obviously, in 30 minutes you won't have time to chill it, but know
that leftovers will taste awesome. If you've got a few more minutes,
grill the shrimp for an extra burst of flavor.

> 1 pound linguine
> 1 tablespoon olive oil
> 1 pound peeled medium shrimp, thawed if frozen
> Fine sea salt and freshly ground black pepper
> ¾ cup prepared pesto
> 1 large red bell pepper, cored and julienned
> ½ cup julienned sun-dried tomatoes, drained if using jarred
> ½ cup pitted black olives
> Shredded Parmesan cheese, for garnish
> Chopped fresh parsley, for garnish

1. Bring a large pot of salted water to a boil over high heat. Cook
the linguine according to the package directions just until al dente.
Drain and rinse with cool water.

2. In a large nonstick skillet, heat the oil over medium-high heat
until shimmering. Add the shrimp and season to taste with salt and
pepper. Sauté until the shrimp turns pink and is cooked through,
about 10 minutes.

3. Place the pasta in a large salad bowl and toss with the pesto,
distributing it evenly. Season to taste with salt and pepper.

4. Divide the pasta among four dinner plates. Distribute the shrimp,
pepper strips, tomatoes, and olives among the plates. Garnish with
Parmesan and parsley and serve.

MAKE IT AHEAD: The salad can be stored in a covered container in the refrigerator for up to 4 days.

#42

A PLACE FOR EVERYTHING

Designate certain spots in your refrigerator for certain ingredients. For instance, we keep condiments in the door and milk on the top shelf. Since most things have a specific spot, no one spends too much time searching for the ingredient he or she needs.

Spiced Berry Bowl

SERVES 4

MEATLESS **GLUTEN-FREE** **MAKE-AHEAD**

Having grown up eating heavily sweetened yogurt, it was a new thing for me to switch to plain yogurt. Now I can't imagine buying anything besides the plain variety. If this is new to you, liven it up with a bit of honey and some warm spices. Use it to top fruit and you'll be hooked.

1 cup plain Greek yogurt
1 tablespoon honey, or more to taste
½ teaspoon ground cinnamon
¼ teaspoon ground ginger
1 pound strawberries, hulled and sliced
6 ounces blueberries

1. In a small bowl, combine the yogurt, honey, cinnamon, and ginger. Taste and adjust for sweetness.

2. Divide the berries among serving bowls. Dollop the yogurt over the berries, and serve immediately.

MAKE IT AHEAD: The yogurt mixture can be stored in a covered container in the refrigerator for up to 2 days. Stir to recombine.

My friends Devin
and Jessika are
excellent guinea
pigs, er, I mean, taste
testers. They are
always willing to try
out one of my con-
coctions, even when
I'm making a mess
of their kitchen. This
meal was the result
of a great weekend
at their house where
I was allowed free
reign of their cup-
boards and backyard
mint patch. It's the
perfect meal for a
hot day: cool, re-
freshing, and full of
flavor.

Turkey and Ham Cobb Salad

SERVES 4

GLUTEN-FREE **MAKE-AHEAD**

The Cobb salad has always been a favorite of mine. This classic
salad typically contains egg, avocado, tomato, chicken, onion, blue
cheese, and bacon. Here, cold cuts stand in for chicken and leeks
play for their close relative, the onion.

4 large eggs
Fine sea salt
4 slices precooked bacon, chopped
½ large leek, sliced (about 2 cups)
¼ cup red wine vinegar
1 tablespoon Dijon mustard
1 teaspoon FishMama Spice (page 162)
⅓ cup olive oil
6 ounces butter lettuce mix
4 ounces smoked turkey, cubed
4 ounces ham, cubed
2 avocados, pitted, peeled, and chopped
2 medium tomatoes, chopped
½ cup crumbled blue cheese

1. Place the eggs in a large saucepan and cover with water. Add a
pinch of salt and bring to a boil. Cover and turn off the heat. Allow
the eggs to sit in the hot water for 12 minutes. Plunge them immediately into a bowl of ice water. Once cool, peel and chop the eggs.

2. In a large nonstick skillet, cook the bacon and leek over medium-
high heat until both have crisped slightly, 3 to 5 minutes. Drain on
paper towels.

3. In a small jar or bowl, combine the vinegar, mustard, and spice
mix. Cap the jar and shake, or whisk to combine. Add the olive oil
and shake or whisk again.

4. Place the lettuce in a large salad bowl. Toss with enough of the
dressing to coat the leaves. Divide the dressed salad among four
plates.

5. Divide the turkey, ham, avocados, tomatoes, bacon-leek mixture,
chopped eggs, and blue cheese among the plates, placing each ingredient on its own section of the lettuce bed. Serve with additional
dressing on the side.

MAKE IT AHEAD: The hard-cooked eggs, sautéed bacon and leeks, and dressing
can be stored in separate covered containers in the refrigerator for up to 4 days.

43

There's a culinary term—a French one, mind you—that makes a ton of sense. *Mise en place* basically means "set up everything you need to create the dish so that you aren't running around the kitchen looking for things and chopping food on a plastic plate when you should be using a cutting board and a good sharp knife." Well, that's a loose translation. Literally it means "set in place"—that is, set up all the ingredients you need at one time in one space. Don't forget a waste bowl. You'll have everything at your fingertips and save time.

Minty Pomegranate Limeade

MAKES ABOUT 8 CUPS

`MEATLESS` `DAIRY-FREE` `GLUTEN-FREE` `MAKE-AHEAD`

This naturally sweetened limeade gets extra flavor from the mint and pomegranate. Be sure to serve it over lots of ice.

¾ cup honey
2 tablespoons chopped fresh mint
¾ cup boiling water
5 cups cold water
1 cup pomegranate juice
1 cup fresh lime juice

1. Place the honey, mint, and boiling water in a heatproof glass jar. Steep for 5 minutes. Strain into a pitcher.

2. Add the cold water, pomegranate juice, and lime juice and stir. Serve with plenty of ice.

MAKE IT AHEAD: The limeade can be stored in the refrigerator for up to 3 days.

MENU

Buffalo Chicken
Salad

Pesto Bread
Sticks

Get ready for your
next game day with
slightly healthier
adaptations of tradi-
tional football food.
Buffalo wings transi-
tion to salad form,
offering a lighter ver-
sion of some great
flavors, while home-
made bread sticks
filled with pesto
stock the bread bas-
ket. The best part is
that the meal comes
together while the
pregame TV cover-
age rolls out.

Buffalo Chicken Salad

SERVES 4

`GLUTEN-FREE` `MAKE-AHEAD`

This buffalo chicken is delightful atop a bed of lettuce, accented
with celery and tomatoes and topped with the traditional blue
cheese dressing.

1 pound chicken tenders
1 tablespoon Tabasco sauce
2 tablespoons butter, melted and cooled a bit
1½ teaspoons garlic powder
1 teaspoon smoked paprika
½ teaspoon fine sea salt, plus more to taste
⅛ teaspoon cayenne pepper
6 ounces mixed greens, spinach, or romaine lettuce
2 celery ribs, chopped
1 cup grape tomatoes
½ cup buttermilk
½ cup mayonnaise
¼ cup blue cheese crumbles
2 tablespoons finely chopped scallion
Freshly ground black pepper
¼ cup chopped fresh cilantro

1. Preheat an outdoor grill for a medium-hot fire or the oven broiler.

2. Place the chicken tenders in a medium-size bowl. Drizzle the
Tabasco sauce and melted butter over the tenders and toss to coat.

3. In a small bowl, combine the garlic powder, paprika, salt, and
cayenne. Sprinkle the mixture over the chicken tenders, tossing to
coat. Allow the chicken to sit for 5 minutes. Cook the chicken on
the hot grill over direct heat or under the broiler until it has reached
an internal temperature of 165°F, 10 to 15 minutes.

4. Tear the greens into bite-size pieces, if necessary. Layer the
mixed greens, celery, and grape tomatoes on each serving plate.

5. In a small bowl, combine the buttermilk and mayonnaise, whisking
until smooth. Stir in the blue cheese crumbles and scallions. Season to taste with salt and black pepper. Drizzle some of the dressing
over each salad. Top the salad with the chicken and cilantro.

MAKE IT AHEAD: The chicken and dressing can be stored in separate covered
containers in the refrigerator for up to 4 days. The chicken is great served cold,
but if you'd prefer, warm it quickly in the microwave.

44

CHICKEN-ZILLA

These days, many chickens are a little too busty! Instead of cooking entire chicken breasts or halves, which seem to be getting larger and larger, fillet them into smaller cutlets. Cutlets cook more quickly and present a reasonable portion.

Pesto Bread Sticks

MAKES 8 BREAD STICKS

MEATLESS **DAIRY-FREE** **MAKE-AHEAD** **FREEZER-FRIENDLY**

I felt such relief when I realized that, unlike other bread doughs, the dough for bread sticks does not have to rise for hours on end. These bread sticks mix up quickly and can be rolled and twisted in a matter of minutes. What fun!

¾ cup warm water
2 tablespoons olive oil
1 tablespoon honey
2 cups unbleached all-purpose flour
1½ teaspoons fine sea salt
1½ teaspoons active dry yeast
1 tablespoon prepared pesto

1. Preheat the oven to 400°F. Line a baking sheet with parchment paper or a silicone baking mat.

2. In a large bowl, combine the water, olive oil, honey, flour, salt, and yeast. Stir well to combine.

3. Turn the dough out onto a lightly floured work surface and quickly knead until smooth, 1 to 2 minutes. Divide the dough into two portions. Flatten each portion into an 8-inch square.

4. Spread the pesto sauce over one piece of dough. Place the second piece over the first and lightly press down. Cut the dough into eight strips.

5. Twist each "pesto dough sandwich" to form a bread twist. Place on the prepared baking sheet. Bake until crisp and golden brown, about 8 minutes.

MAKE IT AHEAD: Cooled bread sticks can be stored in a covered container in the refrigerator for up to 3 days or in the freezer for up to 2 months.

Vegetable
Couscous Salad

Spiced Pita Chips

Couscous and pitas
are natural partners,
since way back in
ancient times. They
meet again here for
a delicious meatless
meal that comes
together quickly.
These recipes also
pair well with all
kinds of grilled
meats.

Vegetable Couscous Salad

SERVES 4

 MEATLESS **DAIRY-FREE**  MAKE-AHEAD

I first learned to cook with couscous when I worked for my university's catering company. Previously, I'd never used the itty-bitty pasta. This salad is based on one that I made for the UCen many moons ago. It's still a favorite at our house, two decades later.

1¼ cups hot water or vegetable broth
2 tablespoons fresh lemon juice, or more to taste
2 tablespoons olive oil, or more to taste
1 teaspoon curry powder
1 teaspoon ground cumin
1 cup whole-wheat couscous
1 (15-ounce) can chickpeas, rinsed and drained
1 medium cucumber, chopped
1 medium red bell pepper, cored and chopped
2 medium Roma tomatoes, chopped
½ cup pitted black olives
¼ cup chopped fresh cilantro
4 scallions, chopped
Fine sea salt and freshly ground black pepper

1. Place the hot water or broth in a heatproof bowl and add the lemon juice, olive oil, curry powder, and cumin. Add the couscous and stir to combine. Cover the dish completely with a lid or plate to allow it to cook. Let sit for 5 minutes. Remove the lid and fluff the couscous with a fork.

2. Add the chickpeas, cucumber, bell pepper, tomatoes, olives, cilantro, and scallions. Season to taste with salt and pepper. Toss the ingredients lightly to combine. Adjust the seasonings, adding more lemon juice, olive oil, or spices as desired, and serve.

MAKE IT AHEAD: The salad can be stored in a covered container in the refrigerator for up to 3 days.

45

There are some days
when your only free
30-minute block for
cooking will occur
at 8 a.m. instead of
5 p.m. Never fear.
Many of the meals
in this book can be
made in advance and
chilled until ready.
While the actual
prep time might not
be shorter, neither
will your fuse be
short later in the day.
You'll have what you
need when it's time
to eat, and you'll by-
pass more costly or
lengthy alternatives.

Spiced Pita Chips

SERVES 4

`MEATLESS` `DAIRY-FREE` `MAKE-AHEAD`

My kids can eat a bag of commercial pita chips in about two seconds flat—and that's allowing time for someone to complain that
someone else got more. It's not cost-effective to buy the commercial brand for something that disappears while my back is turned.
As is so often the case, making your own is cheaper—and tastier.
For a sweet version, you can substitute the olive oil with vegetable
oil or melted butter and the spice mix with cinnamon-sugar.

1½ teaspoons garam masala
1½ teaspoons garlic powder
½ teaspoon fine sea salt
6 pita breads
Olive oil, for brushing

1. Preheat the oven to 425°F. Line a baking sheet with parchment
paper or a silicone baking mat.

2. In a small bowl, combine the garam masala, garlic powder, and salt.

3. Brush a pita bread with some olive oil, and sprinkle it with some
of the spice mixture. Flip it over and repeat. Continue until all the
pita breads are seasoned.

4. Cut the pitas into 8 wedges each and place them on the prepared baking sheet. Bake until lightly browned and crisp, about
10 minutes.

MAKE IT AHEAD: Store cooled chips in an airtight container at room temperature
for up to 3 days.

THE ULTIMATE SNACKY DINNER

At our house, the snacky dinner is an all-time favorite. It's a combination of all kinds of no-cook foods that we love: vegetables and dips, cheese, bread and charcuterie, fruit and nuts.

The mélange is sure to please without taking much time or effort on the part of the cook. You can make this meal meatless, dairy-free, or gluten-free, depending on your preferences. It's so versatile and can be made differently every time. Our family loves a snacky dinner.

It's also ideal to serve as a casual get-together with friends. Be sure to offer your favorite wines, beers, and nonalcoholic sparkling drinks to make the meal festive.

Bread
Sliced French baguette and/or crackers

Cheese
Two or three cheeses of different textures and intensities of flavor (such as Brie, Gruyère, and a soft herbed cheese, like Boursin)

Charcuterie
Deli-sliced ham, salami, roast beef, and/or turkey

Vegetables and Dip
Baby carrots, celery sticks, cucumber slices, blanched green beans, zucchini spears, and/or snap peas

Creamy Buttermilk Ranch Dressing (page 129), Blue Cheese Dip, (page 151), Red Pepper Hummus (page 198), or your favorite dip

Fruits and Nuts
An array of dried and fresh fruits and nuts, such as fresh apples, grapes, figs, and clementines; dried apricots, raisins, and cranberries; and almonds and cashews

Pickles
Preserved condiments like cured olives, dill pickles, and pepperoncini

As the mother of six children, I've been to many a baby shower, whether mine or those of friends. This meal is perfect for a lunch with the girls—and you won't have to spend all morning in the kitchen. It's equally delicious served at a family supper. My husband and his friend were initially skeptical about this "chick food," but both were handily won over.

Curried Chicken and Apple Salad

SERVES 4

`DAIRY-FREE` `GLUTEN-FREE` `MAKE-AHEAD`

I've fallen in love with the flavors of India. This salad boasts not just Indian spices, but also the fruits and nuts grown there. This is an amazing salad, if I do say so myself. Even folks who aren't curry fans (like my husband) love it.

1 teaspoon garlic powder
1 teaspoon curry powder
1 pound chicken tenders
Fine sea salt and freshly ground black pepper
¼ cup plus 1 tablespoon olive oil
2 tablespoons mayonnaise
2 tablespoons fresh lime juice
6 ounces baby greens
2 apples, such as Braeburn, cored and chopped
½ cup golden raisins
½ cup roasted unsalted cashews
4 scallions, chopped
¼ cup chopped fresh cilantro

1. In a small bowl, combine the garlic powder and curry powder. Sprinkle the mixture over both sides of the chicken tenders. Season the chicken with salt and pepper to taste.

2. In a large nonstick skillet, heat 1 tablespoon of the oil until shimmering. Add the chicken and sauté until the juices are clear, about 10 minutes.

3. In a small bowl, whisk together the mayonnaise and lime juice until very smooth. Season to taste with salt and pepper. Add the remaining ¼ cup olive oil and whisk to combine.

4. Divide the greens among four serving plates. Divide the apples, raisins, cashews, and scallions among the plates. Add the chicken, and top with the cilantro. Serve with the dressing on the side.

MAKE IT AHEAD: The chicken and dressing can be stored in separate covered containers in the refrigerator for up to 4 days. The chicken is great served cold, but if you'd prefer, warm it quickly in the microwave.

46

I'm a huge, huge fan of homemade. However, I know that buying some convenience items can save me valuable minutes in the kitchen. Sure, it may not be my favorite way to do something, but it can make the difference between eating at home or eating somewhere else and paying more money.

Parmesan Puffs

SERVES 4

 MEATLESS MAKE-AHEAD

Puff pastry is a quick cook's best friend. You will feel like a rock-star chef when you pull these airy cheese puffs from the oven.

> 1 sheet frozen puff pastry dough (from a 17.5-ounce package), thawed
> 3 tablespoons shredded Parmesan cheese
> Freshly ground black pepper

1. Preheat the oven to 425°F. Line a baking sheet with parchment paper or a silicone baking mat.

2. Lay out the pastry on the prepared sheet. Sprinkle generously with the Parmesan cheese and black pepper.

3. Cut the pastry into 1-inch squares. Separate the squares so there's a bit of space between them. Bake until puffy and golden, 5 to 7 minutes.

MAKE IT AHEAD: Cooled puffs can be stored in an airtight container at room temperature for up to 1 day.

Fast Pizzas and Flatbreads

Friday night is pizza night at our house. It's our way to welcome a few days of rest and family fun. I've made homemade pizzas for over 15 years. But, honestly, some Friday afternoons, I'm just too tired to make dough and didn't have the forethought to pull stuff from the freezer.

These quick-fix pizzas come to my rescue on those nights. They are delicious, fun to eat, and unbelievably easy to prepare.

Biscuit Pizza
with Sausage
and Peppers

Marinated Olive
and Tomato
Salad

Traditional home-
made pizza dough
takes a few hours of
prep time, between
making and knead-
ing the dough and
allowing it to rise.
With a biscuit crust,
you can eliminate
all the rise time. Pair
this hearty pizza pie
with a marinated
olive salad for a
simple yet filling
supper.

Biscuit Pizza with Sausage and Peppers

SERVES 4 TO 6

I love the flavors and simplicity of this biscuit pizza. It bakes in a
9 x 13-inch baking dish, making it an interesting combination of
pizza and casserole all wrapped in one. If you can't find whole-wheat
pastry flour, feel free to use unbleached all-purpose flour.

    2 sweet Italian sausage links, casings removed
    1 medium green bell pepper, cored and chopped
    ½ medium onion, chopped (about 1 cup)
    2 cups whole-wheat pastry flour
    1 tablespoon baking powder
    1 teaspoon dried Italian herb blend
    1 teaspoon fine sea salt
    ¼ cup olive oil
    ½ cup buttermilk
    ½ cup tomato sauce
    2 cups shredded pepper Jack cheese

1. Preheat the oven to 400°F. Grease a 9 x 13-inch baking pan with
nonstick cooking spray.

2. In a large nonstick skillet, cook the sausage, bell pepper, and
onion until the sausage is cooked and the vegetables are tender,
about 10 minutes. Drain off the fat.

3. In a large bowl, whisk together the flour, baking powder, herbs,
and salt. Add the olive oil and buttermilk and stir gently, just until
combined. Spread this mixture in the bottom of the prepared pan.

4. Spread the tomato sauce over the biscuit layer. Scatter the meat
mixture over the tomato sauce. Sprinkle the cheese over the top.

5. Bake until the crust is crisp on the bottom and cooked through
and the cheese is melted, 12 to 15 minutes.

47

ZIP IT

Use zip-top plastic bags for marinating meats and vegetables. The bag seals in the mess and allows you to coat everything well. Less time cleaning the kitchen is more time for other fun things.

Marinated Olive and Tomato Salad

SERVES 4

`MEATLESS` `GLUTEN-FREE` `MAKE-AHEAD`

Jamie's Spice Mix helps these marinated olives come together lickety-split. You could serve them on their own in a bowl as a pre-dinner snack, but turning them into a salad with grape tomatoes adds an elegant touch to a meal with barely any work at all.

¼ cup olive oil
2 tablespoons fresh lemon juice
2 teaspoons Jamie's Spice Mix (page 163)
1½ cups pitted black olives
6 ounces baby greens
1 cup grape tomatoes, halved
¼ cup shaved Romano cheese

1. In a small bowl, combine the oil, lemon juice, and spice mix. Stir well to combine. Add the olives and turn to coat. Let marinate at room temperature for about 10 minutes.

2. Place the greens, tomatoes, and olives in a salad bowl. Toss to coat. Divide the mixture among salad plates and top with the cheese shavings. Serve immediately.

MAKE IT AHEAD: The olives can be stored with their marinade in a covered container in the refrigerator for up to 4 days.

MENU

BBQ Chicken Lavash Pizza

Crudités and Blue Cheese Dip

Pizza is our traditional way to inaugurate the weekend. It's a simple meal that screams, "Fun food!" Make up these BBQ chicken pizzas and a side of veggies and dip and you're ready for a relaxing Friday night.

BBQ Chicken Lavash Pizza

SERVES 4

`MAKE-AHEAD`

Years ago the tortilla pizza became a welcome addition to my repertoire of quick pizza bases. Recently, lavash joined the ranks. Similar to its Mexican cousin, the lavash is an Armenian flour and water flatbread. It makes a super simple pizza base. Buy a few packages to stash in the freezer for quick pizza nights.

1 tablespoon olive oil
8 ounces boneless, skinless chicken breast, cut into bite-size pieces
1½ teaspoons Jamie's Spice Mix (page 163)
4 large lavash breads
¾ cup favorite barbecue sauce
2 cups shredded mozzarella cheese
1 small red onion, sliced
½ cup chopped fresh cilantro

1. Preheat the oven to 400°F.

2. In a large nonstick skillet, heat the oil over medium-high heat until shimmering. Season the chicken generously with the spice mix. Sauté the chicken in the hot oil for about 7 minutes.

3. Place the lavash on baking sheets. Spread 3 tablespoons of the barbecue sauce on each one. Divide the chicken among the four pizzas. Top each with ½ cup mozzarella cheese and a thin layer of onions.

4. Bake until the crust is crisp and the cheese is melted and browned in spots, about 7 minutes. Sprinkle with the cilantro and serve.

MAKE IT AHEAD: The cooked chicken can be stored in a covered container in the refrigerator for up to 3 days.

48

Strategize your meal prep. Look at the lineup of dishes you're making tonight. Begin with the thing that will take longer to prep or the item that can cook hands-free. For instance, start the rice cooker and then work on the main dish. While it cooks, toss together the salad. You'll be more efficient in the kitchen when you prioritize the different recipes you're going to make.

Crudités and Blue Cheese Dip

SERVES 4

`MEATLESS` `GLUTEN-FREE` `MAKE-AHEAD`

Crudités is just a fancy word for cut-up raw veggies, but doesn't it sound so much more *ooh la la*? You can easily and quickly prepare a delicious side of fresh, crunchy vegetables with homemade tangy blue cheese dip that will slap any of those prepackaged trays silly. Double the recipe if your diners are big dippers.

½ cup mayonnaise
½ cup sour cream
1 scallion, chopped
1½ teaspoons chopped fresh basil
½ teaspoon minced garlic
½ teaspoon freshly ground black pepper
⅓ cup crumbled blue cheese
Assorted veggie dippers, such as baby carrots, snap peas, celery sticks, cucumber slices, and baby zucchini

1. In a small bowl, combine the mayonnaise and sour cream until smooth. Add the scallion, basil, garlic, and black pepper, stirring to incorporate the seasonings throughout. Gently fold in the blue cheese.

2. Serve with the veggie dippers.

MAKE IT AHEAD: The dip can be stored in a covered container in the refrigerator for up to 3 days.

MENU

Cheesesteak
French Bread
Pizza

Caesar Salad

As a teenager, I worked at a grocery store and would often pick up a frozen French bread pizza for my late-night snack. Back then I thought it was cool. Today I think: Blech! Why buy a commercial product when you can make a better homemade version in almost the same amount of time? This pizza and salad combo will rock your mealtimes with very little work.

Cheesesteak French Bread Pizza

SERVES 4

MAKE-AHEAD **FREEZER-FRIENDLY**

I love the flavors of a cheesesteak sandwich, so I figured they'd taste great on a pizza. And they do! Please note one important variation from its namesake: There's no Cheez Whiz here, just rich, gooey mozzarella. Feel free to use provolone, if you like, to get closer to the spirit of an authentic cheesesteak.

1 tablespoon olive oil
½ medium onion, sliced
4 ounces white mushrooms, sliced (about 1 cup)
1 teaspoon minced garlic
Fine sea salt and freshly ground black pepper
1 large French bread loaf, split horizontally
¾ cup Last-Minute Pizza Sauce (recipe follows)
8 ounces sliced roast beef, chopped
1 roasted red bell pepper (from a jar), julienned
1 cup shredded mozzarella cheese
½ cup shredded pepper Jack cheese

1. Preheat the oven to 475°F.

2. In a large nonstick skillet, heat the oil over medium-high heat until shimmering. Add the onion, mushrooms, and garlic and sauté until tender, about 5 minutes. Season to taste with salt and pepper.

3. Place the two bread halves on a large baking sheet. Spread pizza sauce over both. Distribute the meat over the sauce, followed by the onion-mushroom mixture, and then the pepper strips. Sprinkle both of the cheeses over the top.

4. Bake until the bread is crisp, the toppings are hot, and the cheese is bubbly, 10 to 15 minutes.

MAKE IT AHEAD: The sautéed onion-mushroom mixture can be stored in a covered container in the refrigerator for up to 4 days.

#49

ROLL WITH IT

A rotary pizza cutter comes in handy for quickly cutting all kinds of things, including pastry, quesadillas, and, of course, pizza.

last-minute pizza sauce

MAKES A SCANT 1½ CUPS

`MEATLESS` `DAIRY-FREE` `GLUTEN-FREE` `MAKE-AHEAD` `FREEZER-FRIENDLY`

I rely on this delicious sauce as a super quick alternative to long-simmered pizza sauce. It's ideal for those days when you don't have time to run to the market, because it relies on regular pantry staples.

1 (6-ounce) can tomato paste
¾ cup water
1½ tablespoons Jamie's Spice Mix (page 163)
1 tablespoon olive oil

In a bowl, whisk together the tomato paste and water. Add the spice mix and stir well. Stir in the olive oil, whisking until well combined.

MAKE IT AHEAD: The sauce can be stored in a covered container in the refrigerator for up to 3 days or in the freezer for up to 2 months. Thaw in the refrigerator before using.

Caesar Salad

SERVES 4

There are few salads that I don't love, but some I love more than others. I have always had a special place in my heart for the classic Caesar salad. It's easy to make from scratch and full of all kinds of powerful flavors. Here, I omit the traditional anchovy paste, a mono-tasker in my opinion, and use the more versatile fish sauce. You get similar flavors but can put the ingredient to good work in other recipes besides Caesar salad. If you are concerned about egg safety, purchase pasteurized egg yolks.

1 egg yolk
3 tablespoons fresh lemon juice
1 teaspoon minced garlic
1 teaspoon fish sauce
Freshly ground black pepper
¼ cup olive oil
1 head romaine lettuce, chopped
1 cup croutons
½ cup shredded Parmesan cheese

1. In a small blender or food processor, combine the egg, lemon juice, garlic, and fish sauce. Blend until smooth. Season to taste with pepper. With the machine running, add the olive oil in a slow, steady stream and continue to blend until well incorporated.

2. In a large bowl, combine the lettuce, croutons, and Parmesan. Add the dressing and toss to coat. Serve immediately.

Goat cheese pizza
has always been a fa-
vorite of mine. When
we go out to eat and
order individual piz-
zas, invariably I turn
to goat cheese for a
topping. This rendi-
tion atop puff pastry
is easy to pull to-
gether and feels just
a little bit fancier
than your average
slice of pepperoni
and cheese.

Tomatoes and Goat Cheese on Puff Pastry

SERVES 4

MEATLESS

Frozen puff pastry is, for sure, a convenience item that God invented so that we could enjoy the delectable layers of pastry without all the hassle that comes with preparing it. The pastry bakes up puffy and light, with a delicate tomato and goat cheese topping. You will impress and amaze the folks around your table with this fancier style of pizza.

1 (17.5-ounce) package frozen puff pastry, thawed
3 medium tomatoes, seeded and chopped
¼ cup chopped fresh basil
1 teaspoon minced garlic
½ teaspoon dried thyme
1 cup crumbled goat cheese
1 cup shredded mozzarella cheese

1. Preheat the oven to 400°F. Line two baking sheets with parchment paper or silicone baking mats.

2. Lay out each puff pastry sheet on a lined baking sheet and cut it in half crosswise; separate the two halves slightly. Prick each portion all over with a fork, leaving a ½-inch border around the edges. Bake until lightly golden brown and puffy around the edges, about 10 minutes.

3. In a small bowl, combine the tomatoes, basil, garlic, and thyme. Toss gently to combine.

4. Divide the tomato mixture among the four baked crusts. Sprinkle with the goat cheese and mozzarella cheese. Bake until the toppings are hot and the cheese is slightly melted and brown, 5 to 7 minutes.

50

Pizza can be made on all kinds of ready-made bases. Consider substituting traditional pizza crust with focaccia, pita bread, tortillas, naan, bagels, or English muffins.

Power Greens with Golden Raisins

SERVES 4

`MEATLESS` `DAIRY-FREE` `GLUTEN-FREE`

One of my favorite bagged items in the produce aisle is "power greens," a mixture of baby kale, chard, and spinach. They taste great in scrambled eggs or as a hearty salad. If you can't find the bagged variety, feel free to use a mixture of chard, kale, and/or spinach for a dish that's healthful and super flavorful.

3 tablespoons fresh lemon juice
1 tablespoon balsamic vinegar
Fine sea salt and freshly ground black pepper
2 tablespoons olive oil
1 (5-ounce) bag baby "power greens"
⅓ cup golden raisins
⅓ cup slivered almonds

1. In a small jar or bowl, combine the lemon juice, vinegar, and salt and pepper to taste. Cap the jar and shake, or whisk to combine. Add the olive oil and shake or whisk again.

2. Place the greens in a large salad bowl and toss with enough of the dressing to coat the greens. Divide among salad plates. Top each plate with an equal portion of raisins and almonds. Serve with additional dressing on the side.

MENU

Pepperoni
Pizzadillas

Chopped
Antipasto Salad

Just about every
culture has its own
flatbread: tortillas
from Mexico, pizza
from Italy, pita bread
and lavash from the
Middle East, crêpes
from France, and
even my Norwegian
relations have their
lefse. Using alterna-
tive flatbreads as a
pizza base makes
for a fun, American-
style mix of cultures.
Plus, it's fast! This
meal is a mash-up of
pizza and quesadil-
las with an easy side
salad, making for a
no-brainer, quick,
and tasty dinner.

Pepperoni Pizzadillas

SERVES 4

What do you get when you use pizza toppings to make a quesadilla?
A pizzadilla, of course! My family gobbles these down almost faster
than I can make them—which is pretty quickly!

8 burrito-size flour tortillas
1 cup tomato sauce
2 cups shredded mozzarella cheese
5 ounces pepperoni, coarsely chopped
2 tablespoons chopped fresh basil

1. Heat an electric griddle or a large nonstick skillet over medium-
high heat.

2. Lay out four tortillas on a work surface. Spread ¼ cup tomato
sauce on each. Scatter ¼ cup cheese over the sauce on each tortilla. Divide the pepperoni evenly among the pizzadillas. Sprinkle the
basil evenly over each. Scatter another ¼ cup cheese on each. Top
each pizzadilla with another tortilla.

3. Cook the pizzadillas on the hot griddle or skillet, flipping once,
until the cheese is melted and the tortillas are crisp, about 5 minutes. Cut into wedges and serve hot.

51

Prepping lettuce for a salad can take mere minutes. Slice the head of romaine or other leaf lettuce in three or four long cuts lengthwise through the leaves. Then slice across into 1-inch slices. Toss the cut greens into a salad spinner, rinse and spin, and you're ready to go.

Chopped Antipasto Salad

SERVES 4 TO 6

MEATLESS **GLUTEN-FREE** MAKE-AHEAD

Chopped salads are the quick cook's best friend. Get out the cutting board and a knife, and in just a few minutes, you have a delicious salad that's full of flavor and crunch.

¼ cup red wine vinegar
1 teaspoon dried Italian herb blend
1 teaspoon minced garlic
Pinch of sugar
Fine sea salt and freshly ground black pepper
¼ cup olive oil
6 ounces romaine lettuce, chopped
1 (15-ounce) can chickpeas, rinsed and drained
1 cup grape tomato halves
1 medium cucumber, chopped
1 red bell pepper, cored and chopped
½ cup chopped pepperoncini
¼ cup finely chopped sweet onion (such as Vidalia)
¼ cup sliced black olives
¼ cup shredded Parmesan cheese

1. In a small jar or bowl, combine the vinegar, herbs, garlic, sugar, and salt and pepper to taste. Cap the jar and shake, or whisk to combine. Add the olive oil and shake or whisk again.

2. Place the lettuce, chickpeas, tomatoes, cucumber, bell pepper, pepperoncini, onion, olives, and cheese in a large salad bowl and dress to coat. Divide among salad plates. Serve immediately.

MAKE IT AHEAD: The salad and dressing can be stored in separate covered containers in the refrigerator for up to 3 days.

Caramelized Onion and Feta Flatbreads

Roasted Vegetable Salad

The classic combo of pizza and salad can take so many different forms that boredom should never enter the equation. This menu isn't necessarily what comes to mind when you think of common pizza toppings—or go-with salads, for that matter—but it's delicious nonetheless. Start the vegetables first so that they can cool to room temperature while the flatbreads bake. You'll be able to manage their cooking temperature differences better that way, too.

Caramelized Onion and Feta Flatbreads

SERVES 4

MEATLESS

Onions and feta cheese are each packed with flavor, and when combined, they really bring it. No boring pizza here! And yes, greens on a pizza are fantastic. Trust me! This is a pizza you can feel good about.

1 tablespoon olive oil
½ medium onion, sliced
1½ teaspoons soy sauce
Fine sea salt and freshly ground black pepper
4 pita breads
2 cups baby "power greens" (or a mixture of chard, spinach, and/or kale)
2 medium tomatoes, chopped
½ cup crumbled feta cheese
2 cups shredded Monterey Jack or mozzarella cheese

1. Preheat the oven to 475°F.

2. In a large nonstick skillet, heat the oil over medium-high heat until shimmering. Add the onion and sauté until tender, about 5 minutes. Add the soy sauce, turn the heat to low, cover, and cook for another 5 minutes. Season to taste with salt and pepper.

3. Lay out the pita breads on a baking sheet. Divide the greens among the four breads. Top with the onion, tomatoes, feta cheese, and Jack cheese.

4. Bake until the toppings are hot and the cheese is melted and browned in spots, about 8 minutes.

52

When you're in a rush or know you'll be pressed for time during dinner prep, don't hesitate to buy pre-chopped vegetables, like broccoli or cauliflower. Often these even come in bags appropriate for microwave cooking. You may pay a little more at the checkout stand, but you'll gain it back in time. Time is money, as they say.

Roasted Vegetable Salad

SERVES 4 TO 6

MEATLESS **DAIRY-FREE** **GLUTEN-FREE**

This is a different kind of salad: the vegetables are roasted, served warm, and dressed lightly with olive oil and lemon. It's delicious and easy to prep. Leftovers are equally tasty the next day, even served chilled right out of the fridge.

1 (12-ounce) bag broccoli florets or 1 head broccoli, cut into florets
12 ounces asparagus, trimmed and chopped
6 ounces white mushrooms, sliced (1½ cups)
⅓ cup olive oil
Fine sea salt and freshly ground black pepper
Juice of 1 lemon

1. Preheat the oven to 400°F. Line a large baking sheet with parchment paper or a silicone baking mat.

2. Spread out the broccoli, asparagus, and mushrooms on the prepared baking sheet. Drizzle with the olive oil and season to taste with salt and pepper.

3. Roast the vegetables until tender, 10 to 15 minutes. Drizzle with the lemon juice and toss to coat. Adjust the seasonings and serve hot, warm, or at room temperature.

MAKE YOUR OWN SPICE BLENDS

One of my favorite ways to save time in the kitchen is to create custom spice blends. They add huge flavor to dressings, meats, rice mixes, and vegetables and make quick work of preparing dinner. No measuring out little bits of this and that; just grab a scoop and go. Store it in a shaker jar and then go to town, sprinkling on flavor.

You can certainly buy commercial spice mixes, but it's cheaper to make your own, and you can customize the flavors and control the sodium level. Buy spices in bulk and combine them in different ways. When using fresh citrus zest or fresh herbs, be sure to store the blend in the freezer. I store my spice mixes in half-pint canning jars. Here are five of my faves.

cajun spice blend
MAKES ABOUT 5 TABLESPOONS

This Cajun-style mixture offers just enough heat to keep things exciting. Use it for Shrimp Chowder (page 95) and Cajun Fish and Chips (page 262), or anywhere you need a little pizzazz.

- 1 tablespoon onion powder
- 1 tablespoon garlic powder
- 1 tablespoon kosher salt
- 2 teaspoons paprika
- 2 teaspoons dried thyme
- 1 teaspoon freshly ground black pepper
- ½ teaspoon dried oregano
- ¼ teaspoon cayenne pepper

Combine all of the ingredients in a small jar with a lid. Shake to combine well and store in the cupboard.

fishmama spice
MAKES ABOUT 3 TABLESPOONS

This is my own little vanity spice, named after Yours Truly. It's a little bit salty with great herb flavor. I love it in Turkey and Ham Cobb Salad (page 133), Oven-Roasted Green Beans (page 232), Pork Medallions with Sherried Shallot Sauce (page 237), and Easy Chicken and Asparagus (page 240).

- 1 tablespoon fine sea salt
- 2 teaspoons garlic powder
- 1 teaspoon dried oregano
- 1 teaspoon dried basil
- 1 teaspoon dried thyme
- 1 teaspoon paprika
- 1 teaspoon freshly ground black pepper

Combine all of the ingredients in a small jar with a lid. Shake to combine well and store in the cupboard.

jamie's spice mix

MAKES ABOUT ⅔ CUP

This blend is named after my sister in honor of the spice mix that she gave as a party favor at her wedding a few years ago. The celery seeds add a strong, unique flavor; feel free to omit them if you'd rather.

Add a few shakes to salad dressings, meat marinades, or French fries. It also goes well on pizza and in pulled chicken sandwiches. Some recipes that feature it include Roast Chicken and Veggies (page 45), Better than Big Mac's Burgers (page 60),and BBQ Chicken Lavash Pizza (page 149).

2 tablespoons onion powder
2 tablespoons garlic powder
1½ tablespoons paprika
1 tablespoon dried basil
1 tablespoon dried oregano
1 tablespoon fine sea salt
2 teaspoons freshly ground black pepper
1 teaspoon celery seeds (optional)
½ teaspoon grated fresh lemon zest
½ teaspoon cayenne pepper

Combine all of the ingredients in a small jar with a lid. Shake to combine well and store in the freezer.

basic taco seasoning mix

MAKES ABOUT ⅔ CUP

I haven't bought packaged taco seasoning in years, as this is a standard spice blend in my cupboard. It can be mixed into ground beef, shredded chicken, soups, or chilis to give them a little punch. It is also delicious whisked into sour cream as a dip and stirred into marinades and dressings. We love this in Taco Joes (page 68) and Yellow Rice and Beans (page 268).

¼ cup chili powder
2 tablespoons dried oregano
2 tablespoons dried onion flakes
1 tablespoon fine sea salt
1 tablespoon garlic powder
1 teaspoon freshly ground black pepper

Combine all of the ingredients in a small jar with a lid. Shake to combine well and store in the cupboard.

greek spice blend

MAKES ABOUT 6 TABLESPOONS

This all-purpose seasoning goes great on grilled meats and in dressings and dips. Try it in Veggie and Feta Torpedoes (page 74), Steak and Mushroom Skewers (page 274), and Greek Vegetable Rice (page 276).

1 tablespoon garlic powder
1 tablespoon onion powder
1 tablespoon dried parsley
2 teaspoons dried oregano
2 teaspoons fine sea salt
1 teaspoon freshly ground black pepper
1 teaspoon dried thyme
1 teaspoon grated fresh lemon zest
½ teaspoon ground cinnamon
½ teaspoon ground nutmeg

Combine all of the ingredients in a small jar with a lid. Shake to combine well and store in the freezer.

MENU

Mushroom
and Pepper
Quesadillas

Ranchero Salad

A quesadilla is
basically a flatbread
sandwich. It is a
favorite go-to meal
at our house on busy
nights. The littler
kids are satisfied
with plain cheese,
but we more sophis-
ticated folks like
to add chicken or a
vegetable filling, like
this one. Paired with
a salad, it makes a
simple and satisfy-
ing meal.

Mushroom and Pepper Quesadillas

SERVES 4

MEATLESS

I can easily convince my husband to go meatless when the meal
has plenty of flavor and spice, like this one. If you prefer more heat,
add a chopped jalapeño to the vegetable mixture. Want less? Use
Monterey Jack cheese instead of pepper Jack. And feel free to
throw in some leftover chicken or beef if you have it on hand.

1 tablespoon olive oil
8 ounces white mushrooms, sliced (about 2 cups)
1 bell pepper (any color), cored and chopped
1 teaspoon chopped garlic
Fine sea salt and freshly ground black pepper
8 burrito-size flour tortillas
2 cups chopped fresh spinach
4 cups shredded pepper Jack cheese

1. In a large nonstick skillet, heat the oil over medium-high heat
until shimmering. Add the mushrooms, bell pepper, and garlic and
cook until the vegetables are tender and start to brown, about
5 minutes. Season to taste with salt and pepper.

2. Heat an electric griddle or another large nonstick skillet over
medium-high heat.

3. Lay out four tortillas on a work surface. Top each with an equal
portion of the vegetable mixture, the chopped spinach, and the
cheese. Cover each with another tortilla.

4. Cook the quesadillas on the hot griddle or skillet, flipping once,
until the cheese is melted and the tortillas are crisp, about 5 minutes. Cut into wedges and serve hot.

53

PREP YOUR VEGGIES

Try to do all the slicing and dicing that you'll need for the week's meals in one prep session. You only need to clean one knife and one cutting board *one time* instead of every day. This alone will save you time. You can store the prepped vegetables in small containers in the fridge and pull them out when it's time to start cooking. Meal prep will go quickly because you've already done the chopping and slicing. You'll also feel more encouraged to cook since you know the battle is already half fought.

Ranchero Salad

SERVES 4

MEATLESS **GLUTEN-FREE** **MAKE-AHEAD**

This salad is reminiscent of a traditional house salad with ranch dressing, only here the toppings and seasonings have a distinct south-of-the-border twist. It can easily stand alone as a main-course salad by adding grilled chicken or shrimp.

1 head romaine lettuce, chopped
2 Roma tomatoes, chopped
2 avocados, pitted, peeled, and diced
2 scallions, chopped
Handful of fresh cilantro, chopped (about ¼ cup)

DRESSING
½ cup mayonnaise
½ cup buttermilk
2 tablespoons chopped fresh cilantro
½ teaspoon ground cumin
½ teaspoon minced garlic
Pinch of cayenne pepper

1. In a large salad bowl, toss together the lettuce, tomatoes, avocados, scallions, and cilantro.

2. In a small bowl, whisk together the mayonnaise and buttermilk until smooth. Stir in the cilantro, cumin, garlic, and cayenne. Stir well to combine. Pass the dressing at the table.

MAKE IT AHEAD: The salad (minus the avocado) and the dressing can be stored in separate covered containers in the refrigerator for up to 3 days.

MENU

Pesto and Shrimp
Pita Bread Pizzas

The Go-To Salad

Once I discovered
what wonderful piz-
zas could be made
on a pita bread base,
I was hooked! So was
my family. Baking
pizza on pita is one
of the easiest, most
foolproof ways to
make a good pie at
home. We've even
tossed the topped
pitas onto the out-
door grill for a quick
hot-weather meal.
Pair it with my favor-
ite salad and you'll
never need to eat
elsewhere again.

Pesto and Shrimp Pita Bread Pizzas

SERVES 4

Pesto and shrimp are great friends. I love how well they complement one another. This pizza is no exception.

    4 pita breads
    ⅓ cup prepared pesto
    ¼ medium onion, chopped (about ½ cup)
    1 medium tomato, chopped
    2 cups shredded mozzarella cheese
    8 ounces peeled medium shrimp, thawed if frozen

1. Preheat the oven to 475°F.

2. Lay out the pita breads on a large baking sheet. Divide the pesto among the pitas, spreading almost to the edges. Divide the onion among the pitas. Top with equal portions of tomato, cheese, and then shrimp.

3. Bake until the shrimp is cooked, the toppings are hot, and the cheese is melted and browned in spots, 8 to 10 minutes.

The Go-To Salad

SERVES 4

MEATLESS **GLUTEN-FREE**

As the name implies, this is my go-to salad, especially in summertime, when the weather is warmer and I don't feel like eating something heavy. Summer is also the time when I am more cognizant of my eating habits and trying to trim down. I know that with an ounce of cheese, a drizzle of olive oil, some avocado, and all the vegetables I desire, I can stay in a reasonable calorie range while still eating well. Serve this salad as a tasty side if you like, but it can easily make a meal all on its own.

6 ounces favorite salad greens
2 avocados, pitted, peeled, and sliced
1 cup canned chickpeas, rinsed and drained
2 medium tomatoes, chopped
1 cup crumbled blue or feta cheese, or other favorite cheese
½ cup black pitted olives
4 scallions, chopped
4 tablespoons red wine vinegar
4 tablespoons olive oil
Fine sea salt and freshly ground black pepper

1. Divide the greens among four salad plates. Layer on the avocado, chickpeas, tomato, cheese, olives, and scallion in that order.

2. Drizzle 1 tablespoon vinegar and 1 tablespoon oil over the top of each salad. Season to taste with salt and pepper and serve.

MAKE IT AHEAD: The salad (minus the avocados and tomatoes) can be stored in a covered container in the refrigerator for up to 3 days.

MENU

Crispy Pepperoni
and Olive French
Bread Pizza

Spinach Salad
with Honey-
Mustard
Dressing

This French bread
pizza is yet another
way to get pizza on
the table without
resorting to the stuff
from the frozen food
aisle that tastes like
cardboard. A sweet
and savory spinach
salad rounds out the
menu.

Crispy Pepperoni and Olive French Bread Pizza

SERVES 4

My kids could eat pepperoni pizza all the livelong day. I don't think they will ever tire of it. I might, except that there are still fun ways to dress it up and give it a new look, like here, where it gets a little added boost from a three-cheese blend and plenty of black olives.

1 French bread loaf, split horizontally
1 cup tomato sauce
1 teaspoon dried Italian herb blend
½ teaspoon garlic powder
3 ounces sliced pepperoni
½ cup sliced black olives
1 cup shredded mozzarella cheese
1 cup shredded Monterey Jack cheese
¼ cup shredded Asiago cheese
Chopped fresh parsley

1. Preheat the oven to 475°F.

2. Lay out the bread halves on a large baking sheet. Spread the tomato sauce over the cut side of each half and sprinkle with the herbs and garlic powder. Divide the pepperoni between the bread pieces. Top with the olives, cheeses, and chopped parsley.

3. Bake until the crust is crisp and the cheese is melted, 10 to 15 minutes. Slice and serve.

54

WASTE NOT

If it's true that Americans waste an average of 25 percent of their food, then that's a fair amount of time spent purchasing the food, storing the food, and in some cases, prepping it that is also wasted. Not to mention cleaning out the fridge to dump it! If you make a concerted effort to use up leftovers, you will save active time by not having to make a new meal, and you'll also save that passive time that you don't really think about in terms of shopping and storing groceries. It goes without saying that you'll save money, too.

Spinach Salad with Honey-Mustard Dressing

SERVES 4

MEATLESS **GLUTEN-FREE**

Spinach salad can be a great way to get lots of good stuff into your diet. This one features a homemade honey-mustard dressing and a mix of colorful, savory-sweet toppings. It's a veritable explosion of flavor. Love it!

3 tablespoons red wine vinegar
1 tablespoon fresh lemon juice
1½ teaspoons honey
1 teaspoon Dijon mustard
Fine sea salt and freshly ground black pepper
¼ cup olive oil
6 ounces baby spinach
2 oranges, peel and pith cut away, sliced
¼ cup sliced red onion
¼ cup sliced almonds
¼ cup crumbled blue cheese

1. In a small jar or bowl, combine the vinegar, lemon juice, honey, mustard, and salt and pepper to taste. Cap the jar and shake, or whisk to combine. Add the olive oil and shake or whisk again.

2. In a large bowl, toss the spinach with enough dressing to coat. Divide among four salad plates.

3. Top the salads with the oranges, onion, almonds, and blue cheese. Serve immediately, with additional dressing on the side.

MAKE IT AHEAD: The dressing can be stored in a covered container in the refrigerator for up to 4 days.

For many years, Indian food was pretty foreign—and even intimidating—to me. Now that I have crossed the border to deliciousness, I'm thrilled with how the flavors of India work so well in family-friendly dishes, even pizza and salad!

Cheesy Chicken Naan

SERVES 4

Naan is an Indian-style flatbread that is available in the bakery aisle of most grocery stores. I keep several packages in the freezer for a quick and delicious dinner on the fly—even my picky eater loves this "pizza"!

1 tablespoon olive oil
1 pound boneless, skinless chicken breast, cut into bite-size pieces
½ medium onion, sliced
1 teaspoon curry powder
1 teaspoon chopped fresh ginger
Fine sea salt and freshly ground black pepper
4 large pieces naan
2 cups shredded mozzarella cheese
Handful fresh cilantro, chopped (about ¼ cup)

1. Preheat the oven to 475°F.

2. In a large nonstick skillet, heat the oil over medium-high heat until shimmering. Add the chicken and onion and season them with the curry powder, ginger, and salt and pepper to taste. Cook, stirring occasionally, until the chicken is cooked through, about 10 minutes.

3. Place the naan pieces on large baking sheets. Divide the chicken mixture among the naan. Sprinkle on the cheese.

4. Bake until the cheese starts to brown in spots, 6 to 8 minutes. Sprinkle with the cilantro and serve.

#55

LOVE ME TENDER

Got a recipe that calls for chopped boneless, skinless chicken? Use chicken tenders instead of whole breasts. Tenders are thin pieces of white meat from the edge of the breast, usually about an inch thick. Cut right through them to quickly chop the needed amount of chicken.

Kachumber

SERVES 4 TO 6

MEATLESS **DAIRY-FREE** **GLUTEN-FREE**

For this recipe I'm grateful to my friend and colleague Prerna Malik, born and raised in India. Much of what I know about Indian cuisine is thanks to her. I pepper her with questions long-distance via Facebook, and she educates me on Indian cuisine. This cucumber salad is very similar to a Mexican salsa, and it is served frequently in India.

2 medium cucumbers, seeded and chopped
2 Roma tomatoes, chopped
¼ medium sweet onion (such as Vidalia), chopped (about ½ cup)
2 tablespoons chopped fresh cilantro
2 tablespoons chopped fresh mint
1 tablespoon fresh lime juice
Fine sea salt and freshly ground black pepper

In a small bowl, combine the cucumbers, tomatoes, onion, cilantro, and mint. Drizzle with the lime juice and stir to coat. Season to taste with salt and pepper and serve.

Spinach and
Egg–Topped
Tortillas

Feta-Melon Bowl

If you stock your
kitchen with whole-
some, fresh ingredi-
ents, you can throw
together many a
meal on the fly. Eggs,
spinach, cheese,
and tortillas come
together in a sur-
prising way here.
Add a side of melon.
Simple and deli-
cious it is, my young
Padawan.

Spinach and Egg–Topped Tortillas

SERVES 4

MEATLESS

My sister thought I was nuts the first time I cracked an egg onto
my pizza before baking it. It's actually a common—and delicious—
dinner pizza topping in Europe. The resulting sunny-side-up egg
cooks in the oven along with the other toppings and adds a
delicious sauce into the mix. I first saw it done in France, and I'm
so glad I tried it myself! If you prefer a firmer egg, consider breaking
the yolk before it bakes.

    4 burrito-size flour tortillas
    4 tablespoons Last-Minute Pizza Sauce (page 153)
    1 cup baby spinach
    2 cups shredded mozzarella cheese
    4 large eggs
    ¼ cup chopped onion
    ¼ cup chopped fresh basil

1. Preheat the oven to 475°F.

2. Lay out the tortillas on large baking sheets. Spread 1 tablespoon
sauce on each one. Divide the spinach among the tortillas. Sprinkle
on the cheese. Crack an egg in the middle of each. Top with the
onion and basil.

3. Bake until the cheese is melted and the egg is set, 6 to 8 minutes.

56

Create your grocery list according to where things are laid out in the store. Divide your list to represent each department so you won't have to back-track if you miss the potatoes on your list while you're in the produce section.

Feta-Melon Bowl

SERVES 4 TO 6

MEATLESS **GLUTEN-FREE**

This melon salad is unique and flavorful and super easy to put together. To save even more time, buy the melon already chopped from the refrigerated area of your supermarket's produce section.

> 1 personal-size watermelon, peeled and cut into bite-size cubes (about 3 cups)
> 1 cantaloupe, peeled, seeded, and cut into bite-size cubes (about 3 cups)
> ¼ cup chopped fresh mint
> ¼ cup crumbled feta cheese
> Freshly ground black pepper

In a large salad bowl, gently toss together the watermelon, canta-loupe, and mint. Divide among four bowls, sprinkle with feta, and season with black pepper to taste.

Rapid Tacos, Burritos, and Wraps

I don't know that I've ever met anyone who didn't love tacos, burritos, or wraps. They are easy to make, customizable to your heart's delight, and fun to eat. We regularly include at least one of these menus in our weekly meal rotation. Their flexibility allows us to mix and match ingredients or to easily include guests without a lot of fuss. Plus, they taste fantastic!

Taco Tuesday is a
favorite at our house.
Since there are so
many ways to make
tacos, there's no rea-
son for Taco Night to
be boring. Mix and
match several differ-
ent kinds if you can,
or lay out an array
of toppings, fillings,
and bases for a fes-
tive make-your-own
dinner. If you have a
craving for fish with
a south-of-the-bor-
der flavor, this meal
will do the trick.

Quick Fish Tacos

SERVES 4

There's a taco shop a couple of miles from our home that sells
some of the best fried fish tacos around. When I want something a
little more economical, not to mention quicker and healthier, I make
these babies instead. *Viva la homemade!*

1 large egg
¾ cup panko bread crumbs
1 teaspoon ground cumin
1 teaspoon chili powder
1 teaspoon fine sea salt
½ teaspoon dried oregano
12 ounces tilapia, cut into 1-inch strips
12 corn tortillas
Spiced Sour Cream (page 124)
Salsa of your choice, such as Serrano Pico de Gallo (page 189),
    for serving
Shredded cabbage
Lime or lemon wedges, for serving

1. Preheat the oven to 400°F. Line a baking sheet with parchment
paper.

2. Beat the egg in a shallow bowl. In another shallow bowl, combine
the bread crumbs, cumin, chili powder, salt, and oregano.

3. Dip the fish pieces into the beaten egg, allow the excess to drip
off, and then dredge in the seasoned bread crumbs, rolling to coat.
Place on the prepared baking sheet and bake until the fish pulls
apart easily, 10 to 12 minutes.

4. Meanwhile, wrap the tortillas in aluminum foil. Add them to the
oven to warm for the last 5 minutes of cooking the fish.

5. Spread each tortilla with a bit of the sour cream. Add a couple of
pieces of fish. Top each with salsa and shredded cabbage. Serve
with lime wedges on the side.

57

Oftentimes folks choose to eat out merely because the cleanup of home cooking is cumbersome or seems to take too long. Consider how you can reduce your cleanup time: Clean as you go, keep a trash bowl at your prep station, and indulge in disposable serving ware. Paper plates may not be your favorite choice, but the fast-food restaurant uses them, too. Using them at home once in a while allows you a healthier, cheaper dinner choice than fast food.

Corn and Bean Salad

SERVES 4

MEATLESS **DAIRY-FREE** **GLUTEN-FREE** **MAKE-AHEAD**

Corn and beans have been a part of Southwest culture since the beginning of time. Here they combine in a flavorful salad, reminiscent of a salsa. It's so good and filling that I can eat it by the spoonful. Leftovers keep well to use as a burrito filling or salad topping or, yes, even as a salsa for chip-dipping.

2 cups frozen roasted corn, thawed
1 (15-ounce) can black beans, rinsed and drained
1 (4-ounce) can chopped green chiles
2 medium tomatoes, chopped
2 scallions, chopped
¼ cup chopped fresh cilantro
2 tablespoons fresh lime juice
1 teaspoon minced garlic
Fine sea salt and freshly ground black pepper
¼ cup olive oil

1. In a large bowl, combine the corn, beans, chiles, tomatoes, scallions, and cilantro.

2. In a small bowl or jar, combine the lime juice and garlic. Season to taste with salt and pepper. Cap the jar and shake, or whisk to combine. Add the olive oil and shake or whisk again.

3. Pour the dressing over the salad and stir gently to coat well.

MAKE IT AHEAD: The dressed salad can be stored in a covered container in the refrigerator for up to 4 days.

A few years ago,
when I started put-
ting on some extra
"mature woman"
pounds, I reconsid-
ered all the carbs
I was eating. Eat-
ing a few low-carb
meals here and there
turned out to be a
simple way to bring
balance to my diet.
Using lettuce or
cabbage leaves as
wrappers is a great
substitute for torti-
llas or other starchy
accompaniments
like bread, rice, or
pasta.

Gingery Turkey-Vegetable Wraps

SERVES 4 TO 6

`DAIRY-FREE` `GLUTEN-FREE` `MAKE-AHEAD`

These turkey wraps are a huge hit at our house. The portion is generous, thanks to the abundance of vegetables. Leftovers store well
if need be, but my people gobble this down the first time.

1 tablespoon vegetable oil
1 teaspoon minced garlic
2 medium zucchini, shredded
2 large carrots, peeled and shredded
5 medium white mushrooms, chopped
3 celery ribs, sliced
2 scallions, sliced
1 (5-ounce) can sliced water chestnuts, drained
1¼ pounds ground turkey
½ cup chicken broth
2 tablespoons soy sauce
2 tablespoons cornstarch
1½ tablespoons minced fresh ginger
Napa cabbage or large lettuce leaves, for wrapping
Sriracha sauce, for serving
Sweet chili sauce, for serving

1. In a large nonstick skillet, heat the oil over medium heat until shimmering. Add the garlic and cook until aromatic, about 1 minute. Add the
zucchini, carrots, mushrooms, celery, scallions, and water chestnuts.
Raise the heat to high and cook until the vegetables are tender, about
5 minutes. Transfer the vegetable mixture to a dish and tent with foil.

2. Add the turkey to the skillet and cook until no longer pink, 5 to 7
minutes.

3. Return the vegetables to the pan and stir gently to combine with
the turkey.

4. In a small bowl, whisk together the chicken broth, soy sauce,
cornstarch, and ginger. Add this mixture to the pan and simmer until
thickened, about 5 minutes.

5. Serve with cabbage leaves for wrapping. You can spoon the sriracha and sweet chili sauces into the wraps before rolling or dip the
rolled wraps in the sauces.

MAKE IT AHEAD: The filling mixture can be stored in a covered container in the
refrigerator for up to 3 days or in the freezer for up to 2 months. Thaw in the
refrigerator before reheating.

58

We can easily fall into the trap that every meal must be a full-course, orchestrated meal—and if not, we succumb to fast food or junky snack foods. Instead, lean on an array of no-cook whole foods to make the occasional meal. Check out the Ultimate Snacky Dinner on page 141 for inspiration.

Pot Stickers with Sweet and Spicy Dipping Sauce

SERVES 4

`DAIRY-FREE` `MAKE-AHEAD`

Pot stickers are fun little dumplings filled with cooked vegetables and/or meats. The frozen packages typically come with a dipping sauce that is salty but not very tasty. Chuck that and make this one instead.

¼ cup rice vinegar
¼ cup soy sauce
1 tablespoon toasted sesame oil
1 tablespoon honey
1 tablespoon sriracha sauce
1 (1-pound) package frozen pot stickers

1. In a small bowl, whisk together the vinegar, soy sauce, sesame oil, honey, and sriracha until smooth.

2. Cook the pot stickers according to the package directions. Serve the hot dumplings with the dipping sauce on the side.

MAKE IT AHEAD: The sauce can be stored in a covered container in the refrigerator for up to 4 days.

MENU

Tacos Fisher

Tres-Frijoles Salad

Tacos and beans are a traditional Southwestern meal. Here the dynamic duo is healthified with all kinds of good things like spinach, avocado, and whole-wheat tortillas.

Tacos Fisher

SERVES 4

My husband made this dish for me often when we were first dating. I had never had tacos like this; they were unique to him, my Mr. Fisher. (Funnily, in Spanish *tacos fisher* is a construction term. Since my Fisher is a construction guy, the name still fits. These Tacos Fisher are much tastier than a wall plug, though.)

    8 whole-wheat tortillas
    1 tablespoon olive oil
    1 medium onion, sliced from blossom to stem end
    1 pound boneless, skinless chicken breast, cut into bite-size pieces
    1 cup favorite salsa, plus more for serving
    1 cup sour cream or plain yogurt
    1½ cups baby spinach
    1 cup shredded Monterey Jack cheese

1. Preheat the oven to 350°F. Wrap the tortillas in aluminum foil and place them in the oven to warm.

2. In a large nonstick skillet, heat the oil over medium-high heat until shimmering. Sauté the onion until translucent, about 5 minutes. Add the chicken and stir. As the chicken begins to cook, stir in the salsa.

3. Lower the heat to medium, cover, and cook until the chicken is cooked through, about 2 minutes. To assemble the tacos, spread each tortilla with sour cream, and add the chicken, spinach, and cheese. Pass additional salsa at the table.

59

ICE, ICE, BABY

Ice-glazed chicken pieces are a boon to the home cook short on time. Not only do they cook quickly, but they are also individually frozen and packaged in resealable bags. You can grab the exact number that you need without thawing a large package.

Tres-Frijoles Salad

SERVES 4 TO 6

MEATLESS **DAIRY-FREE** **GLUTEN-FREE** MAKE-AHEAD

This three-bean salad offers a fresher alternative to a heavy side of simmered beans. Add the avocado right before serving to avoid browning.

1 (15-ounce) can black beans, rinsed and drained
1 (15-ounce) can dark red kidney beans, rinsed and drained
1 (15-ounce) can chickpeas, rinsed and drained
1 medium tomato, chopped
⅓ cup chopped fresh cilantro
¼ cup sliced black olives
1 jalapeño, cored and finely chopped
1 tablespoon fresh lime juice
1 teaspoon ground cumin
½ teaspoon ground coriander
½ teaspoon dried oregano
1 tablespoon olive oil
Fine sea salt and freshly ground black pepper
1 large avocado

1. In a large bowl, combine the beans, chickpeas, tomato, cilantro, olives, and jalapeño.

2. In a small bowl or jar, combine the lime juice, cumin, coriander, and oregano. Cap the jar and shake, or whisk to combine. Add the olive oil and shake or whisk again.

3. Pour the dressing over the salad and stir gently to coat well. Season to taste with salt and pepper.

4. Just before serving, pit, peel, and dice the avocado, and fold it into the salad.

MAKE IT AHEAD: The dressed salad (minus the avocado) can be stored in a covered container in the refrigerator for up to 4 days.

MENU

Super Secret Subs

Veggie Pasta Salad

An Italian sub–style wrap and a cup of pasta salad is a favorite meal to eat out on the patio or to pack for a picnic. Making your own rather than running to the deli helps you eat more healthfully and economically.

Super Secret Subs

SERVES 4

This sub is "super secret" because it's "under wraps." (Obviously.) A large tortilla takes the place of the bread, giving the classic sub a lighter feel.

    4 burrito-size flour tortillas
    8 slices ham
    20 slices salami
    ½ cup shredded mozzarella cheese or Italian cheese blend
    2 cups shredded lettuce
    2 medium tomatoes, chopped
    ½ small red onion, thinly sliced
    ¼ cup favorite Italian vinaigrette, store-bought or homemade
        (page 129), or more to taste

1. Heat a large nonstick skillet over medium heat and soften and warm the tortillas in the hot skillet for a minute or two. Or, place on a plate and warm them in the microwave for about 30 seconds.

2. Layer the ham and salami down the middle of each tortilla. Sprinkle the cheese over the top. Add the lettuce, tomatoes, and red onion. Drizzle with dressing to taste. Roll up like a burrito and serve.

60

TO THE BRIM

Save time in pot washing as well as cooking by adding fresh or frozen vegetables to the pot of boiling pasta. Adjust for cooking times by starting with the longer cooking item, most likely the pasta, and then adding the vegetables when there's enough time left for them to cook sufficiently.

Veggie Pasta Salad

SERVES 6 TO 8

MEATLESS MAKE-AHEAD

I love this mélange of crisp, colorful veggies mixed into macaroni, and leftovers are great for lunches later in the week. Add some grilled chicken to turn it into a main-course salad.

1 pound elbow macaroni
12 ounces sugar snap peas, trimmed
½ cup red wine vinegar
1 teaspoon dried Italian herb blend
Fine sea salt and freshly ground black pepper
½ cup olive oil
2 cups small broccoli florets
2 cups grape tomatoes
2 medium carrots, peeled and shredded
½ cup crumbled feta cheese

1. Bring a large pot of salted water to a boil over high heat. Cook the elbows according to the package directions, adding the sugar snap peas for the last 2 minutes of the cooking time. Drain, rinse with cool water, and set aside to cool.

2. In a large bowl, combine the vinegar, herbs, and salt and pepper to taste. Whisk in the oil. Add the pasta, peas, broccoli, tomatoes, carrots, and feta. Stir gently to mix. Adjust the seasonings and serve.

MAKE IT AHEAD: The salad can be stored in a covered container in the refrigerator for up to 3 days.

MENU

Super-Rica's #7
Tacos

___

Chips with
Serrano Pico de
Gallo

___

Here's a great way
to welcome friends
and neighbors to a
taco supper. Start off
with chips and a big
bowl of homemade
pico de gallo, along
with cold lemonade,
beer, or margaritas.
Dinner is a hearty
one-dish affair with
easy chicken tacos.
Top it off with a
quick sweet treat
from Desserts on the
Double (see page
294).

Super-Rica's #7 Tacos

SERVES 4

`DAIRY-FREE` `GLUTEN-FREE`

There's a little taco stand on Milpas Street in Santa Barbara. It was Julia Child's favorite; today it is mine as well. The #7 features chicken, mushrooms, peppers, and onions. It is out of this world served on warm corn tortillas. The line at Super-Rica's is usually out the door at mealtimes, but you can avoid the wait and make your own.

12 corn tortillas
2 tablespoons vegetable oil
1 pound boneless, skinless chicken breast, cut into bite-size pieces
½ teaspoon ground cumin
Pinch of cayenne pepper
Fine sea salt and freshly ground black pepper
1 medium onion, cut into 1-inch chunks
1 green bell pepper, cored and cut into 1-inch chunks
4 ounces white mushrooms, sliced (about 1 cup)

1. Preheat the oven to 350°F. Wrap the tortillas in aluminum foil and place in the oven to warm.

2. In a large nonstick skillet, heat 1 tablespoon of the oil over medium-high heat until shimmering. Add the chicken and season with the cumin, cayenne, and salt and black pepper to taste. Sauté until the chicken is cooked through and starting to brown, about 10 minutes. Transfer the chicken to a dish and tent with foil.

3. Heat the remaining 1 tablespoon oil and sauté the onion, bell pepper, and mushrooms until tender and starting to brown, 5 to 7 minutes.

4. Return the chicken to the pan and toss to recombine. Serve the chicken with the warm tortillas. Let diners assemble soft tacos themselves.

61

Just as with time, money, or storage space, folks will keep using something until their supply runs out. If you have 20 dinner plates, chances are your family may be tempted to use all 20 before someone decides to load the dishwasher. Limit your dishes so that you've got a cleaner and more efficient kitchen.

Chips with Serrano Pico de Gallo

SERVES 4

MEATLESS **DAIRY-FREE** **GLUTEN-FREE** **MAKE-AHEAD**

Homemade salsa is the bomb—the stuff in jars and refrigerated plastic containers just can't compare. And believe it or not, with just a little chopping, you can make your own pico de gallo in about five minutes. Why not make the best you can with the time you have? Serve this with tortilla chips for an easy appetizer, but feel free to use it as a topping for the tacos as well. For the best texture, warm the chips in the oven before serving.

4 Roma tomatoes, finely chopped
2 serrano chiles, cored and finely chopped
½ bunch cilantro, chopped (about ⅓ cup)
½ medium sweet onion (such as Vidalia), finely chopped (about 1 cup)
Juice of 1 lime
Fine sea salt and freshly ground black pepper
Tortilla chips, for serving

1. In a medium-size bowl, combine the tomatoes, chiles, cilantro, and onion. Drizzle with the lime juice and season to taste with salt and pepper.

2. Serve with the tortilla chips.

MAKE IT AHEAD: The salsa can be stored in a covered container in the refrigerator for up to 2 days. Stir to recombine before serving.

MENU

Asian Shrimp and Avocado Summer Rolls

Ginger-Cucumber Salad

Summer rolls are a light, refreshing way to get protein and veg in every bite, and the rice papers are such a fun novelty. Mix up a simple cucumber salad to serve on the side for this meal that only looks like you spent a lot of time in the kitchen.

Asian Shrimp and Avocado Summer Rolls

SERVES 4

`DAIRY-FREE` `GLUTEN-FREE` `MAKE-AHEAD`

I first fell in love with summer rolls at an Asian-style café, where they were served as an appetizer. Now my whole family loves them as a light supper, especially in hot weather. Feel free to change up these delightful rolls by varying the fillings with whatever salad ingredients you have on hand.

    12 rice paper rounds, 6 to 8 inches in diameter
    1 pound peeled cooked medium shrimp, thawed if frozen
    2 avocados, pitted, peeled, and sliced
    1 (12-ounce) bag coleslaw mix
    4 scallions, chopped
    ½ cup chopped fresh cilantro
    Favorite dipping sauces, for serving (try Sweet and Spicy Dipping
        Sauce, page 183, and/or Sunflower Dipping Sauce, page 286)

1. Heat a few inches of water in a large skillet over medium heat just until hot to the touch.

2. Soften the rice paper rounds in the water one at a time, according to the package directions. Place a small amount of shrimp, avocado, coleslaw mix, scallions, and cilantro on each one and roll it up cigar-style. After you roll each one, keep them covered with a damp paper towel to prevent them from drying out.

3. Serve the rolls with the dipping sauces.

MAKE IT AHEAD: The rolls can be stored in the refrigerator for up to 24 hours. Pack the rolls in an airtight container, leaving a little space in between them if you can so that they don't stick together. You can tuck a damp paper towel in between if you like.

SHARE AND
SHARE ALIKE

Plan meals through-
out the week that
share common
ingredients. You'll
save time shopping,
you can prep or chop
everything at once,
and you'll waste less.

62

Ginger-Cucumber Salad

SERVES 4

DAIRY-FREE **GLUTEN-FREE**

I've been served this salad in restaurants many times as a side to summer rolls. It's so easy to make at home! English cucumbers are nice to use for this dish since they are usually a bit sweeter and have tiny seeds, if any. If you use a regular cuke with large seeds, halve it lengthwise and scrape out the seeds with a spoon before slicing.

2 tablespoons rice vinegar
1 tablespoon soy sauce
1 tablespoon toasted sesame oil
1 teaspoon chopped fresh ginger
1 teaspoon chopped garlic
2 tablespoons vegetable oil
1 English cucumber, thinly sliced
Sesame seeds, for sprinkling (optional)

1. In a medium-size bowl, whisk together the vinegar, soy sauce, sesame oil, ginger, and garlic. Add the oil and continue whisking to combine.

2. Add the cucumber slices and stir gently to coat. Sprinkle with sesame seeds, if desired, and serve.

In our newlywed
days, a burrito from
Rudy's in Santa Bar-
bara was our quick
fix. The fact that it
was just down the
road from our house
enabled us to eat and
spend more than was
good for us. Now,
making my own veg-
etable fajita burritos
is more economical
and just as quick. A
fruity *agua fresca*
makes it a complete
meal.

Veggie Fajita Burritos

SERVES 4

MEATLESS

I love this mélange of sautéed vegetables, rice, cheese, and salsa.
This dish is particularly good in the summer, when zucchini and
peppers are at their prime. If you have a rice cooker, start the rice
right away. Or, if you've got leftover Tomato Rice Pilaf (page 290) or
Cilantro-Lime Rice (page 293), that would work well here, too. If you
prefer less heat, reduce the amount of pasilla and/or cayenne.

 1 tablespoon vegetable oil
 1 medium zucchini, sliced
 1 red bell pepper, cored and julienned
 1 pasilla chile, cored and julienned
 ½ medium onion, sliced
 4 ounces white mushrooms, sliced (about 1 cup)
 ½ teaspoon ground cumin
 ½ teaspoon dried oregano
 ⅛ teaspoon cayenne pepper
 Fine sea salt and freshly ground black pepper
 4 burrito-size flour tortillas
 1 cup hot cooked white rice
 1 cup shredded cheddar cheese
 ½ cup fresh salsa (such as Serrano Pico de Gallo, page 189),
 or more as desired

1. In a large nonstick skillet, heat the oil over medium-high heat
until shimmering. Add the zucchini, bell pepper, chile, onion, and
mushrooms. Season with the cumin, oregano, cayenne, and salt
and black pepper to taste. Cook until the peppers and zucchini are
tender, the onion turns translucent, and the mushrooms start to
brown, about 10 minutes.

2. Fill each tortilla with an equal portion of hot rice, vegetable mixture, cheese, and salsa and roll them up.

#63

BULK UP

Cook many things at one time as often as possible. Not only will you save on energy costs, but you'll also save time making one big batch instead of many small ones. A large griddle helps me make pancakes, burritos, quesadillas, or grilled cheese sandwiches in short order. There's no way I could feed my hungry crew if I were cooking these items in a skillet. No way, no how. Use bulk-cooking techniques and freeze extras in order to save time—and money, too.

Mango-Strawberry Agua Fresca

SERVES 4

MEATLESS **DAIRY-FREE** **GLUTEN-FREE**

An *agua fresca* is a Latin-style smoothie made of fruit, lime juice, sugar, and water. I've used honey to keep it *au naturel*. Full of rich mango and juicy strawberries, this is a delicious beverage to include in your meal.

2 cups mango chunks
2 cups sliced strawberries
¼ cup fresh lime juice
2 to 3 tablespoons honey
3 cups water

1. Combine the mango, strawberries, lime juice, honey, and a little of the water in a blender. Blend to a smooth consistency.

2. Add the remaining water and liquefy. If your blender doesn't have a liquefy setting, strain the mixture into a bowl, pressing on the solids to extract as much juice as possible. Serve immediately over ice.

When dinner is a
Breakfast Burrito Bar
(see the three B's?),
the FishKids practi-
cally break out in
song and dance. It's
filling and it's fun.
Couple it with the
fruit salad and you'll
have everyone doing
the conga line at
your house.

Triple B

SERVES 4

The bacon adds wonderful smokiness to the onions and hash
browns that fill the burritos. Using precooked bacon really speeds
up your prep time—just toss it in the pan to warm and crisp. Or
cook up some regular bacon if you have a few minutes to spare.

8 slices precooked bacon, chopped
½ medium onion, chopped (about 1 cup)
2 cups frozen shredded potatoes, no need to thaw
½ teaspoon ground cumin
Fine sea salt and freshly ground black pepper
2 tablespoons butter
8 large eggs, beaten
8 burrito-size flour tortillas
2 cups shredded cheddar or Monterey Jack cheese

TOPPINGS
Pickled jalapeños
Diced tomatoes
Chopped fresh cilantro

1. In a large nonstick skillet, heat the bacon, onion, and shredded
potatoes and cook until the bacon is crisp, the onion is translucent,
and the potatoes are hot and starting to brown, about 10 minutes.
Season with the cumin and salt and pepper to taste. Remove from
the heat and tent with foil to keep warm.

2. In a medium nonstick skillet, melt the butter over medium heat.
Add the eggs and cook, stirring and scrambling, until the eggs are
set, 5 to 7 minutes.

3. Assemble the burritos by dividing the potato mixture among the
tortillas. Add the eggs, cheese, and toppings as desired. Roll up
and serve immediately.

64

Don't snub the freezer section. Some frozen vegetables and fruits are fresher than their "fresh" counterparts, being flash-frozen at the peak of the season. Peeled and chopped frozen vegetables will also save you time during your dinner prep.

Tropical Fruit Salad

SERVES 4

`MEATLESS` `DAIRY-FREE` `GLUTEN-FREE`

Regular readers of my Good Cheap Eats blog know how much I love my Monkey Salad, a simple combination of bananas, coconut flakes, and cashews. This salad is an adaptation of that one, only with juicier tropical fruit. It is divine.

3 red mangoes, peeled, pitted, and chopped (about 3 cups)
1 pineapple, peeled, cored, and chopped (about 2 cups)
3 kiwis, peeled and sliced
½ cup roasted unsalted cashews
¼ cup toasted coconut flakes

1. In a large bowl, gently combine the mangoes, pineapple, and kiwi. Divide the fruit among four serving bowls.

2. Sprinkle each bowl with an equal portion of the cashews and coconut flakes and serve immediately.

Greek food is a big
favorite around our
house. There's a
Greek café we oc-
casionally go to, but
a meal there costs
about $50 for our
family and some-
times takes more
time than we have
on a busy night. For
a quick, casual meal,
we can make better
for less at home—
and in half the time.
Duh. Mix up a quick
hummus and enjoy it
with veggie dippers
and pita chips while
the seasoned beef for
the wraps cooks.

Greek Beef Wraps with Tzatziki

SERVES 4

`MAKE-AHEAD`

This wrap was inspired by the flavors of a gyro. It's easy to make
and packs a big flavor punch. Serve this as a burrito bar so folks
can customize their wraps as they like.

    1 pound ground beef
    ½ medium onion, chopped (about 1 cup)
    1 to 2 tablespoons Greek Spice Blend (page 163)
    8 burrito-size flour tortillas
    2 cups baby spinach
    4 medium tomatoes, chopped
    ½ cup crumbled feta cheese
    Tzatziki (recipe follows)

1. In a large nonstick skillet, cook the beef and onion over medium-
high heat until the meat is no longer pink and the onion is translucent. Season with the spice blend.

2. Lay out the tortillas and bowls of the filling options—spinach,
tomatoes, feta, and tzatziki—and allow diners to assemble their
own wraps.

MAKE IT AHEAD: The meat mixture can be stored in a covered container in the
refrigerator for up to 2 days or in the freezer for up to 2 months. Reheat on the
stovetop or in the microwave before serving.

Use pans that are easy to clean. In my efforts to get away from dangerous aluminum and non-stick coatings, I tried using stainless steel cookware. These were a pain to clean and took inordinate amounts of time to scrub. After a little searching, I found a "green pan" that is nonstick and for which cleanup is a breeze. Find good pans to help you cook and clean with ease.

tzatziki

MAKES ABOUT 2 CUPS

`MEATLESS` `GLUTEN-FREE` `MAKE-AHEAD`

Tzatziki is a delightful Greek sauce made from tangy yogurt seasoned with garlic, dill, and cucumber. It's delicious in sandwiches, on pitas, and as a dip.

1 cup plain Greek yogurt
1 tablespoon fresh lemon juice
1 cucumber, seeded and diced
1 teaspoon minced garlic
1 teaspoon dried dill
¼ teaspoon freshly ground black pepper

In a small bowl, combine the yogurt, lemon juice, cucumber, garlic, dill, and pepper. Stir well to combine.

MAKE IT AHEAD: The tzatziki can be stored in a covered container in the refrigerator for up to 3 days.

66

WHAT A WHIZ!

A food processor can be a lifesaver in the kitchen. In fact, it's one of my favorite kitchen appliances, making quick work of mixing dough for pie crusts and biscuits, chopping ingredients for soups and salsa, shredding cheese, or slicing vegetables. I use mine several times a week to speed things up.

Red Pepper Hummus

SERVES 4

`MEATLESS` `DAIRY-FREE` `GLUTEN-FREE` `MAKE-AHEAD`

Hummus doesn't have to be complicated, though with the number of commercial varieties available, you would think that it was. This comes together quickly and deliciously with some very basic ingredients.

1 (15-ounce) can chickpeas, drained
¼ cup tahini
1 roasted red bell pepper (from a jar)
1 teaspoon chopped garlic
5 tablespoons fresh lemon juice
2 tablespoons olive oil
¾ teaspoon fine sea salt
¼ teaspoon ground cumin
⅛ teaspoon cayenne pepper
Freshly ground black pepper
Your favorite dippers, such as carrot sticks, cucumbers, and pita chips

Place the chickpeas in a food processor fitted with a metal blade and add the tahini, roasted pepper, garlic, lemon juice, oil, salt, cumin, cayenne, and pepper to taste. Blend until very smooth. Adjust the seasonings as desired and serve with your favorite dippers.

MAKE IT AHEAD: The hummus can be stored in a covered container in the refrigerator for up to 3 days.

HOW TO MAKE GREAT HOT SANDWICHES

I love my panini press. Upon its arrival in our home, this machine revolutionized my sandwich-making prowess. Since I don't have to flip the sandwich, it allows me to go all Dagwood with the sandwich fillings. Not only that, but the panini press can do the work while you bustle around gathering plates, napkins, and other fancy tableware. Pour a great drink while you're at it! It's the quick-supper fixer-upper.

Consider these requirements for great panini or other hot sandwiches:

1. **Good bread:** Try thick rye, sourdough, onion rolls, or ciabatta.

2. **Tasty meats and cheeses:** Pay a little more at the deli case for higher-quality products.

3. **Savory spreads and toppings:** Mix different sauces and flavored mayos or mustards with spices and herbs. Pile on spinach, tomatoes, onions, and roasted red peppers.

In lieu of a panini press, consider a large electric griddle that allows you to cook many sandwiches at once and gives you ample flipping space. Alternatively, you can wrap sandwiches in foil and toss them into a hot oven to warm.

Some of our favorite ingredient combinations include Brie and bacon; turkey and cheddar; roast beef and provolone; ham and Swiss; and grilled vegetables and pepper Jack.

MENU

Turkey-Avocado
Ranch Wrap

Cranberry-
Carrot Salad

Wraps are more
fun than plain old
sandwiches, and
they're a versatile
mealtime choice
because you can fill
them with practically
anything. This meal
could be called the
All-American, from
the turkey and ranch
dressing in the wrap
to the cranberries
in the salad. It's
delicious and easy
to make, and great
for eating al fresco
on the patio or at
the Little League
ballpark.

Turkey-Avocado Ranch Wrap

SERVES 4

I used to pay upward of $5 for a store-bought or fast-food wrap. Now I make them at home for less than a buck! If you shop well and keep these ingredients on hand, the meal comes together in a blink of an eye—without the high price tag.

¼ cup mayonnaise
¼ cup buttermilk
1 tablespoon dried parsley
½ teaspoon garlic powder
½ teaspoon onion powder
Pinch of cayenne pepper
4 burrito-size flour tortillas
8 ounces sliced turkey breast
2 small avocados, pitted, peeled, and chopped
2 Roma tomatoes, chopped
1 to 2 cups shredded lettuce or cabbage
2 scallions, chopped

1. In a small bowl, whisk together the mayo, buttermilk, parsley, garlic powder, onion powder, and cayenne. Stir until smooth.

2. Lay out the tortillas on a work surface. Assemble the wraps by layering equal portions of the turkey, avocado, chopped tomatoes, lettuce, scallions, and dressing on each tortilla. Roll up and serve.

67

Every meal does
not need to be a big
production. A take-
out order of burgers
and fries certainly
isn't a big deal, but
how often do we turn
to that when we're
not prepared to fix
a feast? Instead,
make peace with
sandwich night. It's
quick; it's easy; it's
more healthful; and
it's delicious. It may
not be a three-course
meal, but it gets the
job done.

Cranberry-Carrot Salad

SERVES 4

`MEATLESS` `DAIRY-FREE` `GLUTEN-FREE` `MAKE-AHEAD`

A carrot salad is an easy way to add sweetness and texture to a
meal. This one gets crunch from the carrots and almonds and a
sweet chewiness from the cranberries. My people just gobble this
down; here's betting yours will, too.

¼ cup cider vinegar
Fine sea salt and freshly ground black pepper
¼ cup olive oil
1 (10-ounce) bag shredded carrots (about 4 cups)
¼ cup dried cranberries
¼ cup slivered almonds
2 tablespoons chopped fresh basil

1. Pour the cider vinegar into a large bowl and season to taste with
salt and pepper. Add the olive oil and whisk to combine.

2. Add the carrots, cranberries, almonds, and basil. Toss to
combine.

MAKE IT AHEAD: The salad can be stored in a covered container in the fridge for
up to 3 days.

Green Chile Burritos

Spiced Grilled Corn on the Cob

Burritos are the spice of life. (Okay, well, if they aren't, they should be.) All the ingredients can be kept on hand in the pantry, fridge, or freezer, and they can be pulled together with little work or planning. Prepared burritos freeze well and reheat easily. What's not to love? Throw some corn on the grill to finish off this delicious, easy-on-the-budget meal.

Green Chile Burritos

SERVES 4 TO 6

MEATLESS **MAKE-AHEAD** **FREEZER-FRIENDLY**

With refried beans, abundant cheese, green chiles, onions, and a little hot sauce, these meatless babies will rival whatever the local burrito joint can make. Plus, they're pretty much guilt-free, made from real food and prepared at home. If you've got a little extra time, make a batch of Spicy Pintos (page 33) to really take these over the top. My life is complete when I have a few dozen of these stashed in the freezer.

12 burrito-size flour tortillas
3 cups canned refried beans
2 cups shredded Monterey Jack and/or cheddar cheese
1 (7-ounce) can chopped green chiles, drained
½ cup finely chopped onion
Hot sauce

1. Lay out the tortillas on a work surface. Spread ¼ cup beans in a line down the center of each. Sprinkle on a small handful of cheese, a spoonful of chiles, and then a teaspoon of onions. Add hot sauce to taste. Roll up the tortillas over the filling, tucking in the sides as you go.

2. Heat a griddle over medium-high heat. Cook the burritos on the hot griddle until the filling is hot and the tortillas are crisp, turning to crisp all around.

MAKE IT AHEAD: The filled and rolled burritos can be placed in a zip-top freezer bag and frozen for up to 2 months. Thaw in the refrigerator before cooking.

68

PLAN A QUICK FIX

The local drive-thru restaurant is less than a mile from my home, but the round trip takes about a half hour—on a good day. Chances are you've got ingredients in your cupboards that could be whipped up into something tasty in less time than it takes to make a run for the border. Make a list of quick-fix meals like eggs, pancakes, tacos, pasta dishes, and quesadillas and keep their staple ingredients on hand so you are never stuck at dinnertime. You'll save money, eat more healthfully, and be able to spend that time savings on things that matter more than sitting in a car waiting for a tinny voice to ask for your order.

Spiced Grilled Corn on the Cob

SERVES 4

`MEATLESS` `GLUTEN-FREE` `MAKE-AHEAD`

I love grilling corn on the cob—there's no fussing with pots of water or passing the butter at the table. Prepare a simple seasoned spread, butter the cobs, wrap them in foil, and leave them on the grill until tender. An outdoor grill will provide a wonderful smoky aroma, but you can cook the wrapped corn on a stovetop grill pan as well.

  4 tablespoons (½ stick) butter, softened
  1 teaspoon chili powder
  ½ teaspoon fine sea salt
  ½ teaspoon dried oregano
  Pinch of cayenne pepper
  4 ears corn, shucked

1. Preheat an outdoor grill for a medium fire or a stovetop grill pan over medium heat.

2. In a small bowl, stir together the butter, chili powder, salt, oregano, and cayenne. Spread the mixture on the ears of corn and wrap each in a sheet of aluminum foil.

3. Cook on the hot grill over direct heat with the lid down or on the grill pan, covered, until tender, about 12 minutes.

MAKE IT AHEAD: The corn can be prepped through step 2 and refrigerated for up to 24 hours.

6 MEALS TO MAKE WHEN THERE'S "NOTHING" TO EAT

While I preach all about the benefits of meal planning, sometimes even I fail miserably to follow my own advice. I forget to thaw. The meeting runs late. My kids ate my homework, I mean, all the tortillas.

It's tempting to say, "There's nothing to eat," and then run for take-out. What I realized a few years ago is that we have a couple dozen favorite meals that I can whip up quickly with ingredients that are almost always in the cupboard and/or fridge. This list of "emergency meals" has proven to be one of the most popular features on the Good Cheap Eats blog. My guess is that we're all in the same boat.

These might not be fancy meals, but they get the job done and they're infinitely healthier (and cheaper) than most take-out. Here are some ideas to get you started:

1. Rice Bowls: Cook up a pot of rice and top with leftover cooked meat, beans, cheese, fresh or sautéed vegetables, salsa, sour cream, or other favorite sauces.

2. Pasta: A simple marinara sauce can be whipped up from a can of crushed tomatoes and a handful of herbs. Serve over hot pasta with a sprinkling of cheese, and offer a steamed vegetable or tossed salad on the side.

3. Quesadillas: All you need are tortillas and cheese. Bonus points for sour cream, salsa, and some leftover cooked meat or veggies.

4. Grilled Cheese Sandwiches: Bread and cheese meld for a quick meal on the run. Grab an apple and you're good to go.

5. Sandwich Bar: The beauty of the buffet is that you don't need a lot of any one thing. By laying out a variety of cheeses, meats, veggies, breads, and spreads, you're providing endless options for creative sandwich making.

6. Quick-Fix Soup: Sauté a chopped onion in a pot. Add broth, tomato sauce, and/or water. Stir in leftover meat or veggies, that last potato, or a handful of rice or pasta and season with a spice mix from the cupboard. Before you know it, dinner is ready to be served.

Snappy Sautés, Skillets, and Other Stovetop Specials

Whether you prefer a cast-iron skillet or an eco-friendly Teflon-free nonstick pan, the frying pan can really be your best friend. It's amazing what magic can happen in a skillet. Folks rave about slow cookers and other gadgets, but the good ol' fry pan has been dishing it up for decades.

These sautés, skillets, and other stovetop specials are sure to delight and surprise you. Some of my favorite meals come together on the cooktop in a snap.

Alfredo Noodles
and Broccoli

Easy Bruschetta

Italian food is always
a crowd pleaser.
It's hard to mess
up, affordable, and
healthy—and it
tastes great! This
meatless meal is
quick and simple
to make. Feel free
to add some grilled
chicken or fish if you
like, but know that
my carnivores are
happily satiated with
this combo as is.
There are never any
leftovers.

Alfredo Noodles and Broccoli

SERVES 4 TO 6

MEATLESS

When it comes to pasta dishes, I invariably choose a creamy
Alfredo-type dish over its tomato-based cousins. This sauce is one
of my go-to recipes. For a really quick fix, I make the sauce in the microwave while the pasta cooks and then toss it with the hot cooked
pasta. Easy peasy. My kids can make it themselves; so can you.

- 1 pound penne pasta
- 3 cups small broccoli florets
- 8 tablespoons (1 stick) butter
- 1 teaspoon minced garlic
- ½ cup heavy cream
- Fine sea salt and freshly ground black pepper
- ½ cup finely shredded Parmesan, Romano, or Asiago cheese

1. Bring a large pot of salted water to a boil over high heat. Cook
the pasta according to the package directions, adding the broccoli
for the last 5 minutes of the cooking time. Drain and set aside.

2. Return the empty pot to the stove, lower the heat to medium, and
add the butter. After it melts, add the garlic and cook until fragrant,
about 1 minute. Stir in the cream and heat through. Add the cooked
penne and broccoli and stir to coat. Season to taste with salt and
pepper.

3. Sprinkle the cheese over the pasta mixture and toss again.
Adjust the seasonings and serve.

69

As you plan your grocery shopping this week, decide which stores to shop and add those to your map of errands. If you lump several stops into one trip, you'll save fuel as well as time. Take a cooler for cold items so that if you need to make another stop after the store, you're keeping things chilled and food-safe.

Easy Bruschetta

SERVES 4

MEATLESS **DAIRY-FREE** MAKE-AHEAD

Tomato bruschetta topping is the Italian version of salsa—at least in my mind, they are happy cousins. Toasted baguette slices topped with chopped fresh tomatoes blended with herbs and garlic are a nice alternative to chips and salsa. To save time, I've added the garlic to the tomato mixture instead of rubbing it on the toasted baguette. I buy bags of baguette presliced from the day-old bread rack at the grocer's to save time and money.

1 baguette, thinly sliced
2 tablespoons olive oil
2 large tomatoes, finely chopped
2 tablespoons chopped fresh basil
1 teaspoon minced garlic
1 tablespoon balsamic vinegar
Fine sea salt and freshly ground black pepper

1. Preheat the oven to 375°F.

2. Lay the bread slices on a large baking sheet. Brush with the oil. Toast in the oven until crisp and light brown, about 10 minutes. Flip the slices and toast the other side, about 5 minutes more. Cool on a rack.

3. In a small bowl, combine the tomatoes, basil, garlic, vinegar, and salt and pepper to taste. Stir gently to combine.

4. Spoon a small amount of the tomato mixture onto each toast and serve immediately.

MAKE IT AHEAD: The toasted baguettes can be stored in an airtight container at room temperature for up to 2 days.

There's a deep sat-
isfaction that comes
from spending just
a half hour at the
stove and having
dinner ready to
serve when you step
away. It's even more
satisfying to have
a glass of some-
thing delicious on
hand, some relaxing
music, and someone
special to chat with
while you cook.

This supper is
quick, elegant, and
delicious, just as ap-
propriate for a cozy
date night as for a
company dinner.

Marsala Fried Chicken

SERVES 4 TO 6

I like to fillet boneless, skinless chicken breasts so that each piece is thinner and quicker to cook. It also helps make portions man-ageable, since so many commercial chicken pieces are supersized these days. The Marsala pan sauce makes this extra special.

2 large boneless, skinless chicken breast halves
1 teaspoon fine sea salt, plus more for seasoning
Freshly ground black pepper
¼ cup buttermilk
1¼ cups unbleached all-purpose flour
1 teaspoon herbes de Provence
½ teaspoon garlic powder
¼ cup olive oil
1 tablespoon butter
½ medium onion, chopped (about 1 cup)
2 cups chicken or vegetable broth
¼ cup dry Marsala wine
Hot cooked rice or egg noodles, for serving

1. Fillet each chicken breast. With the thicker side of the breast facing the knife, hold the meat flat on the cutting board and cut horizontally, creating two thin cutlets. Season the chicken with salt and pepper to taste.

2. Place the buttermilk in a shallow dish. In another shallow dish, combine 1 cup of the flour, the salt, herbes de Provence, garlic pow-der, and pepper to taste.

3. In a large nonstick skillet, heat the oil over medium heat until shimmering.

4. Dip each chicken cutlet in the buttermilk, letting the excess drip off, and then dredge in the flour mixture. Place each piece in the hot oil. Fry the chicken until cooked through and crisp, about 4 minutes per side. Remove from the pan and tent with foil.

5. Add the butter to the pan and allow it to melt. Add the onions and cook until they are translucent. Add the remaining ¼ cup flour to the pan and stir, scraping up any browned bits. Whisk in the broth and Marsala and cook until thickened to sauce consistency, 7 to 10 minutes.

6. Return the chicken to the pan to coat with the sauce and re-warm. Serve over hot rice or noodles.

70

Use a small blender to help you quickly prepare dressings and sauces. Many blender models come with party cups that hold 16 ounces or less, making them perfect for these small mixtures. In lieu of party cups, standard Mason jars attach to most traditional blender bases, meaning you can make your own party cup.

Green Salad with Pesto Dressing

SERVES 4 TO 6

`MEATLESS` `GLUTEN-FREE` `MAKE-AHEAD`

This pesto-inspired vinaigrette comes together quickly in a small blender or food processor. It's a nice complement to the fresh veggies and rich Romano cheese in the salad.

¼ cup red wine vinegar
¼ cup packed fresh basil leaves
1 tablespoon chopped scallions
1 teaspoon minced garlic
½ cup olive oil
1 head romaine lettuce, chopped
1 medium tomato, chopped
1 large carrot, peeled and sliced
5 radishes, sliced
½ medium bell pepper (any color), cored and sliced
¼ cup shredded Romano cheese

1. In a small blender or food processor, combine the vinegar, basil, scallions, and garlic. Blend until smooth. With the machine running, add the oil in a thin stream and continue to blend until emulsified.

2. In a large salad bowl, combine the romaine, tomato, carrot, radishes, and bell pepper. Add enough dressing to coat. Toss gently. Sprinkle with the Romano cheese and toss again. Serve immediately, with additional dressing on the side.

MAKE IT AHEAD: The dressing and salad can be stored in separate covered containers in the refrigerator for up to 2 days. Stir or whisk the dressing to recombine before serving.

MENU

Crispy Sage Chicken Strips

Israeli Couscous with Broccoli

Fried chicken never tasted so good—my kids go crazy over this meal. If you've never tried Israeli couscous, which is larger than regular couscous, wait no longer. The pearl-shaped pasta is delicious comfort food that pairs perfectly with the crispy chicken.

Crispy Sage Chicken Strips

SERVES 4

DAIRY-FREE

These pan-fried chicken strips are delicious and finger-licking crispy, but they are so much more wholesome than the processed "chicken fingers" we too often feed kids. The FishKids are thrilled when I make these.

> 2 tablespoons olive oil
> ½ cup panko bread crumbs
> 1 teaspoon rubbed sage
> ½ teaspoon fine sea salt
> ½ teaspoon paprika
> Freshly ground black pepper
> 1½ pounds chicken tenders

1. In a large nonstick skillet, heat the oil over medium-high heat until shimmering.

2. In a small bowl, combine the panko, sage, salt, paprika, and pepper to taste. Dip the chicken pieces into the mixture and cook in the hot oil until the crust is crisp and the chicken is cooked through, 5 to 7 minutes per side.

Israeli Couscous with Broccoli

SERVES 4

MEATLESS **DAIRY-FREE** MAKE-AHEAD

This dish is a great way to combine vegetables and pasta. Chop the broccoli florets small so that they don't overwhelm the small beads of couscous. It is delicious served hot or cold.

2 tablespoons olive oil
4 ounces white mushrooms, sliced (about 1 cup)
1⅔ cups Israeli couscous
3 cups very small broccoli florets
2 cups vegetable or chicken broth
4 scallions, chopped
Fine sea salt and freshly ground black pepper

1. In a large saucepan, heat the oil until shimmering over medium-high heat. Add the mushrooms and cook until they've lost their liquid and started to brown, about 3 minutes.

2. Add the couscous and cook until lightly browned, 1 to 2 minutes.

3. Add the broccoli, broth, and scallions and bring to a low boil. Cover and simmer until the broccoli is tender and the liquid is absorbed, 10 to 12 minutes. Season to taste with salt and pepper and serve.

MAKE IT AHEAD: The couscous can be stored in a covered container in the fridge for up to 3 days. Serve hot or cold.

Every year at Mardi
Gras time, I pay
homage to the Cajun
South by making a
jambalaya-inspired
dish. It's a family
tradition that every-
one loves—our way
to *laisser les bons
temps rouler*.

Jambalaya Pasta with Sausage and Chicken

SERVES 4 TO 6

One of FishPapa's favorite dishes is this jambalaya-inspired pasta. He prefers it so spicy that you'd think your tongue's afire. I've toned it down just a bit here, but if you like it even milder, use sweet sausage instead of hot. Want to turn up the heat? Add more cayenne pepper.

1 pound penne pasta
1 tablespoon olive oil
8 ounces bulk hot Italian sausage
½ medium onion, chopped (about 1 cup)
8 ounces boneless, skinless chicken breast, cut into bite-size pieces
1 green bell pepper, cored and chopped
1 cup chicken broth
⅓ cup heavy cream
1 tablespoon Cajun Spice Blend (page 162)
Chopped fresh parsley, for garnish

1. Bring a large pot of salted water to a boil over high heat. Cook the penne according to the package directions. Drain and set aside.

2. Meanwhile, in a large nonstick skillet, heat the oil over medium-high heat until shimmering. Add the sausage and onion and cook, breaking up the sausage chunks with a wooden spoon, until it starts to lose its pink color, about 5 minutes. Add the chicken and bell pepper and cook, stirring, until the chicken is almost cooked, about 5 minutes.

3. Add the broth, cream, and spice mix and simmer until slightly thickened, about 5 minutes.

4. Add the cooked pasta to the skillet and toss with the chicken and sausage mixture. Garnish with chopped parsley and serve.

#72

THE RIGHT PAN FOR THE JOB

By using an adequately sized pot or pan, you will be able to cook more efficiently. You won't worry about splashing food all over the stove. You'll have enough elbow room to work, so to speak. And it really isn't much more effort to wash a taller pot or bigger pan. The size of the cooking vessel can make a huge difference in your time investment.

Lemon-Dill Cauliflower

SERVES 4 TO 6

MEATLESS **DAIRY-FREE** **GLUTEN-FREE**

We always told our toddlers that cauliflower stalks were white trees and broccoli florets were green ones. It worked for picky eaters. You won't need special names to get folks to eat this cauliflower, however. It's so delicious that I doubt there will be any left over.

1 head cauliflower, cut into florets
2 tablespoons olive oil
Juice of ½ lemon
½ teaspoon dried dill
Fine sea salt and freshly ground black pepper

1. Place the cauliflower in a large skillet with a lid and add 1 inch of water. Cover and cook over medium-high heat for 5 minutes. Drain the cauliflower and return it to the skillet, pushing it to one side.

2. Add the oil to the skillet and raise the heat to high. Toss the cauliflower with the oil and let it brown slightly. Season with the lemon juice, dill, and salt and pepper to taste. Serve hot.

Mini Meatloaves

Stovetop Mac
and Cheese

Meatloaf and mac
and cheese is a
classic combination.
Many folks rely on
boxed mixes and
canned sauces to
make this vintage
dish, but you can
easily do it all
yourself. Savory
meatloaves are made
miniature so that
they cook quickly.
Old-fashioned
macaroni and
cheese cooks on the
stovetop in about the
same time it takes to
prepare that iconic
blue box. Serve
steamed broccoli on
the side and you've
got a tasty, whole-
foods meal that really
isn't more work than
opening those boxes
and cans.

Mini Meatloaves

SERVES 4

`DAIRY-FREE` `MAKE-AHEAD` `FREEZER-FRIENDLY`

These meatloaves may be Lilliputian in size, but they pack Gulliver-
size flavor. Whiz a couple of slices of bread through the blender or
food processor for quick bread crumbs on the cheap.

    1 pound ground beef
    1 cup fresh bread crumbs (from about 2 slices sandwich bread)
    ½ medium onion, chopped (about 1 cup)
    1 tablespoon soy sauce
    ½ teaspoon paprika
    ½ teaspoon dried thyme
    ¼ teaspoon cayenne pepper
    Fine sea salt and freshly ground black pepper

1. Preheat the oven to 350°F. Grease a 9 x 13-inch baking pan with
nonstick cooking spray.

2. In a large bowl, combine the ground beef, bread crumbs, onion,
soy sauce, paprika, thyme, cayenne, and salt and pepper to taste.
Mix gently, being careful not to overmix.

3. Divide the mixture into eight equal portions. Form each one into
a small loaf or patty, not more than 1 inch tall. Place in the prepared
baking pan.

4. Bake until cooked through, 20 to 25 minutes.

MAKE IT AHEAD: The meatloaves can be made through step 3, covered, and
stored in the refrigerator for up to 1 day or in the freezer for up to 2 months.
Thaw in the refrigerator overnight before baking. Add a few minutes to the baking time to allow for the cold dish.

#73

THINK
OUTSIDE THE
BOX

Processed items are
marketed to make
you think you're sav-
ing time, but many
of them don't really
save you much time
over making it from
scratch. Boxed rice
mixes, macaroni
dishes, and cake
mixes do not save
you time, so stop
paying the high
price in nutrition
or grocery budget.
Not only is the time
savings negligible
or even nonexistent,
but the processed
item is not as healthy
as homemade. Get-
ting sick, gaining
weight, or feeling
tired will eventually
take up your time.
Cut those thieves off
at the pass and stick
to whole foods you
make yourself.

Stovetop Mac and Cheese

SERVES 4 TO 6

MEATLESS

Before the advent of processed foods, most home cooks knew
how to make a simple cheese sauce. It was one of the first recipes
taught in home-ec class. It's also a far cry from powdered cheese
sauce mixes and their gloppy canned cousins of modern times.
Forget that! You'll be making mac and cheese like a boss with this
recipe.

1 pound small macaroni, such as shells or elbows
4 tablespoons (½ stick) butter
¼ cup unbleached all-purpose flour
1½ cups milk
2 cups shredded cheddar cheese
Fine sea salt and freshly ground black pepper

1. Bring a large pot of salted water to a boil over high heat. Cook the
macaroni according to the package directions. Drain and set aside.

2. In the same pot, melt the butter over medium heat. Whisk in the
flour and stir until well mixed, hot, and bubbly, 1 to 2 minutes.

3. Gradually whisk in the milk, stirring until smooth. Add the cheese
a handful at a time, whisking until smooth.

4. Add the cooked macaroni and stir until combined. Season to
taste with salt and pepper and serve hot.

The perfect stovetop supper? How about chicken cooked quickly and partnered with vegetables and a creamy, flavorful sauce. Start the rice cooker, get the carrots ready to go, and start sautéing. Dinner will be ready in a jiffy.

Chicken Sauté with Mushrooms and Spinach

SERVES 4

GLUTEN-FREE

I love this dish, with its aromatic onions and mushrooms, tender chicken, sweet tomatoes, and creamy sauce. The spinach adds flavor and all those good things that make Popeye strong. *Bon appétit!* Serve this over rice, if you like.

1 tablespoon olive oil
½ medium onion, chopped (about 1 cup)
4 ounces white mushrooms, sliced (about 1 cup)
1 pound boneless, skinless chicken breast, cut into bite-size pieces
Fine sea salt and freshly ground black pepper
¼ cup dry sherry
¾ cup heavy cream
¼ cup chopped sun-dried tomatoes, drained if using jarred
1 teaspoon rubbed sage
5 ounces baby spinach

1. In a large nonstick skillet, heat the oil over medium-high heat until shimmering. Add the onion and mushrooms and cook until the onion turns translucent and the mushrooms start to lose their liquid, about 5 minutes.

2. Add the chicken and cook until no longer pink in the center; the vegetables will be very tender. Season to taste with salt and pepper. Transfer to a dish and tent with foil.

3. Add the sherry to the pan, scraping up any browned bits. Simmer until slightly thickened, about 2 minutes. Add the cream, tomatoes, and sage and bring to a simmer.

4. Return the chicken and vegetables to the pan, and then add the baby spinach. Cook until the chicken is warm and the spinach is wilted, about 4 minutes.

74

COOK ONCE, EAT TWICE (OR THRICE)

Make your cooking session do double or triple duty. That means you might cook a huge batch of chicken one night and serve it as a main dish. Make chicken tacos with some of the chicken the next night. And then use up the rest of the chicken in a casserole on the third or fourth night. By doing so, you've saved yourself a ton of time and effort and saved some money, too.

Honeyed Carrots

SERVES 4

MEATLESS **GLUTEN-FREE**

My mom used to make these carrots all the time when I was a kid. It was a favorite side dish back then and still is now—for my kids, too. If you have whole carrots on hand, simply peel and chop into 1-inch chunks or slice on the bias into thick coins.

1 pound baby carrots
2 tablespoons butter
2 tablespoons honey
Fine sea salt and freshly ground black pepper

1. Place the carrots in a medium saucepan and add 1 inch of water. Cover and bring to a boil over medium-high heat. Simmer until the carrots are very tender, about 10 minutes.

2. Drain the carrots and return them to the saucepan. Add the butter, honey, and salt and pepper to taste. Stir gently and heat until well glazed, about 5 minutes.

The beauty of
home-cooked Asian-
inspired dishes
is that they cook
quickly and just
burst with fresh
flavor. This supper
of saucy pork stir-fry
and broccoli-flecked
noodles will have
your crew pulling
out the chopsticks in
no time.

Ginger Pork and Mushrooms

SERVES 4 TO 6

`DAIRY-FREE` `GLUTEN-FREE` `MAKE-AHEAD` `FREEZER-FRIENDLY`

It can be tricky to find a cut of pork that's not too fatty or that doesn't dry out when cooked. I've found that pork tenderloin fits the bill perfectly. It's lower in fat and stays moist, while its thinner shape allows me to cut it up quickly for stir-fries.

2 tablespoons vegetable oil
1 pound pork tenderloin, cut into bite-size pieces
8 ounces white mushrooms, sliced (about 2 cups)
1 medium red bell pepper, cored and chopped
2 teaspoons minced fresh ginger
¼ teaspoon red pepper flakes
1 (8-ounce) can water chestnuts, drained
4 scallions, chopped
1¼ cups chicken broth
2 tablespoons soy sauce
2 tablespoons dry sherry
2 tablespoons cornstarch
Hot cooked rice, for serving (optional)
Sriracha sauce, for serving

1. In a large nonstick skillet, heat the oil over medium-high heat until shimmering. Add the pork, mushrooms, bell pepper, ginger, and red pepper flakes. Sauté until the pork is still just a bit pink and the mushrooms and pepper are tender, about 5 minutes. Stir in the water chestnuts and scallions.

2. In a small bowl, whisk together the broth, soy sauce, sherry, and cornstarch. Add this mixture to the pan and simmer until thickened to sauce consistency, about 7 minutes. Serve over hot cooked rice, if you like, and pass the sriracha sauce.

MAKE IT AHEAD: The cooked dish can be stored in a covered container in the refrigerator for up to 3 days or in the freezer up to 2 months. Thaw in the refrigerator before reheating.

75

Learn the technique of the sauté: quickly cooking meat and vegetables in a bit of hot fat. Serve this over rice, pasta, or another cooked grain for a meal that comes together in short order. The variation possibilities are endless—beef and broccoli over rice, shrimp and snow peas over lo mein, chicken and mushrooms over couscous—so there's never a dull moment even if you use this same technique several nights in a row.

Broccoli Sesame Noodles

SERVES 4 TO 6

MEATLESS **DAIRY-FREE**

This noodle dish is similar to a chow mein, only I've used broccoli slaw mix (shredded broccoli and carrots) instead of cabbage. It's delicious as a side dish, but feel free to add cooked chicken or beef to make it a main course.

6 ounces udon noodles
2 tablespoons vegetable oil
½ medium onion, sliced (about 1 cup)
1 (12-ounce) bag broccoli slaw mix
1 teaspoon minced garlic
¼ teaspoon red pepper flakes
½ cup vegetable broth
1 tablespoon soy sauce
1 tablespoon toasted sesame oil
1 tablespoon cornstarch
Sesame seeds, for garnish (optional)

1. Bring a large pot of salted water to a boil over high heat. Cook the udon noodles according to the package directions. Drain and set aside.

2. In a large nonstick skillet, heat the oil over medium-high heat until shimmering. Add the onion and cook until translucent, about 5 minutes. Add the broccoli slaw, garlic, and red pepper flakes. Cook until tender, about 5 minutes.

3. In a small bowl, whisk together the broth, soy sauce, sesame oil, and cornstarch. Add this finishing sauce to the skillet and cook, stirring, until thickened.

4. Top the noodles with the veggie mix, sprinkle with sesame seeds (if desired), and serve hot.

LEFTOVERS MAKE FOR QUICK (AND DIFFERENT) MEALS

Got leftovers? Put 'em to work! You spent good time and money to prepare that meal. To let it go to waste is to kiss that time and money good-bye. While "reheat and eat" is certainly quick and easy, you can make your leftovers new again with these 10 tricks:

1. Wrap it in a tortilla.
2. Make an omelet.
3. Make soup.
4. Make a stir-fry.
5. Top a pizza.
6. Fill a sandwich or panini.
7. Make a salad.
8. Fold it into a quesadilla.
9. Make a potpie.
10. Freeze it for later.

This supper is oh-so-simple, but oh-so-good. Crisp, juicy sausage and greens rest on pillows of polenta. Comfort food in 30 minutes or less.

Smoked Chicken Sausage and Greens Skillet

SERVES 4

DAIRY-FREE GLUTEN-FREE

Be sure to buy high-quality smoked chicken sausages for this dish—it makes a big difference. Since the apple-studded sausages tend toward the sweet side, I'm generous with the salt to balance it all out.

> 1 tablespoon olive oil
> ½ medium onion, chopped (about 1 cup)
> 4 to 8 smoked chicken and apple sausage links, sliced (about 1 pound)
> 1 medium bell pepper (any color), cored and chopped
> 1 bunch kale or Swiss chard, thick stems removed and leaves chopped (about 6 cups)
> ¼ cup water
> Fine sea salt and freshly ground black pepper

1. In a large nonstick skillet, heat the oil over medium-high heat until shimmering. Add the onion and cook until it starts to turn translucent, about 5 minutes. Add the sausages and bell pepper and cook until the sausages are browned and the pepper is tender.

2. Add the kale and water and cook, stirring, until the greens are wilted, 5 to 10 minutes. (You may have to add the kale in batches, depending on the size of your pan.) Season to taste with salt and pepper and serve.

#76

GO WITH THE GRAIN

Choose quick-cooking grains like quinoa and rice. They pack a hearty punch and cook up in minutes. Couscous, orzo, quick-cooking polenta, and quick-cooking pearl barley are also good carb choices that don't take long to prep.

Quick and Cheesy Polenta

SERVES 4 TO 6

`MEATLESS` `GLUTEN-FREE`

I didn't grow up eating polenta. And the first time I tried it as a newlywed, I didn't like it. On a visit to my favorite Italian restaurant a few years ago, I gave it another go, and fell in love. I guess one's taste buds can mature after all. Even my husband was won over after he turned 50.

    3 cups chicken broth
    1 cup milk
    ½ teaspoon fine sea salt
    1 cup polenta
    4 tablespoons (½ stick) butter, cut into cubes
    ¾ cup shredded Asiago cheese
    Freshly ground black pepper

1. In a medium-size saucepan, combine the broth, milk, and salt. Bring to a low boil over medium-high heat.

2. Stir in the polenta and reduce the heat to a simmer. Cook until thick and creamy, 15 to 20 minutes, stirring occasionally to prevent sticking.

3. Stir in the butter. Add the cheese in small handfuls, stirring between each addition to melt and combine. Season to taste with pepper and serve immediately.

MENU

Spaghetti with
Quick Meat
Sauce

Oven-Roasted
Green Beans

Pasta with green
beans has been one
of my go-to meals
for almost 20 years.
It's fast and simple
and even the picki-
est eaters enjoy it.
It's also easy on the
budget. In order to
control the traffic
on the stovetop, the
beans roast in the
oven while the sauce
and pasta do their
thing.

Spaghetti with Quick Meat Sauce

SERVES 4 TO 6

MAKE-AHEAD FREEZER-FRIENDLY

Meat sauces are fun to make because there are so many variables.
You can switch up the type of tomato product, the kind of meat,
or your choice of vegetables. We could probably create a different
sauce every night for weeks without repeating ourselves. This version, however, is worth repeating. If you're a fan of sweeter sauces,
feel free to stir in a teaspoonful of sugar.

1 pound ground beef
½ medium onion, chopped (about 1 cup)
1 teaspoon minced garlic
1 (15-ounce) can tomato sauce
1 (14.5-ounce) can diced tomatoes, with their juices
1 (6-ounce) can tomato paste
2 teaspoons dried Italian herb blend
1 teaspoon kosher salt
¼ teaspoon freshly ground black pepper
¼ teaspoon red pepper flakes
½ cup beef broth or water (optional)
1 pound spaghetti
Shredded Parmesan cheese, for serving (optional)

1. In a large nonstick skillet, cook the beef, onion, and garlic over
medium-high heat until the meat starts to brown. Stir in the tomato
sauce, tomatoes, tomato paste, Italian herbs, salt, black pepper,
and red pepper flakes. Simmer for 15 minutes. Thin with beef broth
or water if you prefer a thinner texture. Adjust the seasonings.

2. Meanwhile, bring a large pot of salted water to a boil over high
heat. Cook the spaghetti according to the package directions. Drain
and serve topped with the meat sauce and Parmesan, if desired.

MAKE IT AHEAD: The meat sauce can be stored in a covered container in the
refrigerator for up to 4 days or in the freezer for up to 2 months. Thaw in the
refrigerator before reheating.

#77

DOUBLE DOWN

Always cook double the amount of pasta you'll need for one dinner. While you're taking the time to heat that big pot of water, cook enough for two meals. Enjoy half right away with a hot sauce, like the Quick Meat Sauce on page 230. Turn the balance into a chilled pasta salad to enjoy later in the week.

Oven-Roasted Green Beans

SERVES 4

DAIRY-FREE **GLUTEN-FREE**

Roasted green beans are amazingly good. These get a little extra oomph from the bacon, though you can feel free to leave it out if you think the pasta is meaty enough. This recipe works just as well with frozen beans as it does with fresh, so be sure to enjoy it all year round.

    1 pound green beans, trimmed, no need to thaw if frozen
    2 slices precooked bacon, chopped
    1 tablespoon olive oil
    1 teaspoon FishMama Spice (page 162)
    2 tablespoons toasted slivered almonds

1. Preheat the oven to 425°F.

2. Place the green beans and bacon in a 9 x 13-inch baking dish. Drizzle with the oil and sprinkle with the spice mix. Toss to coat.

3. Roast until the beans are tender and browned in spots, about 20 minutes. Sprinkle with the almonds. Serve hot or at room temperature.

Beef and
Vegetable
Stir-Fry

Cilantro-Basil
Noodles

Forget take-out
menus and tipping
the delivery guy.
Save some coin
and eat well with
homemade stir-fry
and chow mein. Yes,
this menu has both
rice and noodles.
But be honest: Who
doesn't get both rice
and noodles when
ordering take-out?
My kids always insist
on both.

Beef and Vegetable Stir-Fry

SERVES 4

DAIRY-FREE **GLUTEN-FREE**

Cook the beef and vegetables quickly in a little bit of fat over high heat. You want the veggies to stay crisp and the meat to be tender.

2 tablespoons vegetable oil
1 teaspoon minced garlic
¼ teaspoon red pepper flakes
1 pound top sirloin steak, cut into thin strips
1 (12-ounce) bag broccoli florets or 1 small head broccoli, cut into
     florets
8 ounces white mushrooms, sliced (about 2 cups)
1½ cups beef broth
4 scallions, chopped
¼ cup dry sherry
¼ cup soy sauce
2 tablespoons cornstarch
Hot cooked rice, for serving

1. In a large nonstick skillet, heat 1 tablespoon of the oil over medium-high heat until shimmering. Add the garlic and pepper flakes and cook until fragrant, about 1 minute. Add the steak and cook until browned, about 5 minutes. Transfer the meat and any juices to a dish and tent with foil to keep warm.

2. Add the remaining 1 tablespoon oil to the pan and heat over medium-high heat. Add the broccoli and mushrooms to the skillet. Cook, stirring, until the vegetables are tender, 7 to 10 minutes. Add the broth and scallions. Bring to a simmer.

3. In a small bowl, whisk together the sherry, soy sauce, and cornstarch. Stir this mixture into the pan and cook until thickened, about 5 minutes. Stir the beef back into the pan and warm. Serve over rice.

78

LOTSA PASTA

Pasta salad makes for a very easy and forgiving impromptu dish. Cook the pasta, drain, and rinse. Toss with oil and vinegar and stir in your favorite veggies, cheese, beans, and herbs. No recipe required.

Cilantro-Basil Noodles

SERVES 4 TO 6

MEATLESS **DAIRY-FREE**

One of my kids' favorite dishes when we get a Panda Feast (a bargain family deal at our local Asian take-out place) is the chow mein. This is my cheater's version, using more easily obtained linguine and preshredded cabbage from the produce aisle.

1 pound linguine
2 tablespoons toasted sesame oil
½ medium onion, sliced
1 teaspoon chopped garlic
1 teaspoon chopped ginger
¼ teaspoon red pepper flakes
2 cups shredded cabbage or coleslaw mix
2 tablespoons soy sauce
2 tablespoons fresh lime juice
¼ cup chopped fresh cilantro
¼ cup chopped fresh basil

1. Bring a large pot of salted water to a boil over high heat. Cook the linguine according to the package directions. Drain and set aside.

2. Meanwhile, in a large nonstick skillet, heat the oil over medium-high heat until shimmering. Add the onion, garlic, ginger, and pepper flakes and cook until the onion begins to turn translucent, about 2 minutes. Stir in the cabbage and cook until wilted, about 3 minutes more.

3. Add the linguine to the pot and drizzle with the soy sauce and lime juice. Stir to distribute thoroughly. Sprinkle with the cilantro and basil and toss to combine. Serve hot or at room temperature.

MENU

Pork Chops
Smothered in
Onions

Skillet Potatoes

Pork chops were
a favorite dish on
my mom's regular
menu rotation, often
served up with rice
pilaf or skillet pota-
toes. This meal is a
spin on that child-
hood favorite. Start
the potatoes first to
ensure they are done
when the chops are.

Pork Chops Smothered in Onions

SERVES 4

`GLUTEN-FREE`

The flavorful onion gravy that envelops these pork chops takes the
meal over the top. To ensure tenderness, don't overcook the pork
chops. They will continue cooking while resting in the hot pan gravy.

> 1 tablespoon olive oil
> 4 boneless pork loin chops (about ½ inch thick)
> 1 teaspoon garlic powder
> Fine sea salt and freshly ground black pepper
> 1 medium onion, sliced
> 4 ounces white mushrooms, sliced (about 1 cup)
> 1 cup beef or chicken broth
> ½ cup dry Marsala wine
> ¼ cup heavy cream
> Chopped fresh parsley, for garnish

1. In a large nonstick skillet, heat the oil over medium-high heat
until shimmering. Season the chops with the garlic powder and
salt and pepper to taste. Cook, turning once, until just a bit of pink
remains, 7 to 8 minutes. Transfer the chops to a platter and tent
with foil.

2. Add the onion and mushrooms to the drippings and cook until
golden and tender, about 5 minutes. Add the broth and Marsala
to the pan, scraping up any browned bits. Simmer until thickened
slightly, about 3 minutes. Stir in the cream and return the pork
chops to the pan to reheat. Sprinkle with parsley and serve.

79

Fresh meat can be a little unwieldy to cut. Freeze it just until firm to the touch. It will be easier and quicker to slice.

Skillet Potatoes

SERVES 4

MEATLESS **DAIRY-FREE** **GLUTEN-FREE**

The trick to cooking these potatoes quickly is to dice them small and not crowd them in the pan. If you are really pressed for time, you can use frozen diced potatoes instead—no need to thaw.

2 tablespoons olive oil
6 medium potatoes, diced very small
1 teaspoon minced garlic
1 teaspoon herbes de Provence
Fine sea salt and freshly ground black pepper

1. In a large nonstick skillet with a lid, heat the oil over medium-high heat until shimmering. Add the potatoes and garlic and toss to coat. Add the herbes de Provence and salt and pepper to taste, and toss again.

2. Cover the pan and lower the heat to medium-low. Cook for 20 minutes, stirring once.

3. Uncover the pan and cook for 5 minutes more, stirring occasionally to crisp up the potatoes.

Pork Medallions
with Sherried
Shallot Sauce

Rebel with a
Cause Smashed
Potatoes

My family loves this
meal so much that
it's become a request
for special occasions.
The pork medal-
lions are great over
smashed potatoes,
but you can easily
serve them over
rice, egg noodles, or
quinoa instead.

Pork Medallions with Sherried Shallot Sauce

SERVES 4 TO 6

GLUTEN-FREE

My boys are meativores. (Their term, not mine.) Their eyes light up when something meaty is on the menu. This dish ranks as a top favorite. Grab pork tenderloin when it's on sale and stash it in the freezer so you can make this meal whenever the mood strikes.

4 tablespoons (½ stick) butter
2 pounds pork tenderloin, cut into ¾-inch-thick slices
1 tablespoon FishMama Spice (page 162)
2 or 3 shallots, sliced, or 1 medium onion, sliced
¼ cup unbleached all-purpose flour
1½ cups chicken broth
½ cup dry sherry
Chopped fresh parsley, for garnish

1. In a large nonstick skillet, melt 2 tablespoons of the butter. Season the pork generously with the spice mix and cook until browned on both sides, 3 to 5 minutes. Transfer to a platter and tent with foil.

2. Add the remaining 2 tablespoons butter to the pan to melt with the drippings. Add the shallots and sauté until tender and lightly browned, about 5 minutes. Sprinkle the flour over all and cook, stirring, for 1 minute. Add the broth and sherry, scraping up any browned bits. Simmer until the sauce is thickened, about 5 minutes.

3. Return the pork medallions to the sauce and let heat for a minute or two. Garnish with chopped parsley and serve.

80

ENJOY SLOW FOOD

While the recipes in this book focus on 30 minutes of active prep and cooking time before serving, don't dismiss the beauty of the slow cooker. There are a number of preparations, likes stews, chilis, and braises, that favor slow cooking. You might spend your 30 minutes (or less) in the morning prepping dinner and then come home to the aroma of a delicious meal.

Rebel with a Cause Smashed Potatoes

SERVES 4

`DAIRY-FREE` `GLUTEN-FREE`

Despite what your grandmother says, these potatoes are meant to have lumps. Don't worry about making them all pretty and smooth. Leave the skins on, even. You're a rebel with a cause: Get some yummy potatoes ready to soak up the gravy from those pork medallions. Leather jacket not required.

2 pounds very small red or gold potatoes, halved or quartered
¼ cup olive oil
½ cup warm chicken broth, or more as needed
Fine sea salt and freshly ground black pepper

1. Place the potatoes in a large pot of salted water and bring to a boil over high heat. Cook until tender, 15 to 20 minutes. Drain and return the potatoes to the pot.

2. With a potato masher, mash the cooked potatoes until more or less smooth, but still with some chunks. Stir in the olive oil. Add enough of the broth to moisten and make the potatoes a little bit creamy. Season to taste with salt and pepper and serve.

Easy Chicken
and Asparagus

Creamy
Mushroom Pilaf

You would think that
this combination of
chicken, asparagus,
and mushrooms was
the fruit of much
labor. It packs a huge
flavor punch, but it's
amazingly simple to
make. It's a perfect
company supper
because it just looks
fancy! Start the rice
first, since it's the
longer cooking of
the two dishes.

Easy Chicken and Asparagus

SERVES 4

`DAIRY-FREE` `GLUTEN-FREE`

This dish hits a home run at my house every time. The chicken is
tender and flavorful and the asparagus perfectly seasoned. You'll
be amazed at how easy it is to prepare. Feel free to change up the
seasoning for variety; choose a custom blend from pages 162
and 163.

> 2 tablespoons olive oil
> 1½ pounds chicken tenders
> 2 teaspoons FishMama Spice (page 162)
> 1 pound asparagus spears, trimmed

1. In a large nonstick skillet, heat the oil over medium-high heat
until shimmering. Sprinkle the chicken pieces with 1 teaspoon of
the spice mix. Sauté the chicken in the hot oil until cooked through,
7 to 10 minutes. Transfer to a plate and tent with foil.

2. Add the asparagus to the pan and cook in the drippings until
tender, tossing, about 5 minutes. If the pan looks dry, add a bit of
water to steam-fry the vegetables. Season the asparagus with the
remaining 1 teaspoon spice mix.

3. Return the chicken to the pan. Toss to combine and reheat as
needed.

81

Have a backup plan for those nights when your meal plan fails. I have a list of at least a dozen meals I can make on the fly as well as the groceries I need to keep on hand to make them. Then when I forget to thaw the chicken (it's happened) or the grill runs out of propane (guilty, again), I have a plan B to turn to. It's always better than running to the store at the last minute or spending extra money on restaurant fare. See page 205 for some suggestions.

Creamy Mushroom Pilaf

SERVES 4 TO 6

MEATLESS **GLUTEN-FREE**

A while ago, I woke up in the middle of the night dreaming of this recipe. I'd never made it, but I knew I needed to, pronto! You know those rice dishes cooked with cream of mushroom soup? They're tasty but kinda full of yucky ingredients. This pilaf one-ups those dishes with quality ingredients and packs plenty of creamy mushroom flavor. My husband says it tastes like Thanksgiving in one dish. How can that not be a good thing? Dreams do come true.

2 tablespoons butter
8 ounces white mushrooms, chopped
2 cups long-grain white rice
½ teaspoon dried thyme
½ teaspoon rubbed sage
2 cups chicken broth
2 cups milk
Fine sea salt and freshly ground black pepper

1. In a large skillet with a lid, melt the butter over medium heat. Add the mushrooms. Sauté until the mushrooms lose their liquid and it starts to evaporate. Add the rice and sauté until it becomes opaque and the mushrooms are lightly browned, about 5 minutes.

2. Stir in the thyme and sage. Add the broth and milk and bring to a low boil. Cover and reduce the heat to low. Cook until the liquid is absorbed, about 20 minutes. Fluff with a fork and season to taste with salt and pepper.

MENU

Vegetable Beef
Ragu

Herbed Polenta

Polenta and meat
sauce is one of my
favorite combos
in the whole wide
world. I'm known
as the "froofiest"
eater in our family.
(Polenta counts as
froofy, apparently.)
But Bryan is becom-
ing more adventur-
ous, as are some of
our kids. While I still
make plain noodles
for some of them,
the rest of us enjoy
this froofy herbed
polenta, topped with
a meaty vegetable
sauce. Serve with a
simple green salad.

Vegetable Beef Ragu

SERVES 4 TO 6

`DAIRY-FREE` `GLUTEN-FREE` `MAKE-AHEAD` `FREEZER-FRIENDLY`

We are inundated with zucchini over the summer, and I am often
at a loss for ideas of what to do with it. This dish puts the zucchini
to good use, in a largish company of other vegetables. This ragu
freezes well, so don't hesitate to make a double batch and take a
night off from cooking later in the month. This also goes well over
pasta.

2 tablespoons olive oil
½ medium onion, chopped (about 1 cup)
1 large carrot, peeled and chopped
2 celery ribs, chopped
1 teaspoon minced garlic
1 pound ground beef
1 small zucchini, cubed
1 (15-ounce) can tomato sauce
1 (6-ounce) can tomato paste
¼ cup dry red wine
1 teaspoon fine sea salt
½ teaspoon dried basil
¼ teaspoon dried oregano
¼ teaspoon dried thyme
⅛ teaspoon red pepper flakes

1. In a large nonstick skillet, heat the oil over medium-high heat
until shimmering. Add the onion, carrot, celery, and garlic and cook,
stirring, until the onion turns translucent, about 5 minutes. Add the
beef and cook until no longer pink, another 5 minutes. Stir in the
zucchini and cook for another 2 minutes.

2. Add the tomato sauce, tomato paste, wine, salt, basil, oregano,
thyme, and red pepper flakes. Add a bit of water to thin the sauce
if you prefer a thinner consistency. Reduce the heat and simmer for
15 minutes. Adjust the seasonings.

MAKE IT AHEAD: The ragu can be cooled and stored in a covered container in
the refrigerator for up to 4 days or in the freezer for up to 2 months.

#82

EVERY LITTLE BIT COUNTS!

Save small amounts of leftovers to incorporate into future meals. A few tablespoons of pizza sauce will disappear nicely into a marinara. That spare piece of chicken can be shredded and stirred into soup. Use the last of the garlic butter you made for bread as a seasoning for grilled meats or even to cook eggs. By using up little bits, you add great flavor to new dishes and waste less.

Herbed Polenta

SERVES 4

MEATLESS **DAIRY-FREE** **GLUTEN-FREE**

Polenta is a great gluten-free, dairy-free side dish or base for Italian meats and sauces. It cooks quickly and offers great texture. If there are any leftovers, try reheating and topping with a soft fried egg. Delicious!

1½ cups vegetable or chicken broth
1½ cups water
½ teaspoon salt
1 cup polenta
½ teaspoon minced garlic
¼ teaspoon dried Italian herb blend
2 tablespoons olive oil

1. In a medium-size saucepan, combine the broth, water, and salt. Bring to a low boil over medium-high heat.

2. Stir in the polenta, garlic, and herbs and reduce the heat to a simmer. Cook until thick and creamy, about 25 minutes, stirring occasionally to prevent lumps and sticking.

3. Stir in the olive oil. Serve immediately.

MENU

Egg and Hash Brown Stacks

Homemade Oven-Baked Turkey Sausage

Breakfast for supper is a huge hit in these here parts. It doesn't matter how crazy the day was—if I've got eggs and some fixings on hand, I can prepare a meal that makes my family happy. This menu—hash browns stacked with eggs, cheese, and toppings, paired with homemade turkey sausage—will make your people smile, too.

To keep your cooking time efficient, start the hash browns in the oven first. Then mix and form the sausage patties and add them to the oven. Get the toppings ready while those components bake. Then scramble the eggs quickly and assemble the plates.

Egg and Hash Brown Stacks

SERVES 4

MEATLESS **GLUTEN-FREE**

These hash brown stacks are filling and hearty, but so simple to make. If you've got a few extra minutes, whip up a batch of Serrano Pico de Gallo (page 189) for a delicious topping.

> 8 frozen hash brown patties
> 8 large eggs
> 1 tablespoon vegetable oil or butter
> Fine sea salt and freshly ground black pepper
> 1 cup shredded cheddar cheese
> 1 avocado, pitted, peeled, and sliced
> Salsa of your choice, for topping
> Sour cream, for topping

1. Bake the frozen hash brown patties according to the package directions.

2. Meanwhile, in a medium-size bowl, beat the eggs lightly.

3. In a frying pan, heat the oil over medium heat. Add the eggs and season to taste with salt and pepper. As the eggs lighten in color around the edges, begin to stir the eggs lightly, bringing the edges to the center and flipping as needed to cook the scrambled eggs. Remove from the heat.

4. Place 2 hash brown patties on each plate. Divide the eggs among the plates. Top with the shredded cheese, avocado slices, and dollops of salsa and sour cream. Serve immediately.

83

Get ready for tomorrow today. Prep the coffeemaker, fill a water kettle or water bottles, get juicing ingredients prepped for juicing, fill to-go cups and bottles. Let's face it: The morning is always rushed, so plan for ways to make it easier on yourself.

Homemade Oven-Baked Turkey Sausage

SERVES 4

`DAIRY-FREE` `GLUTEN-FREE` `MAKE-AHEAD` `FREEZER-FRIENDLY`

In my efforts to healthify my family's diet, I've started making my own breakfast sausage patties. These are a little bit spicy and a lot better than store-bought. Speed up your prep time by using wet hands to form the patties so they won't stick to your hands.

1 pound ground turkey
1 tablespoon chili powder
1 scallion, chopped
1 tablespoon chopped fresh cilantro
1 teaspoon chopped garlic
½ teaspoon fine sea salt

1. Preheat the oven to 400°F. Line a baking sheet with aluminum foil.

2. In a medium-size bowl, mix all of the ingredients until thoroughly combined. Divide the mixture into eight equal portions. Form each portion into a round patty and place on the lined baking sheet.

3. Bake the patties until cooked through, about 15 minutes.

MAKE IT AHEAD: The uncooked patties can be wrapped and stored in the refrigerator for up to 1 day or in the freezer for up to 2 months. Thaw in the refrigerator overnight before cooking.

MENU

Whole-Wheat
Banana Pancakes

Man Candy
Bacon

Pancakes are always
a crowd pleaser.
Who would turn
down a pancake
supper? Pair the
flapjacks with spicy
bacon and maybe
a side of fruit and
you have a simple,
wholesome dinner
that takes mere min-
utes to prepare.

Whole-Wheat Banana Pancakes

SERVES 4 TO 6

MEATLESS **MAKE-AHEAD** **FREEZER-FRIENDLY**

This rendition of the traditional flapjack is sweetened only with
bananas. The whole-grain flour ensures that it provides as much
nutrition as possible. If you can't find whole-wheat pastry flour, feel
free to use unbleached all-purpose flour instead.

3 cups whole-wheat pastry flour
1 tablespoon baking powder
1 teaspoon baking soda
1 teaspoon fine sea salt
1 teaspoon ground cinnamon
2 ripe bananas, mashed
2 large eggs
2 cups milk
⅓ cup vegetable oil
Melted butter, for cooking and serving
Pure maple syrup, for serving

1. In a large bowl, whisk together the flour, baking powder, baking
soda, salt, and cinnamon.

2. In another large bowl, combine the bananas, eggs, milk, and oil.
Stir until smooth.

3. Add the dry ingredients to the wet ingredients and fold to combine. It's okay if there are a few lumps.

4. Heat a griddle over medium heat. Brush a bit of butter on the
griddle. Pour the batter in ¼-cup portions onto the griddle and cook
the pancakes until the edges appear cooked and bubbles start to
pop on the surface, 2 to 3 minutes. Flip and cook the other side for
2 to 3 minutes more. Brush with butter and top with maple syrup.

MAKE IT AHEAD: Assemble the dry ingredients from step 1 in a zip-top plastic
bag. Label with the recipe name and the list of wet ingredients to be added
later. Store in the freezer until ready to use. Cooked pancakes can also be
cooled, wrapped, and frozen for up to 2 months. Rewarm in the microwave (for
softer pancakes) or the toaster oven (for crisper pancakes).

84

BRINGING HOME THE BACON

One of my favorite quick touches is to use precooked bacon in recipes. You can find conventional brands as well as uncured bacon in precooked form. It freezes well and is typically packaged so you can pull out just what you need. I was a skeptic at first, but the flavor is great, and the convenience can't be beat.

Man Candy Bacon

SERVES 4

DAIRY-FREE GLUTEN-FREE

This type of spicy candied bacon is served as an appetizer at a local restaurant. The first time I tasted it, I knew it could easily be done at home.

Adjust the levels of cayenne and red pepper flakes if you don't like yours quite as hot, but retain some spice to balance the sweetness of the maple syrup. Using precooked bacon speeds the prep time, meaning you'll be enjoying man candy bacon in the blink of an eye.

12 slices precooked bacon
2 tablespoons pure maple syrup
¼ teaspoon dried thyme
¼ teaspoon ground ginger
¼ teaspoon dry mustard
⅛ teaspoon cayenne pepper
⅛ teaspoon red pepper flakes

1. Preheat the oven to 350°F. Line a baking sheet with parchment paper.

2. Lay out the bacon slices on the lined sheet. Brush them on both sides with the maple syrup.

3. In a small bowl, combine the thyme, ginger, mustard, cayenne, and red pepper flakes. Sprinkle the mixture all over the bacon. Bake until glazed and crisp, 5 to 7 minutes.

I used to think
that I wouldn't like
Indian food. I knew
my friend Jessika
loved it, but I was
hesitant even to try
it. My mind changed
when I finally tasted
chicken tikka ma-
sala at an Indian
restaurant. Delish! I
created this quicker
version of the tradi-
tional chicken dish
and paired it with a
tasty coconut rice.
When I texted Jess
the picture, she said
she had been wait-
ing for this moment
for years! Ha! Now
we can enjoy Indian
food together—and
so can you!

Chicken Tikka Masala

SERVES 4

`GLUTEN-FREE` `MAKE-AHEAD` `FREEZER-FRIENDLY`

The first time I made this, my husband requested it again—the very next night! It is so yummy and easy to make. Special thanks to my friend Prerna, who lives in India, for her long-distance advice and guidance. Serve this alongside or over the coconut rice.

2 tablespoons olive oil
2 tablespoons butter
1 pound boneless, skinless chicken breast, cut into bite-size pieces
½ medium onion, chopped (about 1 cup)
1 teaspoon minced garlic
1 teaspoon chopped fresh ginger
1 serrano chile, cored and finely chopped, or more if you like it
  very spicy
1 (15-ounce) can petite diced tomatoes, drained
1 (8-ounce) can tomato sauce
2 teaspoons garam masala
1 teaspoon curry powder
½ cup heavy cream
Handful of fresh cilantro, chopped (about ¼ cup), for garnish

1. In a large nonstick skillet, heat the oil and butter together over medium-high heat until the butter is melted. Add the chicken, onion, garlic, ginger, and serrano chile. Sauté until the chicken is mostly cooked and the onion is translucent, about 7 minutes.

2. Stir in the tomatoes, tomato sauce, garam masala, and curry powder. Reduce the heat and simmer for 10 minutes. Stir in the cream and heat for another 5 minutes. Garnish with the cilantro and serve.

MAKE IT AHEAD: The chicken mixture can be stored in a covered container in the refrigerator for up to 2 days or in the freezer for up to 2 months. Thaw in the refrigerator overnight before reheating.

85

Use food-safe stor-
age containers for
grains and flours
instead of their origi-
nal packaging. You'll
spill less than if you
were scooping from
the original bag, and
it will be easy to see
how much you have
left. Plus, they'll stay
fresher longer.

Coconut Rice

SERVES 4

MEATLESS **DAIRY-FREE** **GLUTEN-FREE**

I first started using different coconut products when I went dairy-
free for a time; coconut milk can provide the same creamy texture
as milk or cream. I love the flavor coconut brings to different foods,
particularly this coconut rice.

2 tablespoons coconut oil or other vegetable oil
2 cups long-grain white rice
3 cups water
1 cup canned light coconut milk
Fine sea salt and freshly ground black pepper
½ cup coconut flakes, toasted

1. In a large skillet with a lid, heat the oil over medium-high heat.
Add the rice and sauté until it becomes opaque, about 5 minutes.

2. Stir in the water and coconut milk and bring to a low boil. Cover
and reduce the heat to low. Cook until the liquid is absorbed, about
20 minutes. Fluff with a fork and season to taste with salt and pepper. Sprinkle the coconut flakes over the top and serve.

MENU

Eggs and Sweet Potato Hash with Brussels Sprouts and Mushrooms

Spiced Drop Biscuits

The diner classic of eggs and hash makes a filling and flavorful meal. Serve a side of biscuits and you've got the ultimate quick-fix comfort food, good any time of day or night.

Eggs and Sweet Potato Hash with Brussels Sprouts and Mushrooms

SERVES 4

MEATLESS **DAIRY-FREE** **GLUTEN-FREE**

I often make my eggs in a skillet on a bed of greens. But one can only eat so much spinach, so here I switch it up and cook the eggs on a bed of sweet potatoes, Brussels sprouts, and mushrooms. It's tasty as well as nutritious.

2 tablespoons olive oil
1 large sweet potato, peeled and chopped (about 2 cups)
1 pound Brussels sprouts, trimmed and sliced
4 ounces white mushrooms, sliced (about 1 cup)
½ large leek, sliced (about 2 cups)
Fine sea salt and freshly ground black pepper
4 large eggs

1. In a large nonstick skillet with a lid, heat the oil over medium-high heat until shimmering. Add the potato, Brussels sprouts, mushrooms, and leek and toss to coat. Season to taste with salt and pepper. Cook, stirring occasionally, until the vegetables are tender, about 10 minutes.

2. Spread out the vegetable mixture to create four small wells. Crack an egg into each well. Season to taste with salt and pepper.

3. Cover and cook until the desired doneness is reached for the eggs, 5 to 8 minutes. Serve immediately.

86

Label the pantry shelves to save yourself some time. If your shelves are labeled, you will be able to enlist help from family members when it's time to put away groceries. You will also have a better chance at finding the things that are stored in the cupboards. Plus, maybe you can delegate some of the cooking while you're at it, since your people will know where to find everything.

Spiced Drop Biscuits

MAKES 12 BISCUITS

MEATLESS MAKE-AHEAD **FREEZER-FRIENDLY**

With the aid of a food processor, scratch biscuits come together almost as quickly as opening one of those vacuum-packed cartons. Plus, these taste better. *Way* better. These biscuits are not overly sweet, which allows the spices to shine through. If you prefer a bit more sweetness, serve with honey or your favorite jam.

2 cups unbleached all-purpose flour
1 tablespoon baking powder
1 tablespoon sugar
1 teaspoon fine sea salt
½ teaspoon ground cinnamon
½ teaspoon ground ginger
½ teaspoon ground nutmeg
4 tablespoons (½ stick) cold butter, cut into pieces
1 large egg, beaten
1 cup buttermilk

1. Preheat the oven to 450°F. Line a baking sheet with parchment paper or a silicone baking mat.

2. Combine the flour, baking powder, sugar, salt, cinnamon, ginger, and nutmeg in a food processor fitted with a metal blade. Add the butter and pulse a few times, until coarse crumbs form. Add the egg and buttermilk and process just to mix.

3. Drop the batter in 12 equal mounds onto the lined baking sheet. Bake until golden brown, about 10 minutes. Let cool slightly on a rack, and serve warm.

Going meatless is
a great way to cut
costs, improve your
health, and trim
cooking times. These
huevos rancheros
are so filling and
delicious that you
won't think twice
about the fact that
they're meatless.
My husband sure
doesn't.

Huevos Rancheros

SERVES 4

MEATLESS DAIRY-FREE **GLUTEN-FREE**

There are lots of ways to vary "rancher's eggs." Some folks use
salsa, others use enchilada sauce. Some include beans, some
don't. All variations include corn tortillas and fried eggs. This version, quite frankly, is so good that I wake up craving them—in the
middle of the night!

> Vegetable oil, for frying
> 8 corn tortillas
> 2 cups Spicy Pintos (page 33) or 1 (15-ounce) can refried beans
> 1 cup favorite enchilada sauce, heated
> 8 large eggs
> Fine sea salt and freshly ground black pepper
> 1 avocado, pitted, peeled, and sliced
> 2 Roma tomatoes, chopped
> Hot sauce, for serving (optional)

1. In a small nonstick skillet, heat ½ inch of oil until shimmering.
Fry the tortillas until lightly crisped, about 1 minute each. Drain on
paper towels, reserving the oil in the skillet.

2. Heat the beans and enchilada sauce separately on the stovetop
or in the microwave.

3. In a large nonstick skillet with a lid, heat a small amount of the
leftover frying oil over medium-high heat. Crack the eggs into the hot
oil and season to taste with salt and pepper. (The whites will over-
lap a bit; if you prefer to have each cook separately, simply make
two batches or use two pans.) Cover and cook until your preferred
doneness, 3 to 5 minutes.

4. Lay out two tortillas on each plate. Spread each with an equal
portion of beans and enchilada sauce. Top each tortilla with a fried
egg. Top each egg with avocado slices and chopped tomatoes.
Serve immediately, with hot sauce on the side for those who want it.

#87

JUST CAN IT

Canning jars are great for more than just canning. Use them as quick measuring cups for large recipes like soups or sauces. (A pint jar is 2 cups, while a quart jar holds 4 cups.) Another great use of a small canning jar is a quick vinaigrette. See the basic recipe on page 129, then grab a half-pint Mason jar; pour in vinegar or citrus juice; add some herbs, spices, jam, garlic, and/or mustard; and give it a good shake. Add the oil, then shake again. *Voilà!*

Spicy Cabbage Salad

SERVES 4 TO 6

`MEATLESS` `DAIRY-FREE` `GLUTEN-FREE` `MAKE-AHEAD`

This spicy cabbage salad offers a nice, fresh counterpart to the hearty egg dish. It can also stand alone as a filling main-dish salad if you add avocado and grilled chicken or shrimp. To make things go even quicker, use a bag of coleslaw mix in place of the cabbage and carrots.

> 1 (12-ounce) bag shredded cabbage or coleslaw mix (about 5 cups)
> 2 carrots, peeled and shredded
> 1 bell pepper (any color), cored and julienned
> 1 medium tomato, chopped
> Handful of fresh cilantro, chopped (about ¼ cup)
> 2 tablespoons unsalted dry-roasted sliced almonds
> 2 tablespoons fresh orange juice
> 2 tablespoons fresh lime juice
> 1 tablespoon finely chopped seeded jalapeño, or to taste
> ½ teaspoon ground cumin
> Pinch of salt
> ¼ cup olive oil

1. In a large bowl, combine the cabbage, carrots, bell pepper, tomato, cilantro, and almonds.

2. In a small jar or bowl, combine the orange juice, lime juice, jalapeño, cumin, and salt. Cap the jar and shake, or whisk to combine. Add the olive oil and shake or whisk again.

3. Pour the dressing over the salad and toss to distribute the dressing throughout.

MAKE IT AHEAD: The salad and dressing can be stored in separate covered containers in the refrigerator for up to 2 days.

QUICK-CHECK TIPS AND TRICKS

My first job as a teenager was bagging groceries at the local Lucky Supermarket. Two years later I worked at an amusement park. The contrast was striking. The uniforms were still lame, but the mood was different.

Not everyone visits Magic Mountain, but pretty much everybody has to grocery shop, whether they want to or not. It can get pretty tricky to navigate crowded stores, bumping elbows with disgruntled and often hungry shoppers.

Your shopping trips—and mine—can be much more pleasant and efficient when we follow these tricks:

Know your stores.
Within a 5-mile radius of my house, there are 10 grocery stores, and some are duplicates within the same chain even. I know which stores offer the best deals on the things that we regularly buy. I know when they have sales. I know where everything is located in the aisles.

Since I truly know my stores, I can get in and out without a lot of fuss. It saves me time because I don't have to ask where a certain item is located or when the sale price will end. By educating myself on these things, I've bought myself some time. Get to know your store and you will, too.

Limit yourself to one or two shops.
I have been known to shop at up to 10 stores in a week in order to get the best deals on food. However, when time is precious, I choose one store and let the rest go. I may pay a little bit more to buy everything I need at that one store, but the time savings is worth it.

Make a list.
Making a list saves me time because I don't end up short on items that we need. I don't overbuy and I don't end up making extra trips for things I forgot.

Shop in the quiet hours.
I have gone grocery shopping at 6 in the morning during the busy holiday season and had the entire store to myself. The whole place is quiet and calm, meaning I feel that way, too. I find that shopping when the crowd is thin helps me to enjoy the experience more—and to do it more quickly.

Let someone else do the shopping or have it delivered.
It's a hard thing to let go control over something I enjoy doing. I'd much rather let someone else clean my toilets. But, the reality is that having my husband stop at Costco on his way home from work saves me time and gas money. It's on his regular route, and he doesn't mind doing it. The same goes for having our produce box delivered each week. It's one less thing that I need to think about.

Chances are there are other little tricks you can implement in your own grocery shopping routine that will save you time and money.

MENU

Summer
Vegetable Sauté

Strawberry
Fields Salad

Summer is the best time to enjoy fresh produce. This menu, bursting with vegetables and fruit, is perfect after a morning stop at the farmers' market. Feel free to add grilled meat to the sauté, or top it with a handful of chickpeas or cannellini beans.

Summer Vegetable Sauté

SERVES 4

MEATLESS **DAIRY-FREE** **GLUTEN-FREE**

My dad has grown vegetables in his backyard for over 40 years now. His is not a huge yard, but he makes the most of his space. This is the kind of sauté he whips up often with his homegrown bounty. It's delicious served either hot or at room temperature.

2 tablespoons olive oil
1 medium onion, sliced
8 ounces white mushrooms, sliced (about 2 cups)
1 pound green beans, trimmed and chopped
1 red or yellow bell pepper, cored and chopped
1 medium zucchini, sliced
1 teaspoon chopped garlic
¼ cup chopped fresh basil
Red pepper flakes
Fine sea salt and freshly ground black pepper
Hot cooked rice, for serving

1. In a large nonstick skillet, heat the oil over medium-high heat until shimmering. Add the onion and mushrooms and cook until the onion is translucent and the mushrooms give up their liquid, about 5 minutes.

2. Add the green beans, bell pepper, zucchini, and garlic and toss to coat. Sauté until the green beans are tender and all of the vegetables start to brown a bit.

3. Add the basil and season to taste with red pepper flakes, salt, and black pepper. Serve over rice.

88

Little drops of water fill a mighty ocean. If you've got any time throughout the day, do some chopping or prepping in advance. Taking advantage of your "little minutes" will help you get dinner made in a jiffy.

Strawberry Fields Salad

SERVES 4

`MEATLESS` `GLUTEN-FREE` `MAKE-AHEAD`

FishPapa doesn't typically like either sweet dressings or feta cheese, but he loves this salad. Go figure. The combination of flavors is truly out of this world.

2 tablespoons fresh orange juice
1 tablespoon strawberry jam
1 tablespoon balsamic vinegar
1 teaspoon poppy seeds
½ teaspoon Dijon mustard
¼ teaspoon dried tarragon
⅛ teaspoon red pepper flakes
Fine sea salt and freshly ground black pepper
¼ cup olive oil
1 head red leaf lettuce, torn into bite-size pieces
8 ounces strawberries, cored and sliced
2 oranges, peel and pith cut away, sliced
¼ cup slivered almonds
½ cup crumbled feta cheese
2 scallions, chopped

1. In a small jar or bowl, combine the orange juice, jam, vinegar, poppy seeds, mustard, tarragon, red pepper flakes, and salt and pepper to taste. Cap the jar and shake, or whisk to combine. Add the olive oil and shake or whisk again.

2. Place the lettuce in a large salad bowl. Pour the dressing over the salad and toss to distribute the dressing evenly. Divide the dressed greens among four salad plates.

3. Distribute the strawberries, orange slices, almonds, feta cheese, and scallions evenly among the plates. Serve immediately.

MAKE IT AHEAD: The dressing can be stored in a covered container in the refrigerator for up to 2 days.

Fish and chips are a
favorite at our house.
For the longest time
we would go out to
Harbor Fish Com-
pany and try to feed
six kids without
going broke. But
now? Now we make
it ourselves at home.
Sure, the technique
for frying great fish
takes some finesse,
but with practice,
you, too, can be a fry
master.

Cajun Fish and Chips with Rémoulade Tartar Sauce

SERVES 4

`DAIRY-FREE`

This crunchy batter coating, flecked with Cajun seasoning, gives the
entire dish a little kick. Use one of the milder white varieties of fish,
like tilapia, pollock, flounder, or cod. They're cheaper and their flavor
won't get lost under the spicy coating. Be sure to serve plenty of
tartar sauce on the side.

> 1 (1-pound) bag frozen French fries
> Vegetable oil, for frying
> 1½ cups unbleached all-purpose flour
> 1 tablespoon Cajun Spice Blend (page 162)
> ½ teaspoon baking powder
> 1 cup beer
> 1 pound boneless cod fillets
> Rémoulade Tartar Sauce (recipe follows), for serving

1. Preheat the oven according to the package directions for the
French fries. Start the French fries baking.

2. In a deep skillet, heat 1 inch of oil to 350°F on a candy/deep-fry
thermometer, adjusting the flame as necessary to maintain a steady
temperature.

3. In a large bowl, whisk together 1 cup of the flour, the Cajun seasoning, and the baking powder. Stir in the beer.

4. Place the remaining ½ cup flour on a plate. Dredge the fish fillets
in the batter and then in the flour, letting the excess drip off. Fry the
fish in the hot oil in batches until crisp and cooked through, turning
once, about 6 minutes. Drain on paper towels.

5. Serve the fried fish and French fries with the rémoulade tartar
sauce on the side.

rémoulade tartar sauce

MAKES ABOUT ⅔ CUP

`MEATLESS` `DAIRY-FREE` `GLUTEN-FREE` `MAKE-AHEAD`

½ cup mayonnaise
2 tablespoons chopped dill pickles
2 teaspoons fresh lemon juice
1 teaspoon minced garlic
1 teaspoon Dijon mustard
1 teaspoon Cajun Spice Blend (page 162)

In a small bowl, stir together all of the ingredients.

MAKE IT AHEAD: Store the tartar sauce in a covered container in the refrigerator for up to 3 days.

Broccoli Slaw

SERVES 4 TO 6

`MEATLESS` `DAIRY-FREE` `GLUTEN-FREE` `MAKE-AHEAD`

Broccoli slaw is a great way to get all the nutrition of broccoli in an easy and fun salad form. Leftovers are just as good the next day.

½ cup mayonnaise
2 tablespoons cider vinegar
1 teaspoon minced garlic
½ teaspoon dried dill
Fine sea salt and freshly ground black pepper
1 (12-ounce) bag broccoli slaw mix
2 tablespoons chopped fresh parsley

1. In a large bowl, whisk together the mayonnaise, vinegar, garlic, dill, and salt and pepper to taste until smooth.

2. Add the broccoli slaw mix and the parsley. Toss well to distribute the dressing. Serve.

MAKE IT AHEAD: Store the dressed salad in a covered container in the refrigerator for up to 2 days.

Grilled Fare in a Flash

A grilled dinner can be one of the tastiest and quickest to prepare as long as you keep things simple. No overnight marinades or brines or beer cans allowed. Cooking out is a great way to escape a hot kitchen on a summer day, too. The flavor the grill imparts is an added plus. If the weather prevents you from cooking out of doors, consider investing in a stovetop grill pan so you can grill whenever you want.

The main course in each of these menus is cooked on the grill while the side is prepped on the grill, stove, or countertop.

Grilled Mahi-Mahi with Pineapple Salsa

Yellow Rice and Beans

This meal is like taking a trip to the Caribbean or parts of South America. It's full of flavors that you might not see combined on the typical American plate, but I don't see why not. They are so delicious! Fire up the grill, start the rice, season the fish, and stir up the salsa. This meal comes together pretty effortlessly and packs a big punch.

Grilled Mahi-Mahi with Pineapple Salsa

SERVES 4

`DAIRY-FREE` `GLUTEN-FREE`

Fruit salsa is like the cranberry sauce of summer, mixing sweet and savory to good effect. This salsa is best made with fresh fruit, so grab a pineapple and a mango the next time you see them on sale and whip up this supper.

1 teaspoon garlic powder
1 teaspoon chili powder
1 teaspoon ground cumin
½ teaspoon fine sea salt
¼ teaspoon freshly ground black pepper
4 mahi-mahi fillets
Olive oil, for brushing
Pineapple Salsa (recipe follows)

1. Heat an outdoor grill for a medium-hot fire or a stovetop grill pan over medium-high heat.

2. In a small bowl, combine the garlic powder, chili powder, cumin, salt, and pepper.

3. Place the mahi-mahi fillets on a baking sheet and brush them all over with oil. Season them generously on both sides with the spice mix. Cook the fish on the hot grill over direct heat or in the grill pan until it is cooked through and pulls apart easily, 10 to 15 minutes. Serve with the pineapple salsa.

#90

WATCH THE STOCK

As your budget allows, keep your pantry stocked with items you use on a regular basis. You'll spend less time shopping or trying to find substitutes when you run out of time.

pineapple salsa

MAKES ABOUT 3½ CUPS

`MEATLESS` `DAIRY-FREE` `GLUTEN-FREE` `MAKE-AHEAD`

This salsa is excellent over grilled fish and meats, but it's also tasty as a dip for tortilla chips. If you prefer spicier salsa, leave some seeds in your jalapeño.

> ½ fresh pineapple, peeled, cored, and chopped (about 2 cups)
> 1 red mango, peeled, pitted, and chopped (about 1 cup)
> ¼ cup chopped red onion
> 2 tablespoons chopped seeded jalapeño
> 2 tablespoons chopped fresh cilantro
> 1 tablespoon fresh lime juice
> Fine sea salt and freshly ground black pepper

In a small bowl, combine the pineapple, mango, onion, jalapeño, cilantro, and lime juice. Season to taste with salt and pepper. Stir gently to combine.

MAKE IT AHEAD: The salsa can be stored in a covered container in the refrigerator for up to 2 days. Remove from the refrigerator about 30 minutes before serving to take the chill off.

91

Cooking is a fun and tasty experience. Don't stress too much about your meal prep. That leads to accidents and unsafe kitchen practices. Take a deep breath and enjoy the ride.

Yellow Rice and Beans

SERVES 4 TO 6

MEATLESS **DAIRY-FREE** **GLUTEN-FREE**

This rice pilaf offers a lovely contrast to the spicy and sweet fish and salsa, but you can also use it as a filling for burritos or a side dish for other cooked meats. Or add a fried egg on top. An avocado and tomato garnish adds great color to the plate.

    2 tablespoons vegetable oil
    2 cups long-grain white rice
    1 tablespoon Basic Taco Seasoning Mix (page 163)
    1 teaspoon ground turmeric
    1 teaspoon fine sea salt, plus more to taste
    4 cups vegetable or chicken broth
    1 (15-ounce) can black beans, drained
    Freshly ground black pepper
    Sliced avocado, for topping
    Diced tomato, for topping

1. In a large skillet with a lid, heat the oil over medium heat. Add the rice and sauté until opaque, 2 to 4 minutes.

2. Stir in the taco seasoning, turmeric, and salt. Add the vegetable broth and bring to a low boil. Cover and reduce the heat to low. Cook until the liquid is absorbed, about 20 minutes.

3. Fluff with a fork and stir in the beans. Cover and allow the beans to absorb some of the heat, about 5 minutes. Season to taste with salt and pepper. Serve topped with sliced avocado and diced tomatoes.

MENU

Herbed Pork Tenderloin

White Bean Salad

Pork and beans get a face-lift with this upscale take on a classic combination. Get the tenderloin started first and then mix up the salad. If you've got room on the grill, throw some veggies on to char, or toss a quick green salad for an additional side.

Herbed Pork Tenderloin

SERVES 4

`DAIRY-FREE` `GLUTEN-FREE` `MAKE-AHEAD`

My husband never really liked pork until I started buying pork tenderloins. They often go on sale, and they cook quickly without getting tough, making for a meaty meal without breaking the bank.

1 teaspoon fine sea salt
½ teaspoon garlic powder
½ teaspoon dried thyme
½ teaspoon rubbed sage
½ teaspoon dried tarragon
½ teaspoon sweet paprika
⅛ teaspoon freshly ground black pepper
1 pound pork tenderloin
Olive oil, for brushing

1. Heat an outdoor grill for a medium-hot fire or a stovetop grill pan over medium-high heat.

2. In a small bowl, combine the salt, garlic powder, thyme, sage, tarragon, paprika, and pepper.

3. Place the tenderloin on a baking sheet and brush it with oil. Season the tenderloin generously with the spice mix.

4. Cook on the hot grill over direct heat or in the grill pan, turning occasionally, until the pork has reached an internal temperature of 145°F, 15 to 20 minutes. Allow to rest for 3 minutes. Slice and serve.

MAKE IT AHEAD: The tenderloin can be prepared through step 3, wrapped, and refrigerated for up to 24 hours. Allow it to warm slightly on the counter before grilling.

92

EYEBALL IT

Don't be afraid to guesstimate on ingredient measures. In baking, exact measurements matter, but for most savory dishes, they are less crucial. Spend time making comparisons to your own hand so you know at a glance how much to put into a dish. For me, a closed handful of fresh herbs is about ¼ cup. A double handful of chopped onions is about 1 cup. A little extra basil never hurt anybody, so don't spend too much time measuring.

White Bean Salad

SERVES 4

`MEATLESS` `DAIRY-FREE` `GLUTEN-FREE` `MAKE-AHEAD`

This side dish is simple, yet packed with flavor and fiber. It's also a great make-ahead if you've got more time in the morning than you do at suppertime. White beans are delicate, so be sure to stir gently.

2 (15-ounce) cans cannellini or Great Northern beans, rinsed and drained
½ cup finely chopped red bell pepper
⅓ cup chopped fresh parsley
¼ cup finely chopped sweet onion (such as Vidalia)
2 tablespoons white wine vinegar
1 teaspoon minced garlic
Fine sea salt and freshly ground black pepper
2 tablespoons olive oil

1. Combine the beans, bell pepper, parsley, and onion in a large salad bowl.

2. In a small jar or bowl, combine the vinegar, garlic, and salt and pepper to taste. Cap the jar and shake, or whisk to combine. Add the oil and shake or whisk again.

3. Toss the salad with the dressing, folding gently so as not to break up the beans. Adjust the seasonings and serve.

MAKE IT AHEAD: The salad can be stored in a covered container in the refrigerator for up to 2 days.

Stuffed and Grilled Potatoes

Grilled steak and potatoes is probably my favorite meal of all. With a little know-how, you, too, can pull together this special-occasion meal in minutes. Start the potatoes, get the steaks going, and then let the potatoes join the steaks on the grill. Add a green side salad to go with your meat and taters.

Seasoned Tri-Tip Steak

SERVES 4 TO 6

`DAIRY-FREE` `GLUTEN-FREE` `MAKE-AHEAD`

Once obscure outside California, the tri-tip is a cut of beef that has seen great popularity in recent years. While a whole tri-tip roast itself can take a while to cook, steaks cut from the roast cook quickly and easily. If you can't find tri-tip in your neck of the woods, feel free to grill up some sirloin steaks. I like to season them with a spicy rub for great flavor.

1 teaspoon fine sea salt
1 teaspoon garlic powder
1 teaspoon onion powder
1 teaspoon chili powder
1 teaspoon ground cumin
1 teaspoon dried oregano
¼ teaspoon freshly ground black pepper
¼ teaspoon cayenne pepper
2 pounds tri-tip steaks (about 1 inch thick)
Olive oil, for brushing

1. Heat an outdoor grill for a medium-hot fire or a stovetop grill pan over medium-high heat.

2. In a small bowl, combine the salt, garlic powder, onion powder, chili powder, cumin, oregano, black pepper, and cayenne.

3. Place the steaks on a baking sheet and brush them on both sides with oil. Season the steaks generously on both sides with the spice mix.

4. Cook on the hot grill over direct heat or in the grill pan, turning once, until the steaks have reached an internal temperature of 145°F, 10 to 15 minutes. Allow to rest for 3 minutes before serving.

MAKE IT AHEAD: The steaks can be prepared through step 3, wrapped, and refrigerated for up to 24 hours. Allow them to warm on the counter slightly before grilling.

93

Don't overcook your
meat. It wastes your
time as well as your
steak. Use a digital
thermometer to pin-
point when the meat
is cooked to your
liking. Then move on
to dinner.

Stuffed and Grilled Potatoes

SERVES 4

MEATLESS GLUTEN-FREE MAKE-AHEAD

Grilled potatoes? You betcha. Instead of heating the oven, bake
these potatoes in the microwave the first time. Once you stuff them,
throw them on the grill to melt the cheese topping and to keep
them warm while the steaks finish cooking. If you can't find jumbo
potatoes, buy four medium-size ones and give each person a whole
potato.

> 2 large baking potatoes or 4 medium russets
> ⅓ cup sour cream
> ½ cup shredded cheddar cheese, plus more for garnish
> Fine sea salt and freshly ground black pepper
> 2 scallions, chopped

1. Heat an outdoor grill for a medium-hot fire.

2. Place the potatoes on a microwave-safe plate. Pierce them all
over with a fork. Bake them on the baked potato setting of your
microwave until tender, 10 to 15 minutes, depending on your microwave's settings.

3. Once the potatoes are cooked, split them in half lengthwise.
Using a quick-release scoop, remove the insides of the potatoes,
leaving a ¼-inch shell. Place the flesh in a small bowl.

4. Mash the potato insides with a fork and stir in the sour cream
and cheese. Season to taste with salt and pepper. Using the
quick-release scoop, refill the potato shells with the potato mixture.
Smooth the tops with a knife and sprinkle with more shredded
cheese.

5. Place the potatoes on the hot grill and allow them to cook until
the cheese is melted and the filling is hot, about 5 minutes. Be sure
to place them over indirect heat on the grill so that the skins don't
burn. Sprinkle with the scallions and serve.

MAKE IT AHEAD: The potatoes can be prepared through step 4, wrapped, and
refrigerated for up to 2 days. Allow them to warm on the counter slightly before
grilling.

MENU

Steak and Mushroom Skewers

Greek Vegetable Rice

Meaty grilled kabobs, vegetables, and rice make the perfect summer meal. This one is packed with flavor yet super easy to pull together. Start the grill, get the rice cooking on the stove, and set the kabobs on the grill. Easy peasy.

Steak and Mushroom Skewers

SERVES 4

`GLUTEN-FREE` `MAKE-AHEAD`

There is much shuffling and jockeying at our buffet table when I serve these kabobs. Be sure to buy steak tips, not stew meat, for this dish. You want a cut that will be tender upon grilling. If you can't find steak tips, buy a top sirloin and cut it into 1-inch chunks. Leave off the tzatziki if you want a dairy-free main course.

> 1 pound beef steak tips or sirloin steak, cut into bite-size pieces
> 8 ounces white mushrooms
> 1 to 2 tablespoons Greek Spice Blend (page 163)
> 1 (6-ounce) bag baby spinach
> 8 ounces grape tomatoes
> Tzatziki (page 197), for serving

1. Heat an outdoor grill for a medium-hot fire or a stovetop grill pan over medium-high heat.

2. Thread four metal skewers alternately with the meat chunks and mushrooms. Season the skewers generously with the spice mix.

3. Cook on the hot grill over direct heat or in the grill pan, turning occasionally, until the meat pieces have reached an internal temperature of 145°F, 10 to 15 minutes. Allow to rest for 3 minutes.

4. Divide the spinach and tomatoes among four plates. Add the skewers. Serve with the tzatziki on the side.

MAKE IT AHEAD: The kabobs can be prepared through step 2, wrapped, and refrigerated for up to 4 hours. Allow them to warm slightly on the counter before grilling.

#94

WHAT'S FOR DINNER?

How many times have you stood in front of the fridge wondering what's for dinner? Or how about the precious minutes making an extra trip to the store because you forgot something? Meal planning will help you save time on both fronts. Plan a week's worth of meals and shop accordingly. Then you'll have a clear idea of what to make as well as the ingredients you'll need to make it with.

Greek Vegetable Rice

SERVES 4 TO 6

`DAIRY-FREE` `GLUTEN-FREE`

This rice pilaf is a healthier alternative to commercial box mixes. It's packed with flavor from the spices and full of color from the vegetables.

2 tablespoons vegetable oil
2 cups long-grain white rice
1 tablespoon Greek Spice Blend (page 163)
4 cups chicken broth
1 cup frozen mixed carrots and peas, no need to thaw
Fine sea salt and freshly ground black pepper

1. In a large skillet with a lid, heat the oil over medium heat. Add the rice and sauté until opaque, 2 to 4 minutes.

2. Add the spice mix and stir. Stir in the chicken broth and bring it to a low boil. Add the vegetables. Cover and reduce the heat to low. Cook until the liquid is absorbed and the vegetables are tender, about 20 minutes. Fluff with a fork and season to taste with salt and pepper.

GET YOUR GRILL ON

Grilling is one of my favorite fast-cooking techniques, particularly since my husband loves to man the barbecue. That means I can prep the meat and pass it off to him while I pull together a salad and side dish.

Prepping meats for grilling doesn't have to be crazy and complicated. Long marinating times and complex preparations (You want me to put the beer can *where*?) aren't necessary for a great meal. Consider these fast and fabulous ways to serve grilled meats without a lot of hassle:

1. Brush with olive oil and season with one of the spice mixes from pages 162 and 163. This is so easy but so flavorful. It's really effortless.

2. Serve grilled meats and fish with a fruit or tomato salsa. Salsas serve as a great garnish and provide a huge boost of flavor. Try the Pineapple Salsa on page 266 or the Serrano Pico de Gallo on page 189.

3. Make a compound butter by mixing softened butter with fresh herbs and spices. Form it into a log and chill until ready to serve. Top your cooked meat or fish with a few rounds of butter. It melts into a delicious sauce with practically no effort at all. The spiced butter for corn on page 204 goes great on cooked meats as well.

4. Foil or parchment paper packets are great for cooking grilled meats, and you can toss a few chopped vegetables or herb sprigs into the packets to flavor the meat as it cooks. They also save time on cleanup.

5. Use a grill pan, wok, or basket to prevent smaller items from falling through the grates of the grill itself. This is super helpful when cooking smaller bits of meat or vegetables. The grill pan also allows you to quickly and effortlessly remove the dish from the grill so that you can take it right to the serving table.

I often order my
burger "protein
style" (*sans* bun) at
restaurants in order
to curb calories. At
home I find that a
grilled portobello
mushroom serves
as a great stand-in
for the bun, adding
flavor and fiber. This
supper of burgers,
mushrooms, and
barley is healthy
and hearty. Throw
together a quick side
salad to complete
the meal.

Burgers with Marsala-Marinated Portobello Mushrooms

SERVES 4

DAIRY-FREE GLUTEN-FREE

Where's the bun? These aren't your traditional burgers. Nor are they portobello mushroom burgers. Served open-face, beef patties sit atop flavorful marinated mushrooms.

With its umami character, the large, overgrown portobello mushroom is a great alternative to meat. (Here it's a great addition!) Feel free to leave off the beef patties and toast some good rolls alongside the mushrooms on the grill to make vegetarian burgers, or serve the marinated, grilled mushrooms with or on top of salad greens.

½ cup dry Marsala wine
2 teaspoons minced garlic
2 teaspoons herbes de Provence
Fine sea salt and freshly ground black pepper
⅔ cup olive oil
4 large portobello mushrooms, trimmed
1 pound ground beef
2 teaspoons FishMama Spice (page 162)

1. Heat an outdoor grill for a medium-hot fire or a stovetop grill pan over medium-high heat.

2. In a gallon-size zip-top plastic bag, combine the Marsala, garlic, herbes de Provence, and salt and pepper to taste. Add the oil. Seal the bag and shake or massage the bag to combine the ingredients.

3. Place the mushrooms in the marinade, sealing the bag and massaging to coat the mushrooms. Allow to marinate at room temperature for 5 to 10 minutes.

4. Divide the ground beef into four thin patties. Make a depression in the center of each to prevent it from bulging. Sprinkle with the spice mix.

5. Cook the patties and mushrooms on the hot grill over direct heat or in the grill pan, turning once, until the burgers are cooked through and the mushrooms are tender, about 10 minutes. Serve the burgers atop the mushrooms, open-face style.

95

Buying in bulk can be a great technique for saving money as well as time. If it's an item you use frequently, save time shopping by buying the larger portion or buying several smaller packages when you see them on sale.

Barley Pilaf

SERVES 4

DAIRY-FREE

Why rely only on rice as a quick-fix grain when there are others to try? Here quick-cooking barley plays the starring role in a pilaf. I've found two kinds of quick-cooking barley: one that looks just like standard pearl barley and one that looks (and tastes) like rolled oats. Be sure to buy the former. The beef broth here complements the burgers, but you can use chicken or vegetable broth to serve this with other main courses.

2 tablespoons vegetable oil
½ medium onion, chopped (about 1 cup)
2 cups beef broth
1 cup quick-cooking barley
¼ teaspoon paprika
⅛ teaspoon freshly ground black pepper, plus more as needed
Fine sea salt
Chopped fresh parsley, for garnish (optional)

1. In a large skillet with a lid, heat the oil over medium-high heat until shimmering. Add the onion and sauté until translucent, about 5 minutes.

2. Add the broth, barley, paprika, and pepper and stir. Bring to a low boil. Cover and reduce the heat to low. Cook until the liquid is absorbed, about 20 minutes.

3. Fluff with a fork. Season to taste with salt and pepper and sprinkle with parsley, if desired.

Salmon and sweet
potatoes are two
great superfoods
that we could all get
a little more of in our
diets. This meal is a
lovely way to do it.
Marinate the salmon
in a gingery orange-
soy mixture for a few
minutes for a bit of
extra flavor. Serve up
a favorite vegetable
side or salad along
with these sweet
potato hash browns.
Healthy never tasted
so good.

Ginger-Scented Grilled Salmon

SERVES 4

`DAIRY-FREE` `GLUTEN-FREE`

I never liked fish until I tried salmon. Even now that I've expanded my seafood repertoire, I'd still probably choose salmon over any other kind. Categorized as an oily fish, thanks to all those healthy omega-3 fatty acids, it's hard to overcook, making it a perfect fish to throw on the grill. Here it gets a boost from OJ, ginger, and soy sauce. Yum-o!

¾ cup fresh orange juice
2 tablespoons soy sauce
2 tablespoons dry sherry
1 teaspoon honey
1 teaspoon chopped fresh ginger
¼ teaspoon red pepper flakes
4 (6-ounce) salmon steaks or fillets
Chopped fresh cilantro, for garnish (optional)

1. Heat an outdoor grill for a medium-hot fire or a stovetop grill pan over medium-high heat.

2. In a gallon-size zip-top plastic bag, combine the orange juice, soy sauce, sherry, honey, ginger, and red pepper flakes. Shake gently to combine the ingredients.

3. Slip the fish into the bag. Seal it and massage to coat the fish with the marinade. Allow to marinate at room temperature for 5 to 10 minutes.

4. Cook the fish on the hot grill over direct heat or in the grill pan, turning once, until it turns opaque and pulls apart easily, 10 to 15 minutes. Serve with a sprinkling of cilantro, if desired.

Sweet Potato Hash Browns

SERVES 4

MEATLESS **DAIRY-FREE** **GLUTEN-FREE**

These look like regular white potato hash browns, but they are really a powerhouse of nutrition in disguise. White sweet potatoes are less sweet than their common counterpart, the garnet "yam." They also cook up a little more crispy than the orange-red variety, which is, of course, the goal of delicious hash browns.

2 tablespoons olive oil
1 large white sweet potato (about 1 pound), peeled and shredded
1 teaspoon garlic powder
Fine sea salt and freshly ground black pepper

1. In a large nonstick skillet, heat the oil over medium heat until shimmering.

2. Add the shredded potato and spread in an even layer in the pan, pressing down on it. Season with the garlic powder and salt and pepper to taste.

3. Cook until tender and browned on the bottom, 5 to 7 minutes. Flip (either all in one piece or in sections, depending on your flipping skill) and continue cooking on the other side for another 3 to 5 minutes. Serve immediately, either cut into wedges or scooped into serving portions.

WEEKLY FOOD PREP

Spend a few minutes at the start of the week prepping foods to use in recipes over the next few days. You'll be amazed at what a time savings this is and how much fun it makes dinner prep. Consider prepping these items to stash in the fridge in covered containers:

shredded cheese

sliced cheese

homemade croutons

vegetable dippers

salad greens

salad toppings

chopped onions, bell peppers, and carrots

hard-cooked eggs

fresh salsa

homemade baking mixes

Check GoodCheapEats.com/printables for a printable checklist to help you keep track of your weekly kitchen prep.

The beauty about
grilling is that every
culture has some
great food to throw
on the barbie. Take
a virtual trip to
Southeast Asia with
this menu of grilled
spicy chicken, rice,
and a crunchy snow
pea salad. This meal
is always a huge hit
with kids of all ages.

Spicy Chicken Satay

SERVES 4

DAIRY-FREE **GLUTEN-FREE**

Originating in Indonesia, satay is made by grilling cubes of spicy
meat on skewers and serving with a nutty sauce. I've streamlined
the prep time by using chicken tenders instead of cutting the meat
into smaller pieces. We use sunflower seed butter in our dipping
sauce to accommodate for a nut allergy in the family, but peanut
butter is traditional.

¼ cup soy sauce
1 teaspoon chopped fresh ginger
1 teaspoon chopped garlic
½ teaspoon ground turmeric
½ teaspoon ground cumin
¼ cup vegetable oil
1 pound chicken tenders
Hot cooked rice, for serving
Sunflower Dipping Sauce (page 286)

1. Heat an outdoor grill for a medium-hot fire or a stovetop grill pan
over medium-high heat.

2. In a shallow bowl, combine the soy sauce, ginger, garlic, turmeric,
and cumin. Stir well. Add the vegetable oil and stir again. Add the
chicken to the dish and turn to coat. Allow to marinate at room temperature for 10 minutes.

3. Thread each chicken piece onto a metal skewer.

4. Cook the chicken on the hot grill over direct heat or in the grill
pan, turning occasionally, until the meat is cooked through and the
juices run clear, about 15 minutes. Serve with hot cooked rice and
dipping sauce.

sunflower dipping sauce

MAKES ABOUT ¾ CUP

DAIRY-FREE **GLUTEN-FREE**

¼ cup sunflower seed butter
¼ cup canned light coconut milk
1 tablespoon soy sauce
1 tablespoon fish sauce
1 tablespoon fresh lime juice
1 teaspoon chopped fresh ginger

In a small dish, combine the sunflower seed butter, coconut milk, soy sauce, fish sauce, lime juice, and ginger. Stir until smooth and serve with the cooked chicken skewers.

#97

SHAKE YOUR BOOTY

Wash out small jars once you've used up the contents and save them for making homemade dressings quickly and easily. Combine vinegar, garlic, and spices. Cap and shake. Add the oil, cap, and shake again.

Snow Pea Salad

SERVES 4

`MEATLESS` `DAIRY-FREE` `GLUTEN-FREE` `MAKE-AHEAD`

My family members are huge fans of this salad. It's crunchy, spicy, sweet, and refreshing—all in one happy bowl. Rarely do I get my fill because they beat me to it!

1 (9-ounce) package fresh snow peas
1 (8-ounce) can sliced water chestnuts, drained
1 red bell pepper, cored and julienned
2 tablespoons chopped fresh cilantro
2 tablespoons rice vinegar
2 tablespoons soy sauce
1 tablespoon dry sherry
1 teaspoon chopped fresh ginger
¼ cup oil

1. Combine the snow peas, water chestnuts, bell pepper, and cilantro in a large salad bowl.

2. In a small jar or bowl, combine the vinegar, soy sauce, sherry, and ginger. Cap the jar and shake, or whisk to combine. Add the oil and shake or whisk again.

3. Toss the salad with the dressing, folding gently. Serve immediately.

MAKE IT AHEAD: The salad and the dressing can be stored in separate covered containers in the refrigerator for up to 4 days.

Shrimp on the Barbie

Tomato Rice Pilaf

I love the simplicity of shrimp and rice. Both cook quickly, and are perfect partners for creating a delicious dinner. Complete the picture by adding a side salad or steamed or grilled vegetable, if you like.

Shrimp on the Barbie

SERVES 4 TO 6

`DAIRY-FREE` `GLUTEN-FREE`

FishPapa, upon first trying this dish, said, "What did you put on this shrimp?" My confident reply was, "Awesome sauce." He honestly couldn't disagree with me. The simple flavors of the spice mixture complement the smoky shrimp perfectly. This is a favorite at our house. Put another shrimp on the barbie!

2 pounds peeled large shrimp, thawed if frozen
2 tablespoons olive oil
1 teaspoon garlic powder
1 teaspoon paprika
1 teaspoon dried dill
Pinch of cayenne pepper
Chopped fresh cilantro, for garnish
Lemon wedges, for serving

1. Heat an outdoor grill for a medium-hot fire or a stovetop grill pan over medium-high heat. If your grill has widely spaced grates, use a grill pan or wok with small holes so the shrimp don't fall through (or thread the shrimp onto metal skewers).

2. Place the shrimp in a large bowl and drizzle on the olive oil. Toss to coat.

3. In a small bowl, combine the garlic powder, paprika, dill, and cayenne. Sprinkle this mixture generously on the shrimp, tossing to coat.

4. Cook the shrimp on the grill over direct heat or in the grill pan, turning once, until pink and cooked through, about 10 minutes.

5. Transfer to a platter. Sprinkle with cilantro and serve with lemon wedges for squeezing over the shrimp.

98

KEEP THINGS ZESTY

Citrus zest and juice both freeze remark-ably well. If you take a few minutes on a lazy weekend to zest and juice the fruits you have on hand, you can freeze the juice in ice cube trays and the zest in zip-top plastic bags. Then you'll have per-fect portions when you need just a little something to jazz things up.

Tomato Rice Pilaf

SERVES 4

`MEATLESS` `DAIRY-FREE` `GLUTEN-FREE`

This rice dish boasts a little heat, but not too much. It's the perfect spice mélange to complement the onion, bell pepper, and tomato in this simple pilaf.

2 tablespoons olive oil
2 cups long-grain white rice
½ medium onion, chopped (about 1 cup)
½ medium bell pepper (any color), chopped (about ½ cup)
1 teaspoon chili powder
1 teaspoon ground cumin
½ teaspoon dried oregano
3½ cups vegetable broth or water
1 cup canned petite diced tomatoes, with their juices
Zest of 1 lemon
Fine sea salt and freshly ground black pepper

1. In a large skillet with a lid, heat the oil over medium-high heat until shimmering. Add the rice, onion, and bell pepper. Sauté until the rice turns opaque and the onion turns translucent, about 5 minutes.

2. Add the chili powder, cumin, and oregano and stir to combine. Add the broth, tomatoes, and lemon zest and stir.

3. Bring to a low boil. Cover and reduce the heat to low. Cook until the liquid is absorbed, about 20 minutes. Fluff with a fork. Season to taste with salt and pepper.

This meal fools my husband into thinking that he could turn vegan. I don't know that he could do it forever, but this menu combination is so packed with flavor that he really doesn't miss the meat. Going meatless is a great way to economize and cut back on calories, too. And what a delicious way to do it!

Grilled Vegetable Medley

SERVES 4

MEATLESS **DAIRY-FREE** **GLUTEN-FREE**

This vegetable combo is absolutely wonderful. Even my picky vegetable eaters are shocked and amazed at the great flavor imparted by the grill. The medley makes for a tasty meatless meal, but it's also terrific as a side dish.

12 ounces sugar snap peas, trimmed
12 ounces baby zucchini, trimmed, cut in half if largish
2 large bell peppers (any color), cored and cut into 2-inch chunks
8 ounces white mushrooms, halved, quartered, or thickly sliced
½ medium onion, cut into ½-inch-thick slices
⅓ cup olive oil
Fine sea salt and freshly ground black pepper

1. Heat an outdoor grill for a medium-hot fire or a stovetop grill pan over medium-high heat. For an outdoor grill, use a grill pan or wok with small holes so the smaller veggies don't fall through.

2. In a large bowl, combine the peas, zucchini, bell peppers, mushrooms, and onion. Drizzle with the olive oil and toss to coat. Season to taste with salt and pepper.

3. Cook the vegetable mixture on the grill over direct heat or in the grill pan until tender and browned in spots, 15 to 20 minutes, tossing occasionally.

99

CHILL OUT

I'm a big fan of freezer cooking. While it takes an upfront investment of time, cooking in bulk and freezing those meals for future nights is a guaranteed way to save time. Many of the recipes in this book are notated with freezing instructions. Feel free to make a double batch to save yourself more time later in the month. Want more freezer cooking fabulousness? Check out my book *Not Your Mother's Make-Ahead and Freeze Cookbook* for the 411 on cooking to freeze.

Cilantro-Lime Rice

SERVES 4

`MEATLESS` `DAIRY-FREE` `GLUTEN-FREE`

I won the Mother of the Year award with this rice. Not only does it cook quickly, hands-free, in the oven, but it also tastes amazingly like the rice at my kids' favorite burrito restaurant. Score one for the FishMama!

2 cups long-grain white rice
1 teaspoon ground cumin
1 teaspoon fine sea salt
4 cups boiling water
2 tablespoons fresh lime juice
¼ cup chopped fresh cilantro

1. Preheat the oven to 425°F. Grease a 9 x 13-inch baking pan with nonstick cooking spray.

2. Combine the rice, cumin, and salt in the pan and stir to distribute the spices evenly. Spread in an even layer.

3. Pour in the boiling water and lime juice. Cover the pan immediately with heavy-duty aluminum foil, sealing the edges.

4. Bake the rice for 20 minutes. Fluff with a fork and fold in the cilantro.

Desserts on the Double

Dessert is the crowning touch on a great meal. My time in France as a college student transformed the way I looked at the ending of a meal. It doesn't seem complete without a bite of something sweet. It doesn't have to be something super fancy and elaborate. Just a few bites to close a great meal are all I require.

Dessert can be as simple as a dish of beautiful fruit, a cup of coffee and a square of good-quality dark chocolate, or a small piece of pastry. It also doesn't have to take a long time to make. You can pull together any one of these desserts in less than 30 minutes, offering you that little bit of sweet to cap off the evening.

Cinnamon Apple Puffs

SERVES 4

These apple pastries are simple to pull together with packaged puff pastry, applesauce, and cinnamon sugar. I make lots of things from scratch, but puff pastry is not one of them. Impress your people and let them think you did. If you've got time to make homemade applesauce, that will take these pastries over the top.

    5 teaspoons sugar
    1 teaspoon ground cinnamon
    1 (17.5-ounce) package frozen puff pastry, thawed
    1 cup applesauce
    1 egg yolk, beaten with 1 tablespoon water
    Vanilla ice cream, for serving

1. Preheat the oven to 425°F. Line a large baking sheet with parchment paper or a silicone baking mat, and place another sheet of parchment paper on your work surface.

2. In a small bowl, combine the sugar and cinnamon.

3. Lay out the two sheets of puff pastry on the sheets of parchment paper. Cut each puff pastry sheet in half and separate the halves.

4. Spoon ¼ cup applesauce on one end of each rectangle of pastry, leaving a ½-inch border on that end. Sprinkle 1½ teaspoons of the cinnamon sugar over the applesauce. Brush a little egg wash on that border.

5. Fold the empty end of each rectangle over to cover the applesauce mixture. Seal around the edges and press the folded edge down as well so that there is a border on all four sides. Using a fork, crimp all of the borders together. Transfer the two pastries on the work surface to the baking sheet.

6. Brush egg wash over the tops of the pastries. Prick a few holes in the top of each to allow steam to escape.

7. Bake until the pastry is puffed and golden brown, about 20 minutes. Serve warm with ice cream.

Organize your kitchen according to how you use it. You don't have to store all the food in one cupboard and all the appliances in another. Set things up to save yourself some steps. Put all the coffee stuff (cups, filters, coffee, sugar) near the coffeemaker. Store all the baking supplies as well as measuring cups and mixing bowls in another area. Store things near their place of use and you'll save time—and maybe a few brain cells not wondering where something is.

Decadence Sundaes with Caramel-Lime Sauce

SERVES 4

`MAKE-AHEAD` `FREEZER-FRIENDLY`

When we were newlyweds, one of our favorite treats was the chocolate decadence cake, a flourless chocolate cake served with a caramel-lime sauce, at McPhee's Grill. I've re-created that deliciousness in sundae form using vanilla ice cream, so as not to mask the subtleties of the caramel-lime sauce. Use a premium ice cream for the most decadent results.

¾ cup light brown sugar
2 tablespoons butter
2 teaspoons fresh lime juice
½ cup heavy cream
Pinch of salt
1 pint vanilla ice cream
½ cup chocolate cookie crumbs

1. In a large saucepan, combine the brown sugar, butter, and lime juice over medium-high heat and cook, stirring, just until the sugar is dissolved. Then cook without stirring until the mixture is bubbly and thick, 2 to 3 more minutes.

2. Add the cream and decrease the heat to low. Whisk until thickened, about 5 minutes. Remove from the heat. Add a pinch of salt.

3. Scoop the ice cream into four dishes. Top each with 2 tablespoons cookie crumbs. Drizzle with caramel sauce and serve.

MAKE IT AHEAD: The caramel sauce can be stored in a covered container in the fridge for up to 3 days. Warm in the microwave before serving.

Strawberries, Cookies, and Cream

SERVES 4

`MAKE-AHEAD` `FREEZER-FRIENDLY`

I've never been a huge fan of the cookies-and-cream flavor profile—until I tried cookies and real cream. Oh my! This is happiness in a bowl. I make a double batch of this and my kids are in heaven. So am I, actually. If there are any leftovers, which is doubtful, freeze them for a cool treat tomorrow. If you can't find Speculoos cookies (a crunchy spiced shortbread), experiment with your favorite kind of cookie instead.

> 1 cup heavy cream
> 2 tablespoons pure maple syrup
> 1 teaspoon pure vanilla extract
> 1 pound strawberries, sliced
> ½ (7-ounce) box Speculoos cookies, crushed (about 1 cup crumbs)

1. In a large bowl, whip together the cream, syrup, and vanilla until soft peaks form.

2. Fold in the strawberries and cookie crumbs. Spoon into individual dishes and serve.

MAKE IT AHEAD: Prepare as directed and store the individual dishes, covered, in the freezer for up to 2 days. Allow to thaw slightly before serving.

Apple Crowns with Maple Whipped Cream

SERVES 4

GLUTEN-FREE

Years ago, as young parents, we discovered a lovely little food and gift shop down a winding country road in Templeton. There they served apple crowns, delicious concoctions similar to an ice cream sundae, only the apple stood in for the ice cream. If you've got a little extra time, mix up some Caramel-Lime Sauce (page 296) to spoon over the top.

1 cup heavy cream
2 tablespoons pure maple syrup
1 teaspoon pure vanilla extract
4 apples (any kind), cored and cut into wedges
¼ cup Caramel-Lime Sauce (page 296) or favorite purchased
   caramel sauce
¼ cup favorite chopped nuts (optional)
4 maraschino cherries

1. In a large bowl, whip the cream, syrup, and vanilla together until soft peaks form.

2. Arrange the apple slices in a circle on each serving dish. If you use an apple slicer (the kind that cuts it into wedges and removes the core), you can slice the apples right onto the plates, remove the cores, and proceed. You want the apple slices arranged like a crown.

3. Drizzle the caramel sauce around the crown. Dollop the whipped cream in the center. Sprinkle the nuts over all. Top each crown with a cherry.

Black and White Trifle

SERVES 4

MAKE-AHEAD

I love the concept of the trifle: cake, cream, and fruit all jumbled to-gether in layers. What's not to love? It's the perfect solution for the cake that didn't quite cooperate when you flipped it out of the pan. Ask me how I know.

If you don't have a failed cake on hand, don't worry. A purchased angel food cake works in a pinch, as it does in this black and white version, filled with chocolate sauce, chocolate whipped cream, and layers of angel cake. You'll need four 2-cup ramekins or parfait dishes.

    1 cup heavy cream
    2 tablespoons pure maple syrup
    2 tablespoons unsweetened cocoa powder
    8 slices purchased angel food cake or other favorite cake
    1 cup favorite chocolate sauce
    Block of chocolate or mini chocolate chips, for garnish

1. In a large bowl, whip together the cream, maple syrup, and cocoa powder until soft peaks form.

2. Place one slice of cake in the bottom of each ramekin. Pour 2 tablespoons chocolate sauce over each, and top with some of the whipped cream. Repeat the layers.

3. If using a block of chocolate, run a vegetable peeler over the long side to create shavings. Garnish with chocolate shavings or mini chips and serve immediately.

MAKE IT AHEAD: The trifles can be covered and chilled for up to 12 hours.

Don't worry about
having every kitchen
gadget known to
man. Focus on those
that are of good
quality and that help
you get the job done
safely and effec-
tively. One good-
quality knife, pan, or
other tool is better
than 10 mediocre
ones.

Chocolate Fondue with Fruit and Cake

SERVES 4 TO 6

`GLUTEN-FREE`

Chocolate fondue is an easy way to wow people. It's exotic and elegant and pleases everyone—except maybe my mom, the only person on the planet who doesn't like chocolate. She's weird, I know;
let her eat cake. Speaking of which, gild the lily with homemade
cake if you have time; otherwise, store-bought pound cake works
just fine. I like to make this fondue before we eat dinner and keep it
warm in my smallest slow cooker. By the time we're done eating, the
chocolate is ready to be whisked and devoured.

⅔ cup evaporated milk, or more if needed
1 (12-ounce) package chocolate chips
1 pound cake, cut into finger-size strips
Fresh fruit, such as strawberries, apple slices, pineapple spears, and
   banana chunks

1. In a saucepan, heat the evaporated milk until very hot. Remove
from the heat. Add the chocolate and allow it to melt, 4 to 5 minutes. Stir gently until the chocolate is well blended with the milk.
Thin with additional evaporated milk as necessary. Alternatively, you
can place the ingredients in a small slow cooker on low heat for
about 30 minutes.

2. Serve with cake and fruit dippers.

Cherry Mamabars

MAKES 24 BARS

`DAIRY-FREE` `GLUTEN-FREE` `MAKE-AHEAD` `FREEZER-FRIENDLY`

As a girl who used to have a candy bar and a soda for my snack break, I'm the last person one would expect to promote naturally sweetened treats, but it's true. When I can swing it, I want my family to enjoy God's candy instead of processed sugar-coated cocoa bombs. These bars are an alternative that the whole family enjoys. Sweetened with fruit and crunchy with almonds, they never last long.

2 cups dried dates, preferably Deglet Noor
1 cup unsalted toasted slivered almonds
½ cup dried unsweetened cherries

1. Line a baking sheet with parchment paper.

2. In a food processor fitted with a metal blade, process the dates, almonds, and cherries until they are coarse crumbs that will stick together easily.

3. Dump the mixture onto the prepared baking sheet. Cover with plastic wrap and roll it flat with a rolling pin, packing the mixture together tightly. Fold the edges of the parchment paper over the jagged edges and firm them up with the rolling pin. Continue to do this, squaring off the edges and thickening them up so that the bars are in an even layer.

4. Cut into 24 squares and serve.

MAKE IT AHEAD: Wrap and freeze the bars for up to 1 week. Let sit at room temperature for a few minutes to thaw slightly. These bars are great cold as well as at room temperature.

Acknowledgments

Sometimes I try to do too much. Even as a child, I'd pile more on my plate because it all looked so good. My dad was continually saying that my eyes were bigger than my stomach. Yes, I've been cautioned more than once not to bite off more than I could chew.

I have to use that same caution in life since I might try to do it all myself if I'm not careful. I'm super thankful not to be alone in this cookbook-creating endeavor.

Thank you to the team at the Harvard Common Press: to Bruce Shaw, Adam Salomone, and Dan Rosenberg for giving ear to my ideas as well as the space to run with them. To Valerie Cimino, Karen Wise, and Kelly Messier for the most excellent feedback, editing, and correcting. To Pat Jalbert-Levine for her extraordinary attention to detail. To Virginia Downes and Elizabeth Van Itallie for adding style and beauty to the finished product. To Emily Geaman for working so diligently at getting books in the hands of people who will enjoy them.

As always, big thanks go to my agent, Alison Picard, for sharing her expertise and for setting me on this path of cookbook writing.

Thank you to my blog readers at Life as Mom and Good Cheap Eats. Your enthusiasm for and support of my recipes and writing make all the hard work worth it. Thanks to friends and family who offered input and served as recipe testers, specifically Amy, Christie, Janel, JessieLeigh, Jessika, and Michelle.

Thank you to Mom and Dad for being my biggest fans. Love and thanks to my crazy crew of Getskow siblings: Jamie, Janel, John, and Jace; thanks for putting up with me.

Special thanks to my six sweet children. You have been so patient with weird food, late dinners, and all kinds of craziness while I sometimes try to do more than I can really manage with grace.

Deep gratitude goes to my amazing husband, who has encouraged me to follow my dreams so that I would never regret what could have been. You are a wise man to counsel me when I've piled my plate too high. I should listen to you more often.

My ultimate thanks to Jesus, who has given me all good things.

Measurement Equivalents

LIQUID CONVERSIONS

U.S.	METRIC
1 tsp	5 ml
1 tbs	15 ml
2 tbs	30 ml
3 tbs	45 ml
1/4 cup	60 ml
1/3 cup	75 ml
1/3 cup + 1 tbs	90 ml
1/3 cup + 2 tbs	100 ml
1/2 cup	120 ml
2/3 cup	150 ml
3/4 cup	180 ml
3/4 cup + 2 tbs	200 ml
1 cup	240 ml
1 cup + 2 tbs	275 ml
1 1/4 cups	300 ml
1 1/3 cups	325 ml
1 1/2 cups	350 ml
1 2/3 cups	375 ml
1 3/4 cups	400 ml
1 3/4 cups + 2 tbs	450 ml
2 cups (1 pint)	475 ml
2 1/2 cups	600 ml
3 cups	720 ml
4 cups (1 quart)	945 ml
(1,000 ml is 1 liter)	

WEIGHT CONVERSIONS

U.S./U.K.	METRIC
1/2 oz	14 g
1 oz	28 g
1 1/2 oz	43 g
2 oz	57 g
2 1/2 oz	71 g
3 oz	85 g
3 1/2 oz	100 g
4 oz	113 g
5 oz	142 g
6 oz	170 g
7 oz	200 g
8 oz	227 g
9 oz	255 g
10 oz	284 g
11 oz	312 g
12 oz	340 g
13 oz	368 g
14 oz	400 g
15 oz	425 g
1 lb	454 g

OVEN TEMP. CONVERSIONS

°F	GAS MARK	°C
250	1/2	120
275	1	140
300	2	150
325	3	165
350	4	180
375	5	190
400	6	200
425	7	220
450	8	230
475	9	240
500	10	260
550	Broil	290

Note: All conversions are approximate.

Index

Note: Page references in *italics* indicate photographs.

M

Mahi-Mahi, Grilled, with Pineapple Salsa, 266

Mamabars, Cherry, *302*, 303

Mango

    Mangolada Smoothies, 113

    Pineapple Salsa, 267

    -Strawberry *Agua Fresca*, 193

    Tropical Fruit Salad, 195

Maple Whipped Cream, Apple Crowns with, 298, *299*

Marsala

    Fried Chicken, 211

    -Marinated Portobello Mushrooms, Burgers with, 278, *279*

Meal planning tips

    benefits of quick-fix suppers, 54

    budget-friendly pantry items, 41

    golden rules of meal planning, 16

    list of "emergency meals," 205

    prepping recipe foods ahead, 284

    repurposing leftovers, 16, 226

    serving snacky dinners, 141

    shopping tips and tricks, 41, 259

Meat. *See also* Beef; Pork

    grilled, serving ideas, 277

Meatballs, Teriyaki, 39

Meatloaf, Seasoned Turkey, 20

Meatloaves, Mini, 219

Meat thermometers, 13

Melon-Feta Bowl, 175

Mint

    Feta-Melon Bowl, 175

    Minty Pomegranate Limeade, *134*, 135

Muffins, Tomato-Olive, 120

Mushroom(s)

    Bacon and Brie Samwiches, 55

    Beef and Vegetable Stir-Fry, 233

    and Brussels Sprouts, Sweet Potato Hash with, and Eggs, 254, *254*

    Cheesesteak French Bread Pizza, 152, *153*

    Denver Oven Omelet, 22, *23*

    Gingery Turkey-Vegetable Wraps, 181

    Grilled Vegetable Medley, 291, *292*

    Israeli Couscous with Broccoli, *214*, 215

    Minute Minestrone with Chicken, 88

    and Pepper Quesadillas, 164

    Pilaf, Creamy, *241*, 242

    and Pork, Ginger, 223

    Pork Chops Smothered in Onions, 235

    Portobello, Marsala-Marinated, Burgers with, 278, *279*

    Rainbow Ravioli Salad, 116

    Roast Chicken and Veggies, 45, *45*

    Roasted Vegetable Salad, 161

    and Spinach, Chicken Sauté with, 221

    and Steak Skewers, 274, *275*

    Summer Vegetable Sauté, 260

    Super-Rica's #7 Tacos, 188

    and Swiss Chard Sauté, 40

    Vegetable Wonton Soup, 115, *115*

    Veggie and Feta Torpedoes, 74

    Veggie Fajita Burritos, 192

N

Noodle(s)

    Broccoli Sesame, *224*, 225

    Chicken Soup, Simply, 102, *103*

Nuts. *See* Almonds; Cashew(s)

O

Olive(s)

    Carrot Cups, *35*, 36

    Chopped Antipasto Salad, 158

    The Go-To Salad, 168

    and Pepperoni French Bread Pizza, Crispy, 169, *170*

    Pesto Shrimp Linguine Salad, 130, *131*

    Summer Vegetable Salad, 82

    Three-Cheese Enchiladas, 31, *32*

    Tomatoes, and Capers, Farfalle with, 121, *122*

    -Tomato Muffins, 120

    and Tomato Salad, Marinated, 148

    Tres Frijoles Salad, 185

    Vegetable Couscous Salad, 138, *139*

T

About the Author

Sharon Leppellere

Jessica Fisher's two very popular blogs, Life as Mom and Good Cheap Eats, have established her as a go-to authority on cooking for a family cheaply, creatively, and nutritiously.

Good Cheap Eats Dinner in 30 Minutes (or Less!) is Jessica's fourth cookbook. Her bestselling first book, *Not Your Mother's Make-Ahead and Freeze Cookbook*, offers a wealth of clever ideas for feeding a family inexpensively and well. Jessica's second book, *Best 100 Juices for Kids*, brings the juicing revolution home for the entire family, children included. *Good Cheap Eats*, her third book, proves that you can feed a family of four a terrific and tasty dinner for $10 or less.

A widely cited figure in the world of food blogs and "mom blogs," she has also written online for the Kitchn, Life Your Way, Money Saving Mom, $5 Dinners, and the Art of Simple and in print for more than 85 regional parenting publications. Jessica's readers recognize that she walks the talk: She is the mom to, and primary cook for, six children, aged 7 to 18. She lives with her husband and children in the San Diego area.